Synergy:
A Cure for All Ills

by

Easton Hamilton

Published by Easton Hamilton

Copyright © 2014 Easton Hamilton

All rights reserved.

Without limiting the rights under copyright reserved above, no part of this publication may be reproduced, stored, or transmitted in any form or by any means, without prior written permission of both the copyright owner and the above publisher of this book.

Artwork and cover design by Earl Hamilton

Electronic adaptation by Stunning Books

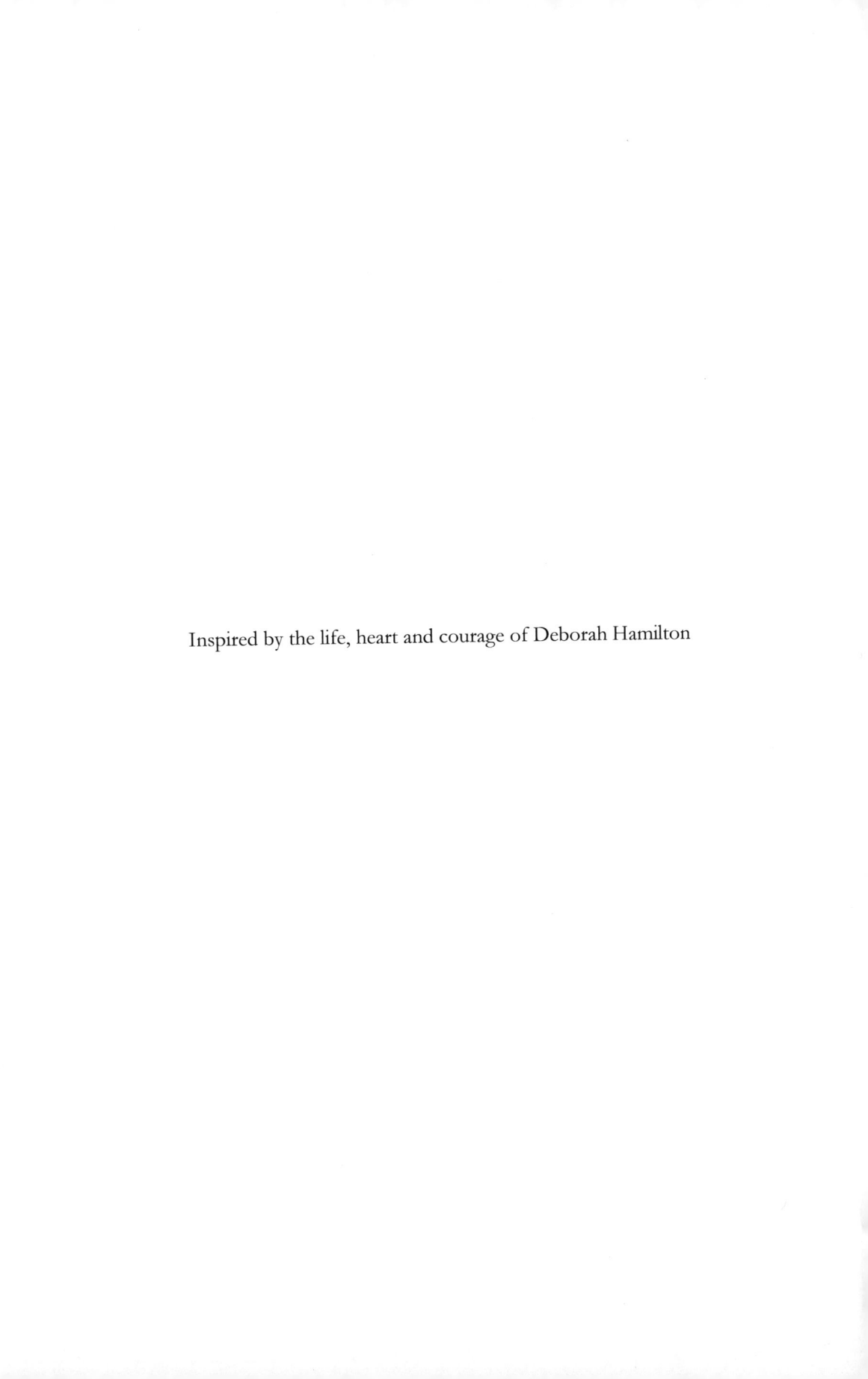

Inspired by the life, heart and courage of Deborah Hamilton

CONTENTS

Preface	i
Acknowledgements	v
Introduction	vii
Chapter 1: The Story of Health	1
Chapter 2: Persuading the Spirit	17
Chapter 3: Persuading the Mind	30
Chapter 4: Persuading the Body	47
Chapter 5: Environment Really Matters	69
Chapter 6: N.O.S.E.	86
Chapter 7: The Three Aspects of Consciousness	106
Chapter 8: The Discipline Dilemma	119
Chapter 9: The Relationship Between the Mind and the Mouth	138
Chapter 10: The Journey of Becoming	155
Chapter 11: Metaphysics – Life's Narrator	178
Chapter 12: Everything is Connected	201
Case Studies	224
Bite Sized Insights	253
Further Reading	257
About the Author	259
Living With Ambivalence	261

PREFACE

The world of counselling, psychotherapy and personal development is full of promises. There is a plethora of models, techniques, interventions and options all offering to 'fix' the problem, each one claiming to be better than the next. No wonder those seeking mental health solutions and recovery are often confused. There is so much competition and choice it's hard to know in which direction to venture.

The same confusion exists within the therapeutic and healing fields, whether it be acupuncture, reiki, herbalism, Qi gong, shiatsu, pilates, yoga, massage, EFT, nutrition, naturopathy, EMDR, hypnosis etc., each claims to address your problem(s) in a unique way, generally better than any other approach. So isn't this what I am also doing, with my claim that synergy is the cure for all ills? I can promise you, I'm not.

The Reach Approach is a unique amalgamation of various schools of knowledge and disciplines from East and West, past and present, delicately and sensitively woven together in a harmonious and colourful tapestry. The Reach Approach is a positive, well thought out and carefully researched response to the reality that we are multifactorial beings. And so, all the answers and solutions to the human condition are unlikely to be found in one place. It is an approach that draws from the 'melting pot' of human experience, giving proper respect and recognition to past ideas, theories and cultures – especially those that have withstood the test of time.

For the sake of integrity and balance the eastern philosophies and traditions are given proper representation in this book. Not as an anti-western stance because such bias would be against my holistic and integrative approach (or philosophy) but because, in my view, history in the developed world, has been unfair in its representation of the eastern contribution to world development. This is especially the case in areas such as the sciences, the arts, mathematics, architecture, language and culture. So most references to the East and the past are merely for the sake of balance and integrity. How can the story of who we are and how we might possibly 'fix' ourselves, be understood if half of the story is missing?

It is the primary proposition of this book that true healing and sustainable recovery cannot be achieved without synergy. Synergy is the concept that the whole is greater than the sum of its parts, and so it's by aligning and where possible, fitting together, seemingly opposing philosophies and ideologies that we can find more lasting solutions. In other words, co-operation is pursued rather than competition. Therefore I dare to suggest that synergy is the panacea the human race needs right now.

Throughout history, especially over the last four hundred years, the spirit of competition has driven us to tremendous achievements and successes. The modern world is a rich testament to these, with its towering buildings, large ocean liners, huge, metal flying machines defying gravity, transporting us across our planet; countless satellites whizzing around the earth providing us with extraordinary telecommunications... the list goes on. Many of these inventions were conceived out of that competitive spirit and unfortunately it is that same competitive spirit that has denied us a clear view of what's really important i.e. synergy. Synergy acknowledges the importance of the 'whole', realizing the limitations of merely focusing on the 'parts' and so it exchanges competition for collaboration. Synergy realizes our answers are best found at the point where all knowledge meets. It's at that confluence that, I believe, facts eventually become truth and information then becomes experience, which in turn leads to positive change. It is at this point of convergence that there is illumination of the self; it is there that the mysteries of life are quietly unveiled.

In order to reach a point of personal sustainability – living an authentic and positive life –we must first understand that the human condition is essentially composed of and influenced by four key aspects. These are: mind, body, spirit and environment – I will explore later in the book what I mean when using these terms, to understand the human story. For now, let's accept that, for the most part, we agree what these classifications refer to. These four main aspects are central to finding therapeutic and life solutions that work and will travel with us, positively influencing our lives.

It's the absence of harmony between mind, body, spirit and environment that keeps most people looking for relief from anger, pain, fear, panic, worry, illness, depression and so much more. As a result we remain tied to the very things we are trying to escape. Whilst we continue to insist on treating the presenting symptoms, the underlying causes continue to keep the seeker ill, either in mind or body or in some cases both. This mistake undermines all therapy; it has done for centuries and continues to do so even today. Carefully consider the following words from Plato.

"The cure of a part should not be attempted without the treatment of a whole. No attempt should aim to cure the body without the soul. If the head and body are to be healed, then you must begin by curing the mind – that is the first thing. Let no one persuade you to cure the head (the body) until they have first given you their soul to be cured, for this is the great error of our day in the treatment of the human body – that the physicians first separate the soul from the body."

Plato (428 BC – 347 BC)

Sadly, we continue not to learn from the kind reminders that history patiently offers up to us. Why? Because our egos have become too big and our ears have become too small! It's a lack of humility that prevents us from learning from our mistakes. If we would only turn our heads slightly and look behind occasionally we might just see what the past and our ancestry have to teach us. To students of history it soon becomes apparent that managing symptoms does not ever in fact treat causes. Furthermore, causes often manifest their symptoms in varied and seemingly unrelated areas of our lives.

For example, you may have a relationship where honest, open communication rarely takes place and yet the problem manifests in your body as repeated headaches or migraines. Or, maybe your physical environment is oppressive in some way – dark colours, inadequate ventilation, poor layout – however, the symptoms turn up in your body as lethargy and fatigue and in your mind as chaos or lack of motivation. Perhaps, your life has no real meaning and purpose, you feel rudderless, unsure of where you're going but your symptoms are again physical – frequent colds and infections, never really ill but never well either – the 'sickly well'. The list of seemingly unconnected causes of physical or emotional symptoms is infinite. I believe Plato was right in his conclusion that mind, body and spirit are inextricably linked and so how can health be attained without respecting these relationships and the interconnectedness of everything? I don't believe it can.

The reason that therapy and personal development, in all their various guises, do not always serve up lasting outcomes is because mind, body, spirit and environment are not equally tended to, as the different systems of healing are often too busy chasing away symptoms rather than properly tracing causes. If I've succeeded, then by the end of this book you will see there are no sustainable solutions without applying the principles of synergy.

So I am going to ask you, as you read on, to undertake a proper inventory of your life in all four areas and there you'll find the problems and - not very far away - you'll also find the solutions. The solutions always live with the problems; this is why if we avoid the problems we struggle to get completely well.

I invite you now to take this unique journey and get really well.

ACKNOWLEDGMENTS

Although I would not have chosen many of the things that have befallen me in this life, the truth is that I owe a huge debt to the enormous challenges I've undergone and the many mistakes that I've made along the way. They have been my best tutors.

They have faithfully held up a mirror for me to look into. Some of the time this has been painful and difficult and at other times it has been insightful and inspiring. Both sets of experiences have been priceless because without them my mind would not have been driven to better understand the complexities of the human condition.

My experience has forced me to ask the difficult questions that I believe at some point pass through all of our minds. The gift of a probing mind has served me well because I've been able to look at and confront those things that I have not liked in others, the world and most of all in myself and in facing my own darkness I have increasingly found refuge and comfort in the light.

I would like to take this opportunity to thank my Mother because in spite of my faults and failings she has always encouraged me, believed in me and taught me, through her guidance, unwavering support and her love. My Father has also been a wise counsel and a close friend who has given me a helping hand whenever I've needed it. They have both taught me the power of kindness and generosity and that giving is its own reward. Thank you both for everything you've done for me - I owe you my life.

Special thanks go to Jo Kilburn, the assistant director of Reach, who has, through her loyal support, hard work and friendship over more than twenty years, made this trilogy possible. At every step she's contributed her energy, time and enthusiasm and this project simply wouldn't have happened without her.

I also need to thank my family, especially my children, Rebecca and Earl, as well as my sister-in-law, Tracy Falconer, all of whom have unconditionally supported and believed in me, through the good times and especially the bad. They have been such wonderful companions.

Special mention goes to the two senior partners of Reach, Elaine Jackson and Judith Madeley, who've been such precious allies and have faithfully walked by my side now for many years. Both have contributed greatly to making Reach an organisation built on conscience and integrity. I am eternally grateful to them for their love, kindness, consistent support and friendship.

I also owe a great debt to my two very special friends, Rashna Walton and Jocelyne Ansorge. They have both, at different points over the years, lent me their eyes, intellects and expertise to enhance this and other written works I have produced. Thank you both for your invaluable contribution, love and friendship.

Given the size of this project, I also gratefully accepted the help of my dear friend, Lisa Shapter, who gave me the gift of her time and played her part in helping me to get the book ready for publication.

Finally, I want to thank the literally thousands of clients who have allowed me to be their special companion on their unique journeys into the self. Each and every one of you has added to me in some way. You've helped me to develop understanding and insights beyond my capacity, to discover levels of empathy and compassion I didn't know I had; you've kept me driving down a path looking for sustainable solutions; you have enabled me to find things that really work and truly last. You all know who you are and I hope by recognising your own virtues and qualities you'll have some idea of the gifts you've given to me.

I hope everyone who chooses to take this excursion will find it rewarding and enriching.

INTRODUCTION

Throughout history many great contributors, leaders and innovators have come with a life-changing message. The list is extensive and would easily exceed the space I have here. My aim is not to get too bogged down with specific examples because even that could miss the point I am trying to make, which is: it's the message that's important, not the messenger.

Having said that though, a few examples would help, for instance: Christ, Buddha, Confucius, Guru Nanak, Lao Tzu and more latterly Gandhi and Martin Luther King all had a significant impact on the world. But how many people do you know who are Christ-like or Buddha-like? How many people do you know who have made or are willing to make enormous personal sacrifices like Gandhi or King, in pursuit of what is right?

I'm not talking about perfection here, because history rarely provides us with 'blemish-free' accounts of the great minds and leaders - past or present. In fact, I am talking about great actions in spite of individual shortcomings and frailties; a greatness that outweighs personal deficiencies. All those I've listed here have been well documented elsewhere and so I have no need to recount their stories, but it's worth restating that they've all offered us examples of a better way. Lao Tzu tried to encourage us to live in alignment with the natural order rather than to battle against it, and Taoism emerged as a result. Guru Nanak, at a time of conflict between Hindus and Muslims, brought a message that sought integration and peace and as a result Sikhism was conceived some five hundred years ago. But despite these great contributors and their messages the world appears to continue in its decline towards spiritual, moral and ethical bankruptcy. Why?

My assessment of the decline in values and the rise of 'me-ism' is quite simple; we have, throughout history, focused disproportionately on the messenger rather than on the message. We become intoxicated by the charisma, delivery and stature of the individual and in so doing the message is not adequately heard and integrated. Although there are some examples of those who have become embodiments of the message, there have been far too few to steer us towards a better course.

It should be said for balance that this is not an attack on the messenger, for s/he is a vital cog in the machinery of positive change. And indeed there is no sin in appreciating the nature, qualities and virtues of that individual. However, history continues to remind us that our attachment and allegiance to the messenger has made us blind to the depth and subtleties of many crucial messages brought to us throughout the ages. This is why so much conflict exists where there is no need for it. Egos, different personalities and the various interpretations that have been overlaid onto the original message(s) have led us away from peace, integrity, forgiveness and truth. Take a look for yourself at the history and evolution of humankind over the last two thousand five hundred years and see what you find – dare I say, what you will often find is our demise, masquerading as progress.

My view is that if the message makes sense to you and sits comfortably in your heart without contradiction, then that is the path you must follow. However, to follow that path means to truly live it. Following takes as much strength as leading – the difference just lies in the starting position. Following means to replicate the message in your own life, in such a way that you in fact become the message. This is what Gandhi meant by his famous entreaty, "Be the change you want to see in the world".

Those familiar with my work and The Reach Approach will notice that we do not deliver our message through a figurehead or primary personality, but through a name that invites us all to 'Reach' for the ultimate prize, 'our truth'. Until we reach inside and find the things that are blocking our progress we will continue to wander the same fruitless paths. Reach is not concerned with the messenger. Our focus is on helping you to 'reach-in', into your heart and mind, to find 'you', in order that you can then 'reach-out', fulfilling your reason for being here. So as an organisation we have no desire for you to remember us, which is why we don't promote ourselves in the conventional ways. However, if our message makes sense to you and 'feels' right then take what you need from it and I am sure you'll find yourself in a better place, one of peace and contentment.

In fact, although I'm the author of this book, if, come the end of it, you are remembering me rather than its message, I will have failed you. This book is not about me - it is about the message contained within its pages.

History is littered with examples of the messenger being hailed above the message and all it has really led to is confusion, conflict and in some cases even war. The religious movements have demonstrated this truth better than just about anything else. Look at Christianity, Islam, Judaism, Hinduism and others and you'll see that time and time again the message in its purest form has often been lost and replaced with countless dogmas, personal opinions and interpretations, followed by internal and then external conflict.

If the message of this book makes sense to you, hopefully it will help you to bring about your own positive transformation, leading you to a place of balance, peace, inner harmony and joy. So please remember the message and not the messenger.

It should be said for the purpose of clarity that this book does not intend to extensively say what's already been said elsewhere, except where it's relevant. This book is really about what hasn't been said. I will touch on many subjects such as: epigenetics, orthomolecular medicine, psychoneuro-immunology, geopathic stress, psychotherapy, metaphysics, neurotheology, spirituality and much more but what I'm concerned with is showing how these things actually fit together and demonstrating their greater effectiveness as a consequence.

As I was writing this book, I realized I could not include everything I wanted to say. Nonetheless, I wanted this to be, as far as possible, a useful handbook, somewhere that most of the things one would need for one's own well-being could be found. I knew that other points of reference would be needed to complement what I've presented, many of which I've alluded to during the course of the book. I should, however, add to that list the Reach website (www.thereachapproach), which is a resource you may find useful in conjunction with this text.

CHAPTER 1: THE STORY OF HEALTH

"The same stream of life that runs through my veins night and day runs through the world and dances in rhythmic measures. It is the same life that shoots in joy through the dust of the earth in numberless blades of grass and breaks into tumultuous waves of leaves and flowers. It is the same life that is rocked in the ocean-cradle of birth and of death, in ebb and in flow. I feel my limbs are made glorious by the touch of this world of life. And my pride is from the life-throb of ages dancing in my blood this moment."

Rabindranath Tagore (1861 – 1941)

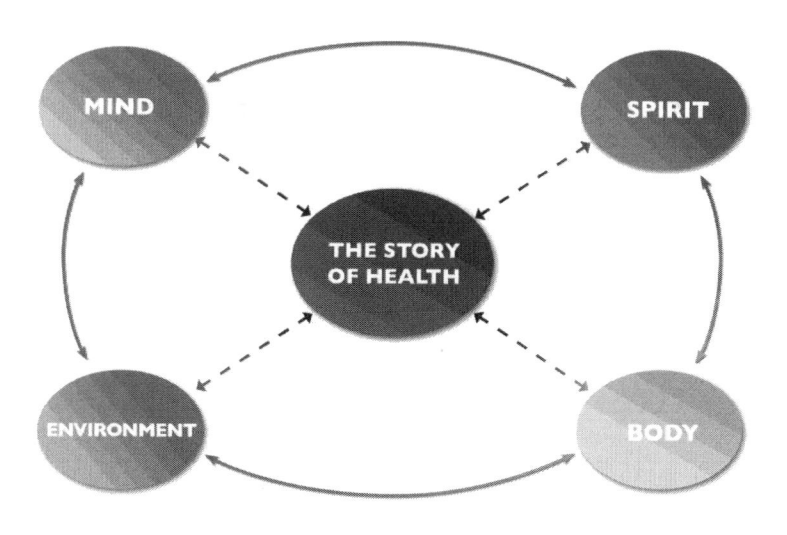

Figure 1: The Story of Health

The missing link?

This book makes what for many will be seen as a grand claim, namely that it offers the panacea, 'the cure for all ills'. A claim that has been made countless times throughout the ages as each discovery promises more than the last. However, this is a claim I stand by and will do my best to demonstrate as this story unfolds, but this claim with its promise to cure all ills means nothing without 'The Story of Health'. The Story of Health is the missing link, it pulls the whole concept of change through synergy together – take it away and this concept, and that claim would simply fall apart. So what is The Story of Health?

The Story of Health summarizes the story of the human condition (see figure 1). It highlights the key characters, mind, body and spirit and the context in which their amazing interplay is expressed, the environment. It's a story of independence, interdependence and cause and effect, as the different energies and forces strive for autonomy and unity in equal measure. The mind, body and spirit are not enemies; in a state of health and well-being they are comrades working for the greater good of the self. However, in the disease state a different dynamic is at play – the three principal characters oppose each other as they now act in a self-interested way, choosing their survival and independence over harmony and interdependence. Why? When the needs of the mind, spirit and body are all being met, co-operation reigns supreme and as a result vibrant health is maintained. But if those needs are not adequately met for any reason, then dis-ease is born and this dis-ease in this tripartheid system eventually leads to disease in either mind or body, or both. So it is our responsibility to understand each character's role in this play and meet their respective needs. Only then can disease be averted or at least better managed.

To better understand this fascinating process, let's look more closely at each character in this story and the stage on which this drama is played out.

Spirit

The debate about spirit continues to rage. Who or what is it? Is it a pure spark of energy bursting with consciousness or is it a beautiful hologram of the body endowed with divine light? Is the spirit a separate, distinct, non-physical energy with its own unique personality and will? Or is it a piece of consciousness attached to a supreme deity and so has no distinctive personality, as it's merely an extension of the divine? I believe these questions cannot fully be answered until we first learn the steps of that beautiful dance called synergy. How can we comprehend the profound when we barely even understand or apply the basics? For the story of health to be truly grasped one needs to understand that the spirit is the principal character in this story, the spirit is the 'feeling' we are left with as a consequence of the decisions and choices we make. It's that 'sense' we have and carry with us at all times. In other words, whether you are sad, happy, depressed, hurt or euphoric, that is actually a description of the spirit – your internal state. So this is what I'm referring to when I use the term spirit – how you are actually feeling, the feeling that best describes your inner world. The debate about the role, construct and form of the spirit is not the primary concern of this literature. Although I have a very clear view of this, born of my own experience, my belief is that the answer to these questions is best arrived at through your own experimentation and exploration.

Mind

The mind is quite simply phenomenal, defying explanation. Its breadth and depth are quite staggering. Whatever I will be saying here or whatever you may have read on the subject elsewhere, simply won't be able to do justice to the 'majesty of the mind'. It truly has magical and mystical powers that have yet to be fully unveiled. In the context of the story of health, the mind is the character that strives to maintain order and where possible deliver positive change. It acts on the feelings of the spirit and seeks out the strategies and solutions to restore balance and peace if they are absent, or maintain them if they are present. The mind is always trying to achieve homeostasis and avoid dis-ease by addressing any lack of balance in the system. It will go to extraordinary lengths to achieve that, which is why, at times, it can unwittingly work against the body in its pursuit of homeostasis. As you can see in figure 1, when this battle between mind and body takes place then it is the spirit that pays the price – as it experiences the resultant neurosis and/or ill health or worse still, psychosis and/or a chronic physical condition.

The mind needs a diet of self-nurturing activities if it is to achieve the peace, balance and harmony it strives for. When its needs are not met then it acts in its own self-interest and anarchy ensues as mind, body and spirit, due to the resulting breakdown in communication, all pull in opposing directions. I will explore the needs of the mind later, but for now it is important to recognize that the mind-body-spirit system never 'knowingly' works against itself. Where this happens it is due to needs not being adequately met and the subtle system of communication between the three breaking down as a result. There are many reasons for this, which will become clear as we go further. But let's continue to sketch the role of each character in what is arguably the most important story of them all.

Body

Just as the mind can defy logic and exceed the boundaries of the imagination, so too is the body worthy of our attention and marvel. The body is busy carrying out four billion activities per second in order to give us the gift of life, such are the miracles it performs from moment to moment. And yet do we ever sit in awe and wonder, appreciating these miracles? Do we give thanks for the countless tasks performed in our names? Rarely, if at all, in my experience. Having worked with thousands of individuals, couples, families and groups over more than thirty years, what has become clear is that the casual neglect of the body is pretty universal. Most of us demand and expect from our bodies great things each day and yet we find little or no time to appreciate and reward this most incredible organism. As with the mind and spirit, if the core needs of the body are not met it begins to act in its own self-interest. Survival and protection becomes the name of the game.

It's worthy of note that in nature all activities, whatever their outward appearance, can be classified in just two ways, growth and protection. I will explore this concept more fully later, but for now it's important to understand that when the body's needs are being met it 'grows' i.e. it is able to fully express itself. Growth means continually producing the energy for life and expressing that potential to the full. When the body's needs are not being met it moves to the protectionist position. Protection is when energy withdraws and shutdown takes place. There is then no fullness of expression, as our energy acts in ways that are only instinctive, essential and life-preserving. This is why if the body does not get at least the ninety nutrients it needs every day (sixty minerals, sixteen vitamins, eleven amino acids and three essential fatty acids) plus the two litres of water, the necessary sleep and the correct acid/alkaline balance it needs through food, as well as regular exercise, and a stress-free life with peace and joy as its foundations, it simply cannot deliver its promise of health and well-being. This is when matter can so easily overthrow the mind and, despite our best efforts, the body's cries for sustenance and help can bring the mind to its knees. So how do we stop this tug of war between mind and matter, non-physical and physical? All will become clear.

Environment

So far the principal characters have been outlined but no drama would be complete without a stage. The environment is the stage – it is the context in which the other three manifest their characteristics and express their purpose. Environment is such a vast subject including as it does both the internal and the external world. It describes the sophisticated interplay between the micro and the macro - and mind, body and spirit all have a continued entanglement with the environment. Its role and importance cannot be overstated because it is constantly impacting on our emotional, psychological, social and biological realities. In fact, the findings at the cutting edge of science (in quantum physics, energy medicine and epigenetics) are almost daily re-writing our understanding of the environment's impact on our genetic expression. Long gone is the simplistic idea that genes are governing our lives and their unfolding is determining our reality. What has become increasingly clear with the help of scientists such as Einstein, Podolsky, Rosen, Temin, Cairns and more latterly Pert, Sheldrake, Lipton and others, is that genetic expression is determined by our relationship with our environments. To be more precise, it's our perception of our environments that determines which genes are switched on or off. This introduces another important aspect to the discussion on the environment, the subject of beliefs.

So we are not merely responding to the obvious environmental factors such as, light, colour, space, smells, shapes, sounds, our various relationships etc. It's more complex than that. It is our relationship to, and perception of these factors that determines not only genetic expression but our reality in general. In other words, consciousness is both shaped and influenced in its expression by our beliefs. This too will become clearer as the story of health comes together, then we shall see that we are not merely responding to environmental factors, we are also equally responding to what we believe, based on those perceptions. This has huge implications for us as human beings and really underlines the importance of free will and the power of choice in this fascinating story. It also makes clear that our relationship to the environment can either enslave or empower us. So how do we move forward from here?

Making sense of the jigsaw?

Having sketched the outline of The Story of Health, I will add some depth and detail about each of the four principal forces in the subsequent chapters. This is because I believe the better each one is understood, the more likely you will be to strive for harmony in all areas of your life. I hope the primary factors and dynamics have been sufficiently understood for now.

It would be easy to fall into the trap of thinking that because the spirit is the principal character, it is somehow more important than the other three elements. This would be a serious mistake because the truth is that in this story no single factor is more important than any of the others. Compare this to a four-legged table, which leg is more important? No matter which leg you remove, the table will topple and fall. Each leg matters equally and in The Story of Health the same is true. If any one of these four aspects, mind, body, spirit or environment were to be removed from this beautiful arrangement, then one's sense of self and experience of reality would collapse.

So as we piece together the jigsaw, think of mind, body, spirit and environment as equals. This is why the table is a perfect analogy for keeping the concept clear in your mind. When all four legs are properly positioned, equal in length, performing their roles as they should, the tabletop is straight, square and stable. This represents a balanced mind, a healthy body and a spirit that is at ease with itself and the environment. However, when the legs are not properly positioned or are not equal for whatever reason, then disharmony quickly follows - so of course we want a stable table, because only then can health in all its full glory be our experience. If you are not experiencing health and well-being then one or more of the legs of your table has been or is being compromised in some way. Until that imbalance or shortfall is addressed then whatever your presenting problem may be, it will continue in one form or another.

How the presenting problem often deceives

For centuries we have pursued the 'presenting problem' believing that in doing so the issue will be resolved. Nowhere is this pursuit more often demonstrated than in the field of medicine. Allopathic medicine in particular has specialized in producing pharmaceuticals that busy themselves arresting the primary symptom(s), usually at the cost of generating secondary ones in the form of side effects. This is often considered a price worth paying, even when at times what is being offered is only temporary relief. Sadly, in some cases, complementary and alternative medicines are now in danger of following the path of the 'magic bullet' approach.

There is a plethora of vitamins, herbs and supplements offered for very specific issues and conditions. This has become confusing for those looking for healthy options and solutions because if one were to follow every piece of advice and purchase every remedy for the countless ailments we experience, one could easily accrue substantial debts in the pursuit of better health. With so much advice and seemingly infinite options where does one even begin? Health, even in areas that claim to be natural in their approach, has on the one hand become too complicated and on the other hand too one-dimensional as supplements and remedies are talked about in very 'issue-specific' terms. In other words, take zinc for this and vitamin A for that. But is this how health really works? Is it actually that simple?

Health cannot be achieved by exclusively homing in on the presenting problem. By all means we have to start there, but we cannot afford to be trapped by the presenting issue, whatever it is, for it is often the symptom and not the cause. Likewise, in the area of personal growth we cannot afford to make the mistake being made in medicine and also, increasingly, in the field of natural alternatives. Taking vitamin A or zinc may bring some relief and temporarily address a set of symptoms, but vitamins and minerals do not work in isolation. In fact, the more you scrutinize everything about health the more you find synergy and co-operation at the heart of what really works. So when considering a particular intervention, whatever its primary focus, we must think of the whole, otherwise we merely displace the problem, shifting it somewhere else in the system. This mistake is being made in almost every area of healing. There are far too many examples to document here but we can look at a few to illustrate the point.

Regularly individuals go to see chiropractors and osteopaths for structural adjustment to their bodies. This is a very good choice if the body is out of alignment in any way, due to an injury, fall or some other trauma. However, if one pursues a successful course of treatment but has not drunk adequate amounts of water throughout the treatment, then the adjustments made to the body's structure can so easily and often do, return to the pre-treated state. This is because water holds the body's messages in place, acting both as a messenger and as memory to the system. So when we are hydrated at the time of treatment the 'message input' from the therapist is held in place by the water. When we are dehydrated the message and the memory have no point of anchor.

We are literally vertical rivers and nothing can work properly in the body without the wonderful properties and skills of water. This is a subject I will discuss at some length later, because the role of water in terms of mental and physical health cannot be overstated.

So if adequate amounts of water are not imbibed (approx. 2 litres per day – but this amount is only an average), then very good bodywork can be and is often undermined. As you will come to understand, water after our need for oxygen is the single most important thing our body requires to fulfill the countless tasks that are performed literally every second we are alive. Even a small percentage drop in the volume of the water in our bodies (less than 2%) can undermine physical and cognitive functions.

Another example of the weakness of the 'one-pronged' approach is that it's very common for clients to pursue counselling and psychotherapy for depression, anxiety and other forms of neurosis, looking almost exclusively at the emotional and psychological factors that have contributed and still do contribute to their dysfunction. That is a perfectly reasonable course of action but as neuroscience and nutritional science is rapidly helping us to see, depression and anxiety almost always have biological undercurrents that contribute to the emotional disturbances.

The works of Dr. A. Hoffer and Dr. Carl C. Pfeiffer, in the 1960s powerfully demonstrated that with schizophrenia, whatever emotional and psychological factors were at play, there was nearly always an obvious vitamin and mineral deficiency in such patients. They particularly found vitamin B3 (niacin) and vitamin B6, zinc (and some other trace minerals) to be consistently low or missing in sufferers of this particular condition. Their successes in applying nutrition in such cases were quite staggering. For those interested, take a closer look at the pioneering work being undertaken by orthomolecular medicine and more latterly nutritional genomics. Also look at the work of Patrick Holford and Dr. Paul Clayton – who are playing their part in putting nutrition on the map of both physical and mental health.

So, based on the research and my own experience, as well as the expertise of clinicians and professionals I work alongside, it has become clear that factors such as nutrition are often relevant to the client or patient's problem and therefore recovery. If this is not considered at the point of assessing the situation, the therapist can easily look beyond the relevance of the individual's diet, nutrition and possible need for supplementation, leading him to draw inaccurate conclusions. I have seen a lot of this misdiagnosis. It should be said that this is done in good faith and is not about the practitioner, it has more to do with their model and approach.

To illustrate my point a little further let's see how, by overlooking the importance of the environment, someone's progress and recovery can grind to a halt. There are still many who dispute the validity and therefore, relevance of geopathic stress and electro-pollution. I believe we need to keep an open mind. When you study the literature you soon see that to ignore these 'very real' physical threats could be dangerous and injurious to our health. Geopathic stress does not claim to cause illness but it does appear to undermine health by weakening our immune systems, therefore compromising the body's ability to fight off viruses, parasites and other infections. These organisms are not just threats to our internal organs, cells and tissues, they also impact on our psychological capacity and well-being. Anything that challenges one part of the mind-body-spirit system automatically takes energy from somewhere else in the system, jeopardizing optimum health.

In simple terms, geopathic stress is linked to the earth's own natural vibration (frequency 7.8MgHz). That frequency has a harmonizing effect on the body and its systems (I will cover this subject in greater depth in Chapter 9). However, many things, both natural and man-made, do impact on and alter the 'earth's song' (vibration). Electro-pollution in its many forms, various electromagnetic fields created by subterranean running water, fault lines, underground cavities and other forms of man-made pollution alter the original optimal vibration. So as the 'earth's song' is distorted our internal frequencies are affected too.

This is why all healing modalities and interventions need to consider the relationship we have with the planet and how its pollution is having a direct effect on all our lives - one cannot fully heal without the other. Is it a reasonable question to ask what can we do about such influences, given many of the things listed here are beyond our control? As I stated earlier geopathic stress does not cause illness but rather creates the conditions for the undermining of one's health. If we are at least aware of this then there is a lot we can do to protect ourselves both in our bodies and our homes. There is also a lot we can all do to protect and promote the health and well-being of our physical environments. I hope by the end of this journey you will be able to see what you can do to protect yourself in all four areas.

These examples go some way to explaining why the presenting problem may well be the departure point but rarely serves to lead one to the destination. That quest requires greater inquiry, more knowledge of the whole and time and patience in equal measure. So beware of a one-pronged approach, which doesn't treat all four factors equally.

Everything is connected?

"A scientific worldview which does not profoundly come to terms with the problem of conscious minds can have no serious pretensions of completeness. Consciousness is part of our universe, so any physical theory which makes no proper place for it falls fundamentally short of providing a genuine description of the world.
Sir Roger Penrose (1931 – present)

By the time you complete this journey I hope to have demonstrated how everything in life is indeed connected. By everything I mean our minds, bodies, relationship to the planet, to each other, to the universe. Life is an intimate and intricate dance of energies, each one playing its unique part and yet dependent on the other. There are four forces that we are aware of in the world of matter, which are an excellent example of this energetic dance, because each has its own quality and virtue and yet all four are connected. They are: electromagnetism, gravity, the strong nuclear force and the weak nuclear force. Everything taking place around us falls into one of these four categories.

Electromagnetism accounts for heat, electricity, light, radio waves, TV, X-rays etc. Gravity makes the world go round and holds the planets and stars in place. The strong nuclear force holds the nucleus together at the heart of the cell. It's the dividing of this nucleus that creates what we refer to as nuclear power, which as we're all aware, is awesome in both positive and negative ways. The weak nuclear force holds the sub-atomic particles together, which in quantum physics is now being referred to as 'information', existing in time and space, serving up unlimited possibilities. These four forces are responsible for all life as we know it and are often referred to as the 'unified field'.

Quantum entanglement has been described as possibly the most important discovery in physics because it demonstrates that everything is indeed connected. For those of you interested in understanding the history and development of entanglement, then much has been written in the scientific literature (I will say more about this topic in the concluding chapters). The initial work that brought this concept to our awareness was undertaken by Einstein, Podolsky and Rosen in 1935 – who used quantum mechanics theory to try and make greater sense of how things that were separated by great distance, 'appeared' to have a 'synchronicity' in terms of their patterns and behaviour. Einstein referred to this concept as "spooky action at a distance". Quantum theory, at this point had already theorized that a scientist or researcher working on a particular project could not be 'neutralized' with regards to their influence on events. In other words, the very act of observing a phenomenon, in some way makes him a part of what is going on. So the concept of entanglement takes this principle a stage further as it relates to localized and non-localized events/situations.

This 'spooky' phenomenon was in fact first described as 'entanglement' by Schrödinger who was an Austrian physicist also specializing in quantum mechanics. He went on during the thirties, forties and fifties to do a lot of work on the aforementioned Unified Field Theory, which has been much developed and commented on since by those who increasingly believe in the relationship between all energies including consciousness. Lynne McTaggart's book, The Field, is an excellent introduction and development of this beautiful idea that nothing exists in isolation. Although it should be said for the sake of balance that quantum entanglement continues to be debated and in some quarters the original hypothesis has been rewritten in parts, there are still many others who have gone on to champion this concept.

The Institute of Noetic Sciences (IONS) is one such example. This institution has spent the last forty years bringing together spirituality and subjectivity, scrutinizing both with scientific rigour. Their primary objective is both to explore and understand consciousness, using science as its primary investigative tool with the hope of building bridges between seemingly opposing perspectives. The Greek term noetic, is an apt description for this scientific endeavor as it is particularly concerned with 'subjectivity' within science - that inner 'knowing' and innate wisdom that is either overlooked, doubted or neglected by the mainstream.

The Institute's involvement with established universities and other leading agencies such as: Stanford University, Cambridge University, Harvard Medical School, Oxford University, the United Nations, The Max Planck Institute and many more conducting a range of existential experiments and investigations, many of which have been peer reviewed and published, has given IONS a credibility that is increasingly being acknowledged elsewhere in the field. Amongst their investigations they have examined the role of consciousness in relationship to entanglement. To find out more, take a look at the work and research they've been involved in, which includes: the role of compassion, prayer, distant healing, intention and extrasensory perception. They continue to build a body of solid research around what many would describe as the esoteric and spiritual, which I believe deserves to be taken seriously, as they are attempting to join up the dots.

The relationship between inner space and outer space is now not just a philosophical discussion - if we are willing to suspend what we 'think' we know then the relevance and importance of the interconnectedness of life does not in any way threaten our existence, it promises to enrich it.

Some of you may be familiar with the Living Matrix movie, which is an excellent documentary pulling together the latest discoveries at the cutting edge of biochemistry, physics, medicine, healing and alternative and complementary medicines. Its contributors include: Rupert Sheldrake Ph.D, Dr. H. Koning MD, Marilyn Schlitz Ph.D, James Oschman Ph.D, Edgar Mitchell Ph.D and many others who have spent their lives trying to demonstrate through research and therapeutic practices, from a wide variety of disciplines, the interconnectedness of the mind-body system. The general premise being offered is that the body is a field of energy and health is a state where that energy field is in harmony with itself and its environment. Disease is where there is a breakdown in communication within that field, leading to disharmony.

There are many things that can and do negatively impact on the body's energy field, such as diet and nutrition, emotional trauma, isolation and lack of social contact, inadequate levels of hydration and arguably most of all our beliefs. What we think really does matter! Thoughts are 'things' – parcels of energy packed with either a positive or negative charge, and so they too impact on the energy field, which in turn impacts on the body's functions and performance. What's interesting to note is that this is not a one-way system, so any disturbance within the body's energy systems, returns back to the mind via the intricate dual carriageways, carrying information both ways between the two systems and if we do nothing to break that negative momentum we are pulled down by that vortex.

We can turn the whole story around by eating the right foods, drinking the necessary fluids, adopting and maintaining healthy relationships – building compassion and kindness into our lives and changing the way we think. Changing our thought patterns and processes as I previously indicated seems a crucial piece in this jigsaw and I will spend more time exploring this in subsequent chapters.

Candace Pert was one of the pioneers in this area of emotions and biochemistry and she coined the phrase 'molecule of emotion' (also the name of her book). She was able to demonstrate through her work how every emotion has a biological/physical consequence and so the metaphysical realm of thought and feeling could not be divorced from the physical (body); they are intimately entwined. Her book lays an excellent foundation for understanding this mind-brain-body connection; where the mind could be seen as the pharmacist and the brain as the pharmacy, as a magical cocktail of neuropeptides, hormones and other biochemical substances are produced in exact measures and proportions reflecting the individual state of mind.

Bruce Lipton's work in this area builds on Pert's contribution and is summarized very effectively in his book The Biology of Belief. There he offers a clear map of how thoughts and feelings are in fact primary factors in the shaping of the genetic material. There is a critical set of genes described as the IEGs (immediate early genes) that have been discovered to be the primary interface between thoughts and feelings and they determine how the genes express themselves. In other words the genes' behaviour and performance is significantly influenced by the thoughts and feelings of the individual (this is another topic I will return to as our journey unfolds). It's interesting to note that these immediate early genes have also been described as immediate 'experience' genes because of the impact of our thoughts and feelings on their expression. Again we can see the mind-body connection and the relationship between the visible and invisible. Nature and life are littered with countless examples like this.

Another fascinating illustration of the interconnectedness of life, demonstrating the depth of the relationship between our beliefs and the environment, can be found in the discoveries being made almost daily in the arena of placebo and its less fashionable partner nocebo. Let me offer a brief introduction to this topic.

Placebos (the use of a simulated medicine or treatment, which is deemed ineffectual and won't cause harm) is not a new topic. John Haygarth was the first to investigate the efficacy of placebos in the 18th century and he clearly demonstrated that what was described as the 'dummy' remedy was often just as effective as the 'real' medicine. This was arguably the first relatively modern demonstration of how important beliefs are in their impact on the disease process. The French psychologist and pharmacist, Émile Coué, wrote a powerful book about his extensive work on this subject in 1920 called Self-Mastery Through Conscious Autosuggestion. He discovered over nearly a thirty year period what Haygarth had seen, but he went much further as he gave positive notes to patients when administering the medicine, praising the efficacy and virtues of each remedy because he'd been able to demonstrate the impact of belief on the healing and recovery process. Since then many have contributed and added to this discussion such as: Cabot, Graves, Beecher and more latterly Dr Lisa Rankin and Professor Irving Kirsch, who have done some good research in this area.

What has been discussed much less is the equally powerful nocebo effect. The nocebo effect also offers a very clear illustration of the role and impact of beliefs, not only in medicine - where some research has demonstrated its effects - but in life generally. With the placebo, a patient is either given what they believe is the 'real' remedy, or they've been exposed (as is the case in double-blind placebo-controlled studies) to a situation where they do not know which of the two remedies they've been given. Equally there are those cases where the patient believes they've had surgery whereas in fact the 'appearance' of a surgical event is all that took place. The nocebo effect on the other hand is where the patient has been told that a remedy or the treatment is unlikely to work, or their prognosis is very poor and so recovery is unlikely, which installs a belief in the patient that then works against the healing and recovery process (remember the I.E.Gs.).

William James, the philosopher, psychologist and physician who is described by many as the Father of American Psychology because of his pioneering contribution in the field during the 19th century, frequently commented on the flaw in medicine, namely its inability to recognize the power of the physician and her role in the transformative process. In other words, whatever else the doctor was prescribing she should also be prescribing hope because within the capacity of hope is a belief that can potentially aid the patient on their journey of healing. This was consistent with his 'pragmatic theory of truth' for which he is renowned.

My interest in the placebo and nocebo effects is that they remind us of the power of the mind to influence and shape biology. They also help us to understand our relationship to the environment and how important perception is in shaping our reality. In addition they remind us that we do not live in a compartmentalized world and everything is indeed connected, in some cases obviously and in other instances less so.

One final illustration for now about the entanglement that we are all a part of is how our bodies behave at a cellular level. The research of Dr. Sondra Barrett into the inner world of our cells has added some useful data to this concept. She has explored extensively the architecture, intelligence and ability of the cells to work in harmony and what happens when there is disharmony. She describes in her book, The Secret of Your Cells, how we are more than an arrangement of chemicals that are haphazardly and fortuitously creating life. She presents clearly the idea of the body as a community of sixty trillions cells working together to create a sanctuary from which consciousness can then express its creative intelligence in the world. When you look at the anatomy of each individual cell, you see a replica of the human structure and functions, as every cell has a brain, a digestive system, reproductive system, circulatory system, immune system etc. - and when those cells are in harmony with themselves and one another we enjoy a state of health and when that harmony is disturbed, disease in the system then becomes disease in one form or another.

I hope from the examples I have given here, that you're beginning to see some of the evidence for the idea that everything is connected. As our journey unfolds I will do my best to add further colour, texture and depth, as I add to this illustration with many more examples and insights.

"When we try to pick out anything by itself, we find it hitched to everything else in the Universe."

John Muir (1838 – 1914)

The arsonist

I described the Story of Health at the beginning as the missing link because without it we continue to be deceived by the presenting problems and issues. We also fail to see how everything is connected. And so to pursue a solution without paying proper respect to this principle is why in my view, despite all our progress, we are in many ways still chasing our tails. When we champion any one thing above the other, we are in danger of missing the point, which is to see how the two things might be connected and together are stronger. Think about this – if as the research suggests, the effectiveness of placebos is somewhere around 35% (interestingly modern medicine is only offering marginally better results at 38%), then imagine if we could use that power of belief proactively with medication and remedies that actually do work. The two bound together must be better than either one on its own. Émile Coué saw in his work the power of the positive message to transcend the effects of the remedy - he discovered how the power of belief could only enhance the outcome. Imagine if we were applying this in the field of medicine generally. We would massively improve the results we're currently getting because both mind and body would be working together and the spirit, that sense of self, would claim the prize.

Our current approach, where we simply follow the trail of the symptoms, is like only ever putting out fires and never catching the one that starts them. Surely it makes more sense to catch the arsonist and persuade him or her that there's a much better way to live than to run around starting fires in the first place. This is the philosophy of The Reach Approach, which by the way, I'm not presenting to you here as the panacea. What I am saying is that The Reach Approach is a signpost towards what needs to be done. Each one's panacea, although there are common elements, will be slightly different because the weaknesses or shortfalls for each person will be different in each of the four areas. And so what is the best 'potion' for you will be unique to you. This is where proper reflection on these matters will be needed and you may even need help to work out exactly what is right for you. This book is an attempt to do just that.

So what is involved in persuading your arsonist? This is where a much deeper insight into The Story of Health is required because until the needs of the mind, body and spirit are fully understood and properly met and the environment is fostered to support those three, fires will continue to rage in our consciousness and our bodies. It's time for a different strategy; I call it the art of persuasion.

There is a need for a conversation between the mind, body and spirit and until we set up the necessary dialogue, what we will find is that the desire we have to be peaceful, happy and whole will elude us. This is arguably the most important journey you will ever take, the journey towards yourself...

"We don't receive wisdom; we must discover it for ourselves after a journey that no one can take for us or spare us."
Marcel Proust (1871 - 1922)

CHAPTER 2: PERSUADING THE SPIRIT

"When you are inspired by some great purpose, some extraordinary project, all your thoughts break their bonds; your mind transcends limitation, your consciousness expands in every direction, and you find yourself in a new, great and wonderful world. Dormant forces, faculties and talents become alive and you discover yourself to be a greater person by far than you ever dreamed yourself to be."

Patanjali (1st-3rd century BC)

A life of meaning and purpose

In order to take the spirit on a journey of renewal, it's important that it finds real meaning and purpose. A life of meaning and purpose is the lifeblood of the spirit. My own clinical experience and research have illuminated what is quite obvious once you stop and think about it and that is so many cases of mental ill health are the result of a life devoid of clear focus and direction, where the individual is trapped in a fog of uncertainty and has no idea where his/her life is going. Over more than three decades I've seen countless patients with schizophrenia, bi-polar disorder, paranoid schizophrenia, multiple personality disorder and borderline personality. Although these conditions have varying classifications and are considered to be at different points on the psychological scales of disturbance and dysfunction, it's interesting to note that in nearly all cases, in my experience, those diagnosed with these illnesses have lives that lack meaning and purpose. It could be said that this lack of meaning and purpose is the inevitable consequence of their condition, but this would be a mistake, because on closer inspection the lack of meaning and purpose nearly always comes first. Sadly our mental health structures and systems do not always take the time to discover this because they are too swift to 'treat' the effect rather than establishing how the individual has arrived at his/her state of disrepair.

Lack of meaning and purpose leads to a loss of focus and direction, which can be brought on by trauma or unexpected life changes. These factors then act as catalysts for change, often dismantling the individual's perspective and with that their beliefs, and very quickly the client/patient can find him/herself overwhelmed by distorted thoughts and feelings, which generate fear, paranoia, delusion and much more. Their moods, attitudes and behaviour also follow suit. Sadly, in most of these cases, conventional wisdom is again busy managing symptoms, usually with medication and possibly small amounts of talking therapy. This approach almost always misses the point and leaves the person spiraling out of control. Isn't it obvious that we need to start where the problem began?

The absence of meaning and purpose is like having a slow puncture in a tyre that you keep pumping up to no effect. Until it's repaired that tyre will never do its job properly. So your first task is to repair your tyre by ensuring your life has meaning and purpose and where it doesn't, it's imperative that you busy yourself finding 'something' that really makes your heart sing.

Finding the song of your heart

It is amazing how varied that 'something' can be for different people. For one person personal satisfaction and a sense of fulfillment can come from volunteering at a shelter for the homeless or working with ex-criminals, helping them to resettle back into the community. Whereas for someone else it might be reclaiming their health and fitness and helping their family or a friend do the same. For yet another it might be becoming active in transforming the fortunes of our planet, lobbying for change, either economically, politically or in some other way. The truth is that meaning and purpose differ widely from one person to the next. It is also the case that some things will drive your motivation for a period of time whilst others may move you for the rest of your life. What is important is that whatever you focus on, truly makes your heart sing.

So go and find what that is, but be patient – the answers don't always come immediately. If you're unsure about your direction and purpose, keep asking yourself the following questions, "What are my skills, talents and abilities best suited to?", "How can I best apply my life experience in my present circumstances?", "Given my personality traits, strengths and limitations, how can I be a force for good in the world?" Keep asking questions like these and then listen for the answer(s). The answer(s) may come in the form of a dream, an interaction with a friend, family member or colleague. They could just as easily come whilst you're watching the TV, listening to a play on the radio or reading something seemingly unconnected. Don't expect a divine revelation, in fact don't expect anything at all. Sitting anticipating a response is an obstacle to you getting a reply. All you need to do is ask your question, with that inner knowing (faith) that a reply is already on its way and you'll recognize it when it comes. This is an art, something the ancient masters and scholars of the past understood and practised. They waited without impatient anticipation because they knew the laws of the universe guaranteed a response.

The nature of a cause and effect world is that whatever we put 'out there' has to come back to us sooner or later. More specifically, it is our intention that defines the nature of the return. There is a growing body of evidence validating the power of intention with regards to the architecture and structure of life. Quantum physics has restored credence to the part intention plays in shaping events and outcomes. It has helped us to understand that even observing an experiment means we are in some way influencing and changing the outcome. We need to understand that our thoughts, feelings and intentions are 'real' forces that have consequences. For those interested in understanding the role of intention in shaping our reality, look at the work of those from the past and present - you'll be spoilt for choice. See the work of Einstein, Sheldrake, Confucius, Dyer, Chopra, Lao Tzu and others.

So always ask your question with a sincere heart and patiently wait, your answer is guaranteed to turn up with the necessary clarification and direction for you… then you can set your ship to sail to the destination of your choice.

What else does the spirit need on this voyage of persuasion?

Altruism as a force for your personal transformation

What I will offer you in the following pages is a greater insight into some of the core needs of the spirit because once these are met, one easily finds the capacity to meet all its other needs.

A vital ingredient for achieving spiritual magnificence is generosity - better still, altruism. There are those who would say there is no such thing as true altruism because there will always be some reward in giving, whether it be adulation or praise or merely the joy and satisfaction that genuine giving brings. Although these can quite rightly be described as some form of gift or return for the giver, this calculation misses the point. Altruism is not about giving and not receiving a reward. In the cause and effect world that drives and underpins our experiences, this would be impossible as giving will always lead to receiving. I'm sure you've heard the biblical reference "As you sow, so shall you reap". This describes accurately the nature of all interaction on the planet. In Hinduism, Buddhism and within the eastern traditions generally, this principle is described as the law of karma and is seen as the overriding principle that equalizes the push and pull of life and in the end ensures that justice and order prevails. The first law of thermodynamics paints the same picture for the world of matter, "To every action there is an equal and opposite reaction". So altruism doesn't concern itself with the receipt of something because it knows it cannot do anything about that. Altruism is beautifully wedded to pure intention, for it knows that it is one's intention that truly categorizes one's action. It's not the outward appearance of what we do that matters, it's what is in our heart when we do what we do that counts.

Altruism is about giving without counting; it's about giving without concern for reward. Altruism knows reward in some form is inevitable but that in no way shapes its motivation. This is true generosity and benevolence and the spirit cannot be optimally well without it. So in order to be whole and truly well, find as many ways as you can to give without counting.

There is now a growing body of research taking place in the study of kindness, which has generated interest in a chemical messenger called oxytocin (see the work of Professor Paul Gilbert and Dr. David Hamilton). You will remember I spoke earlier of how quantum physics has helped us understand that the act of observing an experiment influences the outcome. I will explore this much more fully in the concluding chapters. This underlying principle has been further proven with the work done around the role of kindness in human interaction. It has been found that when kindness is involved in a transaction between two people, both the giver and receiver produce oxytocin. And what's also fascinating is that this effect (the release of oxytocin) is also experienced by anyone witnessing an act of kindness.

Oxytocin has many wonderful benefits on the body, it enhances mood, improves immune function, balances blood sugar, lowers blood pressure and regulates all the major systems of the body with its beautiful chemical fragrance. Such is the subtle power of a generous spirit. Here we see science catching up with the glaringly obvious that being generous and kind has benefits for us all! So why not pursue a life that will not only benefit you but all those around you too?

Forgiveness and gratitude

What else can you do to meet the needs of the spirit and persuade it to be all it can be? There are two contenders for the title in the contest of achieving personal growth way beyond your present belief – they are forgiveness and gratitude. In truth, they can't be separated – both have immeasurable impact on the self and offer a lifetime guarantee of continued growth. So if you want to claim the prize of positive change, get busy in these two areas and make time for both.

When we are unable to forgive, the energy of the self becomes stagnant. This has a negative impact on the mind and body. A spirit troubled by a lack of forgiveness sends a continuous stream of negative thoughts flowing through the mind, which in turn impacts on the neuronal pathways of the brain. The biochemical 'slurry' produced deposits its toxic waste ultimately into the veins, tissues and organs of the body. This stagnant stew keeps the individual stuck physically and mentally, poisoning perception and outlook. A lack of forgiveness has the opposite effect to kindness. Whereas kindness floods the body with oxytocin and other healing hormones, the lack of forgiveness poisons the body with substances such as cortisol and adrenochrome (which is the conversion of adrenalin in the body and is highly toxic). A lack of forgiveness is also able to lower seratonin levels, causing the person troubled by their inability to let go of pain, hurt or anger, to also become anxious or depressed. So there is at least a double tragedy in being unable or unwilling to forgive, as the person not only suffers from the initial event, but is also being slowly poisoned by his own thoughts and biochemistry.

Forgiveness is not primarily about the other person, who may indeed be suffering from their own cycle of pain, hurt, anger or fear, or in fact be in denial of their actions. Forgiveness is about you. When we are able to forgive ourselves and others, everything in our reality improves. Let's explore forgiveness further to illustrate what I mean.

Forgiveness sets you free

It would be a mistake to think that forgiveness is an easy path. For many it will prove the ultimate challenge because so often we cling desperately to our hurts and pains and to the 'righteous' anger associated with them. So the notion of forgiving someone when we have held so tightly to the belief that we are justified in feeling the way we do towards them is not always an easy position to renounce. However, a reluctance or in some cases refusal to forgive actually does more harm to the one who holds onto the anger and the pain. As previously stated, the individual is literally being poisoned with the chemical secretions generated by those mood states. We need to understand that our emotions are either healing or toxic in nature, so when we remain attached to any emotion that makes us feel bad, regardless of the reasons, there is a negative trickle-down of chemical messengers (hormones) from the brain, which pollutes and poisons the body. So not only does a lack of forgiveness poison the mind, it changes behaviour and perception and also contaminates the body. This is why forgiveness needs to be taken seriously as it really is one of the primary antidotes to pain, anger and regret.

It is as we learn to forgive that gratitude and appreciation grow. So, how do we go about the business of really forgiving? Since we cannot give what we do not have, the first thing we need to do is to forgive ourselves. In order to begin our journey of self-forgiveness we need to compile a list of all the things that we have done for which we would want to be forgiven. Once we have compiled that list, which may take several days of thoughtful reflection to complete, we then need to work systematically through the list using the wonderful tool of creative visualization and with a sincere heart, practise the art of 'making amends'.

To achieve this, take one or two things on your list each day, sit in solitude, either in silence or with some gentle music in the background. You may choose to light a candle, although this is not necessary, but to have a focal point of some kind is very helpful. Then using the eye of the mind, see as clearly as you can, the person whom your actions affected or damaged in some way, then, speak to them from the heart. It is important to underline that this has to be a 'heartfelt' activity - it is not an intellectual or mechanical process. Sincerity has to run through the very veins of this endeavour. Remember what was highlighted about intention earlier.

When undertaking this task, say all those things that need to be said and that have probably never been said or if they have, were not said in the right way. This is not a time for justification, or for making excuses for your position. It is a time for making amends. When you feel you have done that in a heartfelt way then bring that particular sitting to a close. (This may take ten to twenty minutes, or maybe longer. Let it unfold naturally).

It is important to remember that you may need to revisit a particular event and person more than once before the feeling of forgiveness in your heart has been achieved. This is a very powerful activity and if you work through your list in this way it will probably take several weeks if not longer to properly make amends for the things you feel you need forgiveness for. The more you do this activity from your heart, the more you will feel like a flower opening, able to spread your fragrance of gratitude in a way that hitherto had not seemed possible.

It might appear that this simple activity is not enough to truly cleanse your heart and mind but the continual evidence of my experience walking alongside those seeking self-improvement clearly demonstrates that it is. However, this is only the first phase in forgiveness because once you have done this you then need to repeat the exercise but this time your starting point is a list of those things that have been done to you. This will require you to give your forgiveness to those who have trespassed against you in some way.

When you truly have made amends within yourself, it is easy to offer the hand of forgiveness to another and when you do that you are able to connect with the very best in yourself. So why not try this exercise over the coming days, little and often. You'll be surprised how things begin to shift. Remember the quality of sincerity is the key.

When the spirit is emptied of the toxic waste accrued from a lack of forgiveness then gratitude comes more easily. It's not that gratitude should not be pursued at the same time as doing forgiveness work, because sometimes the focus on gratitude can speed up the letting go of the hurts of the heart. However, it is equally true that for some there is a block in their ability to be totally grateful until forgiveness work has been adequately pursued. This should come as no surprise because a lack of forgiveness negatively binds the individual to the event, people and feelings connected to what's hurting their heart. This literally creates a blockage in their pathways of consciousness. How can good thoughts and feelings truly prosper in a toxic mind? How can we see the best in ourselves, others and life when our perception has been stained? Remember that until we do something to expand our consciousness, we only ever see the world through the eyes of our experience and opinions. This is a very limited way of looking at the world because it denies us far more than it offers us (this is explored more fully in Chapter 7 - The Three Aspects of Consciousness).

Gratitude coupled with forgiveness is the most effective way to expand your consciousness. I would ask you to not only reflect upon but to practise this worthy mantra – 'a mind full of gratitude has no room for complaint'. If I push away my negative thoughts and beliefs with an appreciative mind, the negative grip of complaint is weakened and the mind becomes healthy, strong and whole.

> *"All that we are is a result of what we have thought."*
> Buddha (563 BC – 483 BC)

From as far back as Buddha, some nearly five hundred years before Christ, it was understood that we become what we think.

The present day work in neuroscience keeps pointing us to this truth again and again (see the work of Nataraja, Greenfield, Pert, Ramachandran and Bolte). We are natural pharmacists and biochemists. With our minds, through our brains and bodies, we are able to carve out a destiny that is unimaginable. Gratitude will enable you to do this in a breathtaking way.

The power of thank you

Expressing feelings of despair and dissatisfaction are useful for one's personal growth as long as it is part of a constructive process. There is limited value in beating the drum of 'how bad everything is' and 'how if it were not for this or that our lives would be so much better'. All we really achieve from this kind of thinking is pollution and stagnation, which prevents growth. This way of being also means we do not see solutions because we spend too much time living in the problem. This magnifies the problem and extends its influence, which also disempowers us, creating a self-limiting prison for ourselves in the process.

It is within this prison that negative beliefs are born. A common sub-conscious belief, that limits so many of us, is that life seems to punish us and reward others, and there is very little we can do about it. This creates a victim consciousness which can be described as 'poor me' but this consciousness can only really be useful if it motivates change. If on the other hand we make this mind-set our home, never daring to venture beyond its walls then we slowly shrink under its influence. This is why taking responsibility for our lives is such a critical component in personal transformation.

The power of thank you is limitless, the more we find things to be thankful about - great and particularly small - then the more growth and well-being flood into our lives. The 'poor me' consciousness simply creates a culture of pessimism and negativity, a culture that overshadows our positive state of being. Whereas the vast vocabulary and the colourful language of thank you creates positivity and a real appreciation of things that are so easily overlooked.

Thank you helps us to savour life and find beauty and truth; it helps us discover our true nature, abilities and talents. Thank you stokes the fire of creativity and introduces us to higher levels of awareness and consciousness. The thank you process motivates us to act because the appreciation that it produces gives us real power. It is a power that inspires, a power that rejoices more and complains less, a power that realizes our lives are dictated most of all by the thoughts we generate in our own minds.

The power of thank you is not an attack on the self-pitying consciousness because self-pity does have a place. The power of thank you is about understanding one way to move out of self-pity and victimhood. It is about realizing that whatever the state of our lives, we do have the power and ability to influence things positively. We do not have to wait for chance, or some miracle to bring change to our circumstances, we can create our own miracles by being more thankful.

Starting from today create some thank you statements. Take a close look at your life and find at least half a dozen things you take for granted, or overlook and never really consider the value and importance of. Then make these thank you statements into affirmations that you can recite throughout the day, particularly before you go to sleep at night and before you get out of bed in the morning. By reciting these thank yous at least twice a day meaningful growth will start appearing in your life and that growth will eventually bear good fruit.

The power of thank you is particularly valuable in the face of life's challenges and if we can find something to be grateful for, something that can be celebrated, we can and do move forward more quickly taking necessary lessons and insights with us. Practice, patience and perseverance guarantee success. So try saying thank you more and watch a different perspective, attitude and set of values and beliefs begin to unfold which will serve to free you from your self-limiting prison.

Below are a few examples to help you on your way, but remember that the more you can personalize these statements, making them relevant to you and your life, the better.

Thank you for the gift of my enemies and for the opportunities to develop forgiveness and kindness.

Thank you for the gift of this moment, as it allows me to fully blossom into the best I can be.

Thank you for the gift of my friendships and for the love and support that they bring.

Thank you for the gift of my challenges, for the insight, growth and wisdom that they offer.

Thank you for the gift of each day and the opportunity for greater peace, joy and happiness.

Thank you for the gift of my body and the countless wonders it performs each day.

Thank you for the gift of a life in which I can serve and benefit others with no desire for myself.

Thank you for the gift of sleep and for the renovation and repair that takes place each night.

Thank you for the gift of tomorrow which, when I allow it to, always adds value and meaning to my life.

Thank you for the gift of silent reflection that offers the unravelling of the mind's many mysteries.

Thank you for the gift of the inner wisdom that lives deep within my heart.

Thank you for the gift of nature in all her wonderful guises and magnificent forms; she's amazing!

Thank you for the gift of my life and the opportunity that each day brings for positive change.

Thank you for the gift of my family, who offer me the chance to develop patience and unconditional love.

This is in no way a definitive list because it hasn't included many of the things we take for granted – the warmth of our beds, our next glass of water, the food on our table, the roof over our heads and those many things that support our lives which we barely give any recognition to. So remember to include these too and the other things you take for granted.

Here's another example of how we can engrave the invaluable benefits of appreciation on our hearts and minds.

An attitude of gratitude

Try this thought out for size: 'My life is perfect. I have everything that I need and I am truly grateful'. Spend a day reciting this thought in your mind over and over again. If it helps, write it down again and again. Just try for twenty-four hours to truly embrace this thought and see what happens. If there's even the slightest improvement in your day or how you feel, make a deal with yourself to do it for another day. And why not keep doing this whilst it continues to work for you?

By now I am sure it will be clear that I passionately believe well-being is a healthy marriage between mind, body, spirit and environment. It's a beautiful dance between all four, where each performs its role gracefully and harmoniously. It's a wonderful contract of interdependence where each aspect performs its function with respect for itself and for the whole organism. In other words, health is a state of non-rivalry. Therefore, anything we do that spoils the dance and corrupts or contaminates the relationships, denies us health and well-being. Complaining does just that. The more we complain, the more we have to complain about. The more we give thanks, the more we will have to be grateful for. This is so simple and in many ways obvious and yet the depth and power of this principle is still not fully understood.

Complaining has many forms. It is not simply the act of 'wittering on' or grumbling to yourself and others. That's the obvious expression of complaint. To complain also means being frustrated with your life, being dissatisfied with your relationships, doubting yourself, your talents and abilities. It's a life of comparing and competing, striving to mask your deficiencies and shortcomings; a life of overcompensating in order to be liked and to fit in. It's a turbulent river of dissatisfaction that runs through the landscape of your life. It eats away at you, telling you you're not good enough, that what you have is not good enough and it propels you to pursue things you don't need, to make you feel better about yourself and your reality. Can you relate to this? Are you complaining and haven't even realized? My clinical experience clearly shows that most people are complaining in some form. They simply aren't aware of it. Why not take a closer look at your life and note how much you pretend, defend, justify and deny (these are just some of the offspring of complaining). Why not stop and check right now how much these habits are dominating your inner landscape.

Take up my challenge. Develop the habit of 'thank you'. An attitude of gratitude will completely change your perception and perspective. Just as a culture of complaint has bent you out of shape by distorting your true nature, the practice of 'thank you' will not only restore your beauty, but will attract everything you need into your life.

Complaining takes you further away from yourself and the truth, whilst 'thank you' brings you into a loving embrace with your purpose and potential. In other words, you stop living as a passenger in your own life, wondering which way the vehicle will take you next. Instead you move into the driver's seat with confidence in what you need to do and where you need to go. It's so satisfying.

So I implore you again to try this thought, 'My life is perfect, I have exactly what I need and for that I am truly grateful'. Even though your life may not be perfect and may not be exactly as you wish it to be right now, by daring to think in this way, you are positively affecting both your psychology and biology. You are what you think you are. Your perceptions and your beliefs do shape your reality.

Find things to be grateful for every day and things to be grateful for will come and find you! The laws of cause and effect relate to everything in our world, so try sending out the right signals and watch the inevitable return of your preferred outcomes (your dreams). This one act will save your life if you let it. Practise the power of thank you faithfully. It has untold depths and it never disappoints.

A life of thank you is a rich and full life. It's kind to you and those around you. It's full of smiles and laughter where a gentle river of insight flows continuously through the mind, touching every cell and sinew. A life of gratitude soothes hurts and pain, evaporates anger and reframes your perspective. If you do one thing today, let it be to say thank you with all your heart.

By applying the principles of both forgiveness and gratitude, as described here, the spirit will be able to take that wonderful journey of personal transformation. Let go of the anger, hurts and bitterness and let in peace, harmony and joy. 'Let go and let in'.

Forgive and give thanks because this is the foundation of your redemption and happiness.

Gratitude bestows reverence, allowing us to encounter everyday epiphanies, those transcendent moments of awe that change forever how we experience life and the world."

John Milton (1608 – 1674)

CHAPTER 3: PERSUADING THE MIND

"Nothing strengthens authority so much as silence."
Leonardo da Vinci (1452 – 1519)

The sacred contract

It is important to state that there is no 'right' order in the task of persuasion. For health to be achieved and then sustained, mind, body and spirit must all have their needs met equally and the necessary adjustments must be made to the environment to facilitate and maintain the 'sacred contract' between the three. Remember, that until the needs of each are adequately met they will continue to compete rather than collaborate, as each will act in its own self-interest. This is why persuading all three to move towards synergy (their natural and optimal position) is the answer.

So how do we persuade the mind? As previously stated, the mind is magical, mysterious and awesomely powerful. It needs a diet of positive, self-nurturing activities to fulfill its potential. It also needs a clear mission (vision) statement. The mind abhors confusion as it stifles its potential and obscures its purpose. As you become more familiar with The Story of Health, it will become increasingly clear that although I speak of the mind and spirit in separate and distinct ways, they are closely and intimately linked. What affects one undoubtedly affects the other. What is true for one is, albeit in a subtly different way, true for the other one too. For example, take my earlier description of the spirit in relation to forgiveness and gratitude, it could appear contradictory to say the mind also needs this activity to create an energetic shift, but it does. The mind needs forgiveness and gratitude too because anything that hurts the spirit blocks the pathways of consciousness. In other words the mind cannot actualize its potential when a lack of forgiveness leads to it operating from a place of deficiency. As soon as a journey of forgiveness is embarked upon both spirit and mind become free, and of course the body too.

The mind is the aspect of the self that drives one's energy and potential, always striving to reach the highest point. It is also that aspect of the self that when not positively fed, or is bound by toxic influences, can hold the rest of the self hostage, which in turn brings the spirit to its knees. The spirit on the other hand is the 'experiencer', that aspect that absorbs life and adjusts itself accordingly. It is left with the net result of its experiences and, depending on the internal position it holds, it is either able to transcend those experiences or unfortunately becomes subordinate to them. The mind is critical in assisting the spirit, which is why it is difficult to talk about the one without referring to the other. I will explore the anatomy of consciousness further in chapter 7.

There are many areas of overlap in the mind-body-spirit-environment system. It is in fact somewhat artificial to speak about the four aspects as if each occupies its own compartment, as they are naturally interconnected and there is also some degree of duplication. However, in the disease state they strive for autonomy and 'act out' as individual forces. But in spite of their connectedness, it is helpful to understand their individual characteristics, for this does help us to discover and highlight what links them so intrinsically. It also offers us insight into their needs and helps us to better meet them, which is how health and well-being are achieved.

So now we understand that forgiveness and the pursuit of gratitude are also essential to the elevation of the mind, in order that the streams of consciousness can flow unhindered. Let's look at what else is pivotal to ensuring the mind becomes and remains an ally to our cause.

The value of silence

Meditation or stillness and solitude of some kind are imperative not only to ensure growth, but more importantly to make contact with one's 'essence', one's true self. This is another place where a deep subtle connection between mind and spirit exists. It's essential for the spirit to remain true to itself, which I call 'honouring the heart', but this is best facilitated via the mind. By taking the mind down a path of introspection, reflection and contemplation, the spirit moves closer to the truth about itself and what's really important.

This is one of the reasons meditation, or some other introspective activity, is vital for the mind to help the spirit realize its potential and find its purpose. It is the silence that comes through stillness and the 'inward looking-ness' of these activities that feeds the mind. The hyperactivity of the mind, which has tremendous value when chanelled, is counterproductive to growth if there is never any respite from it. The mind is an incredible energy system and although for the creative process to take place there needs to be intense periods of combustion, in order that this combustion isn't rapidly followed by exhaustion, energy conservation is vital. Hence the need for meditation, still time, prayer or some other introspective practice.

If you are interested in pursuing introspective practices, you are spoilt for choice. There is a vast array in the area of meditation alone. There is now also a rapidly growing movement under the banner of mindfulness. Both these activities have been around for thousands of years although they have been in some cases 'modernised'. I would also encourage practices such as still-time, creative visualization, invocation and prayer (subject to your faith). For more suggestions see www.thereachapproach.co.uk and take a look at the Healing Habits and Resources pages. Whatever you choose a good place to start is simply practising 'listening in'.

To understand what I mean by this read the following extract and subsequent exercise and begin to practise this beautiful art.

Listening-in

The journey of personal growth depends on listening. Listening is the critical ingredient in the positive change process; without it we simply remain stuck in the very things we are desperate to leave behind. If, despite your best efforts, you keep going round the same loop, and continue to be bullied by old familiar habits, patterns and moods, then there is 'something' missing. There is 'something' you haven't seen, heard or understood and until you find out what that is you will remain frustrated and trapped. It is generally at this point we look to blame other things, or people for our predicament, but the truth is usually found in the mirror – that is, in you! Although you may find some temporary comfort and relief in the game of blame, all you really achieve is inertia, as you are unable to move away from all that holds you back.

Blame is a mirage that promises you much but in the end provides you with an illusion because none of your answers and solutions will ever be found in that place. Look closely at your life and be really honest with yourself and you'll see blame is an excuse that distracts you from the real problem, which lives within you. You will find under closer scrutiny that the real problem lies somewhere in your shame, fear, doubt, anger, guilt, pain and resentment. In order to respond to what's really going on and discover what's missing, the journey needs to begin with listening. Sadly this is a journey few have taken. Ask yourself this question, "am I really listening or simply waiting to speak?" If you're honest, far too often you're simply waiting to speak – you're waiting for your turn because it's when you next speak 'they' are bound to understand that you're indeed right!

If you look even closer you'll begin to see that most of your conversations are actually with your own assumptions and projections; you're not even able to hear the other person because you're too busy listening to your own internal dialogue. It's this absence of listening that most keeps you stuck. Not only do you not hear what is being offered from the outside world, but even worse you are unable to hear the whisperings of your own heart. This 'waiting to speak' is a destructive habit that is largely a defence mechanism. It is either driven by your desperation to be right or your fear of being found out. Essentially it is about fear and shame.

'Listening-in' requires finding time regularly to sit in solitude, even five or ten minutes will do, but it must be regular otherwise you simply won't develop the rapport with yourself. Listening to what is going on in your inner world, then decoding and understanding its many messages takes time. So sit often, but without expectation. This is critical. Listening has no expectation, it's too busy absorbing what it can hear, even if it's only silence – for it knows even silence has a language all of its own. The more you practise sitting and listening to your mind, heart and body the more you will make 'conscious contact' with yourself. When there is conscious contact your body will tell you what its needs are. In fact it's doing this all the time but if you check carefully, you'll find that you're rarely paying attention. And yet the body continues to patiently work in your best interests. If you could hear your body's cries, you would support it and work with it rather than against it. Your heart (feelings) offers an unlimited set of insights, a 'knowing' beyond the limitations of logic and yet you ignore its cries too. Your heart is your best internal guidance system, it's like a compass pointing you in the right direction, but without learning to listen you'll rarely hear what it advises. The mind is a powerhouse of potential and opportunity; it hungrily feeds off knowledge in an attempt to fuel its hopes and endeavours. The mind is, as I've said, a magician ready to disclose its secrets but without the practice of 'listening-in' we become confused because we don't know which of our thoughts to trust. But if you sit still and really connect to the moment, your heart will reveal its secrets to you.

Listening-in recognizes that what we know, by itself, will never free us. It's what we do that counts. Doing what needs to be done comes from the power of realization. Knowing is to have the information within your grasp and therefore the possibility of change, whereas realization is to understand the deep significance of that information and to apply its meaning to your own life. So to know means very little but to realize means everything. Realization depends on both listening to the world and 'listening-in' to the sounds of the heart and mind. This takes practice.

Find five to ten minutes every day, or at least every other day, to sit with the question, "dearest heart and mind, what more is there for me to see, understand and learn?" Let this question gently resonate inside you. Don't force it; be patient and keep reciting it every minute or so. Don't be concerned about getting answers, they will come in their own time. Let your concern be to give yourself this gift of listening-in. You could also say, "dearest heart and mind, probably for the first time I'm really listening, I'm not afraid or unwilling to hear your secrets, so please tell me what I need to know". Practise this simple drill and you'll find 'listening-in' will also enhance your 'listening-out', which in turn will deepen your insights and reveal even more secrets; it's a beautiful, eternal loop.

Here's another wonderful example of listening-in that I use in my work. I call it Old Friend, Dear Friend. See if it appeals to you. Firstly, read the brief introduction, followed by the guided commentary

Progress is such a paradoxical process. Just as we think we may have cracked it or tamed the beast of adversity another challenge comes and questions our beliefs, our focus and resolve. Before we know it we're on our backs again, looking up at the sky wondering how our 'best' efforts have brought us back to this point?

If only we would accept that relapse is part of the growth process our journeys would be made so much easier. Relapse does not come to harm us; it offers us deeper understanding and further insight. In fact every relapse is a gift, it's simply a matter of perception. I invite you to try a new approach. The next time you find yourself standing in the old and familiar, surrounded by the unpleasant odour of that which you would rather leave behind, rather than sighing in disgust and sitting in that seat of defeat and victimhood, try changing your thoughts in this way....

Old friend, dear friend what have you come to teach me? ... I've been so busy 'doing' that I haven't really been listening... I've only just begun to realise that personal growth starts with listening... I promise from today to really listen... I know you have a message for me if only I'd be still long enough to hear your sweet words... I've been so consumed with the challenges I face that I've fallen into the trap of becoming a victim... But no more... I'm tired of contributing to my own demise... generating my own confusion because I'm too busy 'doing' rather than 'being'... I'm beginning to understand that the ultimate in doing is to 'be', that 'being' is the most beautiful act I can perform and it's time to do just that... It's time to be... Old friend, dear friend, what have you come to teach me?... Probably for the first time I'm really listening... Please whisper your sweet truths into my welcoming heart and mind...

This is not a script that you're expected to learn and recite, it's merely a template, illustrating how you can set up such a dialogue with yourself. You will find your own words, words that best express your sentiments. Try to 'feel' your way through this kind of dialogue; it's not meant to be a well-constructed speech, it's an expression of the heart.

Every experience affords you the opportunity to grow. Often what may be deemed to be the worst of these experiences offers you the greatest learning. And so, if you set up a dialogue between your mind and whatever experiences you may be facing as illustrated above, magical insights begin to unfold. You need to be patient though; it often takes time for these insights to fully blossom, but blossom they will. Do not fear relapses; embrace each one as an old friend bringing you priceless gifts. Sit with that old friend and keenly ask what gifts have they brought this time. Offer your time, attention and appreciation. Most of all ask what lesson(s) do you still have to learn and listen with all of you. Your insights and personal revelations, as I said before, will come to you in many forms, such as: dreams, reading inspirational material, a seemingly unrelated conversation, listening to or watching a play, a sporting achievement, or something else that moves you. Whatever form it takes, if you're listening you'll recognise it when it turns up. When it does turn up remember to always give thanks.

Try this approach and you will see how quickly your perception shifts. Your world will make more sense and rather than being a slave to events you'll slowly become a master. This is an easy way to create humility. Ego is so busy battling and defending itself it simply isn't able to recognise the truth. Humility, on the other hand, is a place of openness, eternal learning; its love for truth means all mysteries eventually unveil themselves without even being asked.

Choose humility and you'll find you are choosing clarity, peace and wisdom. Remember when you're next struggling with uncertainty, pain, or feeling confused, staring into a life that seems to have little meaning, have the thought: "Old friend, dear friend what have you come to teach me?"… and really listen.

Listening-out?

Listening is a quiet, gentle, attentive skill. The more you practise it the more it becomes an art which enables you to see life with all its depth and subtleties. Listening makes the complex simple, it makes the unknown visible, and it explains the 'un-said', leaving no mystery unresolved. Listening offers you the 'gift of truth' but it requires your patience and attention. Without these it will not offer up its countless revelations and secrets.

'Listening-out' is the willingness to hear what the world is saying to you. Much more can be learned by listening and then cross-referencing what you hear with the sounds of your own heart and mind. It is not possible for one person to experience everything in one lifetime but it is possible to 'understand' everything in your lifetime if there is sufficient humility.

Humility is not a weak and submissive virtue, it offers you real power, incredible depth and the keys to wisdom. The kind of wisdom that takes a three hundred and sixty degree look at one's self and reality. It's the willingness to listen to what life and others are really saying that gives you access to all you need to know. Humility does not need to be right, in fact it is so obsessed with truth it doesn't concern itself with needing to be right, or with the fear of getting it wrong and even looking silly. Humility knows that denial, justification and generating smoke screens to conceal the self are a prison that never offers parole.

So free yourself by 'listening-out'. There is so much to learn and your journey can't really begin until you do. It must be also said that 'listening-out' without 'listening-in' will eventually lead you down blind alleys and crooked paths. You must have both practices sitting side by side. One who only 'listens-out' will never develop the discrimination to know what should be embraced and what should be discarded. Without discrimination you will be deceived, manipulated and lose your own identity in order to fit into a world that demands constant change from you. The fact is, that as necessary and valuable as 'listening-out' is, it must be balanced with 'listening in' to ensure you don't lose your way.

For the sake of balance and clarity it should also be said that if we only listen-in we can also be deceived. To only 'listen-in' can mean we become trapped in believing those things we've inherited which have lived in our minds for so long that we've come to believe them. What you believe, you make true, so don't fall into the lethal trap of simply believing your thoughts. 'Listening-in', as well as 'out', enables you to properly vet the heart and mind and discern what's real and true from what is fake and habitual. Both kinds of listening will free you from this prison of limitation, ignorance and victimhood. All that is needed is practice, little and often, and your life will open up in ways you couldn't even have imagined.

When there is a balance between creation and conservation the on-going health of the mind is guaranteed. This is why the mind needs stimulation but also relaxation if it is to deliver its best. Under those circumstances it is able to find the clarity and focus it needs to fulfil its potential. When the mind moves in a rudderless way, there is great expenditure of energy and very little to show for it. It is at these times that the individual speaks of being depressed, anxious, lacking direction, feeling lethargic, temperamental, angry or confused. In fact, the beginnings of neurosis are often conceived in this phase and if left unattended, can easily become psychosis.

The primary difference between neurosis and psychosis is that someone who is neurotic 'knows' they are out of control and feels unable to do anything about it and will often seek help for their condition. Someone who is psychotic doesn't 'know' that they have lost their way and has become subservient to negative drives and patterns. Furthermore, they can reach a point where they believe it is everyone else who has 'lost the plot' as they alone remain the true bastions of sanity.

This is why I would enthusiastically encourage you to come up with your own personal mission (vision) statement because it's the rudderless mind that moves unwittingly towards neurosis and psychosis. In my work I call it a personal prayer but you can call it what you like. The name isn't important, it is its purpose that matters. I've found this approach extremely powerful when working with children, particularly those with behavioural issues. It also works beautifully with those struggling to find value and meaning in their lives. When I've used it in groups the creative energy, reciprocation and countless suggestions that come out of the 'womb' of many minds focused in one direction is such a joy to behold too. So I highly recommend you create a personal prayer that best suits you.

Personal prayer – your own mission statement

A prayer is a composition of words directed to the Divine, which could be God, a Deity or some other object of reverence or worship. In this context, however, the composition of words that you are invited to create is directed to the part of you that is divine.

The journey from pain to power is a journey based on the understanding that despite your current experience and challenges, no matter how difficult life might be or how insurmountable things may seem, there is a part of you that remains untainted and free from the damage and distortion that life might have inflicted on you. That untainted part is your divinity, your essence and the whole point to the journey of personal empowerment is to enable you to reclaim it. Composing a personal prayer is one of the most effective ways to unleash what currently lies dormant within and is in need of expression.

A personal prayer speaks to the subconscious mind, the power-house. This is the part of the self that is busy driving your affairs based on the beliefs you hold about yourself. Generally what you believe about yourself is bound up in your history and your life experiences. These beliefs are often flawed because they are a mixture of your own perceptions and the perceptions that others have of you. Within that mixed bag of consciousness, there is often no clear sense of self, or at best there exists a contradictory position where you think of yourself as one thing in one moment and in the next as something else. This ambiguity simply serves to dilute who you are, robbing you of clarity, stability, peace and balance.

The subconscious mind is like the crew on a ship, ready and waiting to take instructions from the captain (the conscious mind). If the captain is lying drunk on the bridge, confused about which route to take, then the crew has to act without supervision and guidance, which inevitably leads to chaos. So, for example you may well have half the crew wanting to take the ship in one direction and the other half wanting to go the other way. The consequence is either the ship goes round in circles or is split in half! Either way the destination is never reached. So you need to give your sub-conscious mind (the crew) a clear map, with a clear set of instructions, which will allow it to support you in your endeavours to reach your desired destination.

It is important to understand when composing your prayer that your motivation is pivotal in determining the outcome. In other words, the reason(s) for your invocation has the biggest influence in determining the end product. The more you want what is in your heart for the right reasons the more your ambition and vision will materialise in your life. What is meant by the right reason(s)? Simply, it's to want something without causing harm to another. It's to pursue a goal not driven by the force of selfishness. To be selfish is to pursue whatever is in your heart without care or concern for others - a motivation (drive) that will quite happily walk over others in the name of its attainment.

Selfishness will happily justify any action it takes in order to achieve its objectives. These are not the right reasons. Of course there will be a 'sense of self' driving what is in our hearts but that 'sense of self' (meeting one's own needs) should not cost someone else anything at all. One cannot build happiness on other people's misery. This could be likened to building a house on sand. Sooner or later it will collapse. So if your motivations are not right it will be very difficult, even if you attain your heart's desire, to sustain it. Pursue what's in your heart with self-respect, self-esteem and self-confidence, but also maintain a social conscience. Nothing is worth attaining if it overlooks one's fellow human beings and causes them sadness, misery or pain.

Find some time when you can sit and reflect on your heartfelt desires and aspirations. Pull together the things you most wish for and compose a prayer that would take about two to four minutes to read aloud. Do not write the prayer as a hope, a wish or a desire but write it as if this is already your reality. It needs to be composed with a sense of certainty enshrined in every line. For the sub-conscious mind to co-operate with you in your endeavour it needs language that is clear and determined. The sub-conscious mind is one of the most powerful forces on earth and like a magnet, it will pull into your personal orbit that which you focus upon. It is the intensity of your focus and the purity of your intention that will most influence the outcome. A quiet stream of determination needs to flow through your mind, combined with a repetitive focus on what you want and need in your life in order to feel complete and content.

Once you've composed your personal prayer, it is something you need to read at least two or three times a day, which given its length is, in reality, a small commitment of some six to twelve minutes per day. So listen to your heart and compose those words that best relate to the needs of the divine part of you and you will see that out of your pain comes the joy of personal power.

A prayer for all occasions

The power of personal prayer should not be underestimated. To feed the subconscious mind consistently and clearly with elevated instructions that match your heart's deepest desires is probably the greatest gift you can give to yourself. The more you become the captain of your ship, giving clear, precise instructions to the crew, the more your authority will be respected, understood and adhered to. The subconscious mind aches for positive instructions but when there is a void or a vacuum, familiarity, habit and old past patterns will rush in to fill that void. "Nature abhors a vacuum", and we need to realize we are working with the laws of nature. If we sow good seeds and nurture them they will bear good fruit. So make your personal prayer part of your everyday life. Don't see it as a chore to be executed but as a wonderful opportunity to create peace, clarity and joy in your life. Give yourself the gift of a personal prayer every single day and watch how quickly your life changes direction as the crew (your subconscious mind) acts in your very best interests, manufacturing what you desire and aspire to.

Although there may only be one single prayer that embraces everything within your heart and could be described as your mission/vision statement, or Mother Prayer, there can be some value in having a number of prayers.

So you may choose to have a prayer that only focuses on the nature and quality of your relationships or the direction of your career or work, or a prayer that deals with how your personal life interfaces with your social life. In fact you can compose a prayer around any aspect of the self, your life or what's happening in the world. So if you prefer to have more than one prayer that embraces everything I would recommend in addition to your Mother Prayer that you develop a few more (three or four is sufficient) to deal with other aspects of the self and your life. But remember, let your prayers invoke a better life for us all.

For what you give out will come back and find you, so through your personal prayer invoke the very best for yourself and the world.

Start today by thinking about aspects of your life you want to change, how you can improve your key relationships and what contribution you could make to the atmosphere of the world to make it a better place. Compose your prayers from your heart and recite them daily, then both self-transformation and well-being will come and sit comfortably alongside you.

A personal prayer introduces you to the 'meditational mind', it slows you down and focuses your energy on what really matters and as a result, gives you access to your 'unlimitedness'

"In meditation it is possible to dive deeper into the mind, to a place where there is no disturbance and there is absolute solitude. It is at this point in the profound stillness that the sound of the mind can be heard."
A.E.I. Falconer (1926 - present)

A meditational mind is unwavering and uncompromising in its pursuit of peace, balance and harmony because it understands that you can't give what you haven't got. So if the mind continues to overtrade, it cannot from a position of negative equity ever reach its destination. This is why forgiveness and gratitude, a clear mission statement and the refuelling power of introspective practices are imperative for positive change.

However to sustain these and other good practices a set of non-negotiables is needed. These are antidotes to your bad habits and undesirable tendencies. Experience has taught me that if you don't come up with a set of your own non-negotiables positive change is unlikely to occur, and even if it is achieved it will be unsustainable. For those of you looking for a formula that works, marrying The Story of Health to Non-Negotiables is that formula. The Story of Health demands mind, body, spirit and environment are all equally tended to. A set of non-negotiables is the method by which this is achieved.

Non-negotiables - the way forward

The current climate of personal development and uplifting of the human spirit seems to be offering a plethora of magical solutions. The fact that more and more of us are beginning to look inside rather than outside for our solutions is wonderful. Unless we turn within we will continue to be run ragged by the rat race of the twenty first century. Most of our answers are to be found in inner space, not outer space.

Unfortunately, the expansion of consciousness that is unquestionably taking place has also brought with it a worrying trend, which is the idea that little effort is required in order to achieve our goals. The growing culture of concepts that appear to offer a 'quick fix' is worrying, as they seem to suggest that anything that doesn't generate results quickly should somehow be viewed with some skepticism. Although, undoubtedly for some people and for some issues, there can be a quick fix, I believe that the idea that all problems regardless of their origins can be resolved with a few simple 'techniques' laughs mockingly in the face of wisdom.

The quick fix culture is a symptom of our 'immediate' society - everything has to be delivered now! This immediate expectation that hovers in the air is increasingly being practised in all walks of life but at what price? My experience and belief is that quality, conscience, compassion and humanity are withering on the vine of 'I must have it now'. So much therapy, especially since the beginning of this century, has bent itself out of shape to fit in with this demand of modern life.

This is not an advert or a promotion for long-term therapeutic work or strategies. On the contrary, it's a request to work with nature and time and not against them. Personal development and therapeutic work, whatever its complexion, ought to follow the rule, 'it takes as long as it takes'. There is no official end date that is agreed at the start and must be met by any means necessary. This approach to complete things according to a method rather than the method fitting the person does a lot of damage. It leaves individuals feeling they have failed when they can't fit into the structure and specifications they've been given.

It's time to understand that if we do want sustainable solutions that work tirelessly for our well-being then we need a set of non-negotiables. Non-negotiables are those activities that create health. They are 'life-givers'. They serve up health again and again. If we would only worship at their altar, all our prayers would be answered. In essence, the four key areas (mind, body, spirit and environment) need equal attention and we need to create a set of non-negotiables for each of these areas. These non-negotiables are promises to ourselves, promises we do not break because they guarantee us stability, peace and happiness, whatever our life serves up.

It's time to realize quick fixes rarely last. The solutions are more often found in lifelong pledges to the self, underpinned by activities that travel and grow with you, adapting along the way to meet your needs. There are many such activities, like creative visualization, focusing with faith, personal prayer, forgiveness and gratitude, the power of thank you, just to name a few. I have already touched on some of these, and will return to them and much more as we continue.

So take some time now to look at your life; where are you going wrong? What's missing? What could you do differently or better? As the answers become clear, formulate a strategy that addresses the deficiencies you uncover and put in place those things that will help rebuild your life. It's time to make a deal with your heart - it's time to be 'non-negotiating' in your pursuit of happiness.

With your chosen non-negotiables firmly in place, a voyage of certainty awaits you. Certainty doesn't mean a voyage without challenge, because challenge in its various guises is certain. Certainty means that, regardless of what life presents you with, you'll always be equal to it. It requires courage and faith, it is a life imbued with integrity. A beautiful quote that has kept me safe and strong on many occasions springs to mind.

"The boat of truth may rock and shake but it will never sink"
Dada Lekhraj (1876 – 1969)

I think this quote offers a mantra for life and certainly is a principle that underpins my own life. It has provided me with much comfort in my own hours of need – which have been many. And I would encourage you to really embrace it too.

The following extract describes how I've incorporated this principle of truth into my work - see if it appeals to you. If so, find a way to incorporate it into your life as it will certainly help your mind fulfill its potential.

The only destination is right action

Our obsession with the destination has blinded us from the truth. We are so attached to the 'outcome' that there are very few rules we won't break in order to achieve that desired outcome. We have sadly reached the point where we readily silence our conscience and compromise our own values and principles just so we can win and claim the prize. But is this winning? If, in order to cross the line, we have had to trade away a little bit of ourselves, have we really won? Of course the answer is no.

How can it be of benefit to surround oneself with kudos, status, material possessions and those things that our modern world holds dear, if in doing so the ultimate prize, 'an awakened self', has been lost? There is no attainment that can even begin to equal the 'awakened self'. So ask yourself what destination are you heading towards; is it even a place you want to be? Will it really make you happy and content? Will it give you clarity and peace of mind? The 'awakened self' offers you this and so much more.

People who are 'awake' do not blindly pursue the 'trappings' of the material world. They are not averse to money, possessions, status, etc; they simply are busy pursuing other things. Their focus is on living ethically; they are concerned with values and principles. If as a consequence of this approach, wealth, possessions and status emerge then they will happily accept these things without ever allowing them to become a focus in their lives. They understand that to do this is to give away the most precious of gifts - the self.

True happiness and wealth are not found in things, they are found in treasuring and nurturing oneself. The more we cultivate our inner landscape the more abundant its harvest will be. The 'things' that matter the most will then bear splendid fruits. The fruits are the gifts, talents and qualities we already have that simply need our attention and love to grow. Instead they are left to go rotten on the vine because they are rarely picked, as we are so busy chasing the wrong 'things'. It's time to wake up. An 'awakened self' knows the only destination worth pursuing is 'doing the right thing' because then the outcome takes care of itself. In fact the desired outcome comes and finds us.

What follows next may appear to be a contradiction - as the truth often appears paradoxical - but on closer inspection you will come to understand the depth of its message. Here's the paradox - whilst it is important to focus on 'doing the right thing' and not on the destination it is equally important to know where you are going. If you don't know where you are going you are unlikely to get there. So on the one hand I am asking you to not be attached to the outcome and not be a 'destination junkie' and on the other hand I am also saying the destination does matter and you need to have a clear vision of it. So which is it? Actually it is both.

Both requests do quite comfortably co-exist. It is imperative to have a sense of where we are going so you can point your efforts and actions in the right direction. Once you have a clear vision of where you're going, you need to turn your attention to what's required to get there. Here comes another twist - if part of that 'getting there' requires you to regularly visualize being 'there', isn't that being a 'destination junkie', continually focusing on the goal? Isn't that being attached to the outcome? Yes it is but this is a destination you want to be attached to; more accurately, you need to be fully focused on. This is not a focus that takes you away from the self or from those things that really matter. The prize on offer here is clarity, peace, love, happiness, personal power and much more. As you peel back the layers you will see there is not really a contradiction here at all, there are simply different layers of understanding that you need to become aware of and appreciate. Practise being still often and quietly reflect on this conundrum and it will all become clear.

The only destination is 'right action' and 'right action' means to focus on the 'right things' and to do what is necessary to make 'conscious contact' both with yourself and your dreams. Be obsessive about this and the pointless messages of the modern world (i.e. acquire this, become that, you're incomplete until you have one etc.) will pass you by as you become ethically driven, morally focused and concerned only with right thought, word and action, for they are the ultimate prize.

I need to say that performing the right action does not mean taking up a punitive consciousness when we get things wrong. Mistakes are bound to be made on this journey and it's important, when they are, that we are kind to ourselves and we invite the lessons in. If we are to persuade the mind to be an ally to our personal transformation, then condemning ourselves for our mistakes will deny us its magic and potential. Being compassionate is not weakness as it allows us to see what we need to do to pursue the right course, whilst at the same time offering the hand of forgiveness, which allows the spirit to be free and the mind to function in healthy ways. Learning to live with this ambivalence is so wonderfully liberating.

As I said in the introduction, following the messenger and losing sight of the message is the mistake we have kept making throughout history. This mistake is still being made today, which is why the message of co-operation keeps being drowned out by the overpowering stampede of competition. Competition has a place and value but never at the expense of co-operation. This has been our collective blind spot. We need a new culture, one based on appreciation and gratitude, where we look for the best in ourselves and in each other. And then we need to hold hands in a spirit of co-operation and march forward together to create a better world. This is the real meaning and purpose that our spirit and mind ache for.

"The only true source of knowledge is experience."
Albert Einstein (1879 – 1955)

CHAPTER 4: PERSUADING THE BODY

"As I see it, every day you do one of two things: build health or produce disease in yourself."
Adelle Davis (1904 – 1974)

The first person

Often, the first 'person' you need to persuade in order to achieve and sustain self-transformation is your body. This is a very deep and, once understood, truly liberating concept. Describing the body as a person is simply a way of helping you to conceptualize the relationship between spirit, mind and body. Far too often the healing traditions compartmentalize the self in packages that are more convenient for their theories and ideologies but which bear little resemblance to the true story of the self. This is actually a story of fluid integration, a system where each aspect has its own particular role and whilst playing its part, intuitively understands its relationship to the whole organism. When understanding the self, there are no nice neat compartments with definite beginnings and endings. This is also true for the body. What you have are various systems that cannot and do not stand alone. For example, how would the endocrine system (responsible for the production of hormones) carry out its role without the digestive system to provide a nutrient and energy basis for it to function? How would the immune system (responsible for our biological defences) function if the lymphatic (detoxifying) system were not removing waste? In fact the more you look at the whole organism, the more you see that each system is completely dependent upon what the other systems of the body are doing.

The secret of health is the removal of waste

So much of modern/allopathic medicine is about 'putting something in' the body/system to rectify a problem. Sadly, alternative and complimentary medicine seems to be going down a similar path. Most healing modalities seem geared towards what we need to 'put in' to respond to the dysfunctions thrown up by the body (and equally the mind). There is a very serious flaw in this approach. In fact, the secret to health is the removal of waste. The primary mission in restoring health is firstly about taking things out of the system. If we understood the disease process we would see that nothing else makes sense. Let's examine this further.

The body is made up of approximately sixty trillion cells. Each day thirty billion dead cells are produced as a result of simply being alive. These cells are no longer efficient or useful and they create a large cell debris. They include nitrogen compounds, uric acid, lactic acid, sulphates, ammonia etc. Under normal conditions the lymph and the blood swiftly remove these materials from the fluid that surrounds the cells (the connective tissue). In addition to these excretions, which are the by-products of cell metabolism, the blood dumps blood plasma proteins into the connective tissue. These include albumens, globulins, fibrinogens and other regulatory proteins.

If these naturally occurring waste products and the blood proteins are not removed promptly, they build up in the body, eventually causing congestion. Once 'stored' waste has reached a certain threshold, it simply impairs the functions of the affected parts of the body. Amongst the organs undermined are the intestines, liver, kidneys, gall bladder, appendix and reproductive organs. Under these conditions, the body busily tries to restore health. It is important to understand that the body is always trying to restore health with all the materials it has at its disposal. The body is never really working against itself.

Once the build up of waste has reached a critical mass, the body employs oxygen free radicals, enzymes, fungi and even destructive bacteria to try and break down the mixture of dead cells and metabolic waste. It is also at this stage of what is the body's attempt to heal itself that the immune system becomes engaged trying to remove waste matter and other toxins as well as any weak and damaged cells. This response is commonly known as inflammatory disease. However, if you understand that the body is always trying to make the best of the situation, given the resources available to it, you begin to see that what we generally are referring to as diseases are in fact the body's attempts to survive the onslaught of waste. Both inflammation and infection are not strictly diseases. They are really part of the body's first line of defence.

Various organs and systems in the body are designed to deal efficiently with the daily waste products. So disease is often conceived out of some obstruction to these organs performing their tasks. Here are some of the miracles our bodies perform each day in an attempt to keep us free from waste:

The liver breaks down cellular components and detoxifies drugs, alcohol and various noxious substances.

The lungs remove the highly acidic metabolic waste product carbon dioxide and other toxic gases.

The kidneys and bladder remove excessive blood plasma as well as uric acid, ammonia and other waste matter delivered by the liver.

The colon excretes faecal matter, mucus, dead bacteria and parasites.

The hair and nails remove proteins, excessive mineral salts, pigments and oil.

The skin through sweating eliminates 40-60% of all waste in the body.

The lymphatic system is continuously patrolling the body, dealing with the waste loaded lymph fluid, which is a key player in the detoxification process.

This is just a small insight into the countless tasks the body is performing moment by moment and it is when these tasks are undermined in any way that our health becomes compromised.

For these invaluable activities to take place, we need copious amounts of water. The greatest enemy to the body is dehydration. When the body becomes dehydrated, the blood becomes thickened. To try and compensate for this the blood will attempt to draw water from nearby cells. However, in doing this, the blood does become thinner but the connective tissues surrounding the cells and the cells themselves are losing the very water they need to remove metabolic waste. So again, we see the body striving to achieve balance but without water so many of its attempts prove to be in vain.

The many wonders of water

Apart from oxygen, water is the most vital substance we put into our bodies. Thankfully nature takes care of oxygen for us otherwise given our track record with hydration most of us wouldn't see out the day! Given that water along with oxygen is involved in almost every aspect of human health it seems crazy that we largely speak of it in an incidental way, without proper respect and reverence for all that it does in our names.

For many who come to our doors at Reach, the thing they are least expecting to be told when they have an emotional and psychological concern is that they must drink more water. For most clients and indeed therapists, drinking water would simply not seem to be an important part of any strategy or solution when dealing with emotional and psychological issues. However, it's our lack of understanding about the mind-body connection that would have us believe this lie. Plato was right, three hundred and fifty years before Christ, when he said you cannot fix the mind without fixing the body and you cannot fix the body without fixing the mind (I'm paraphrasing – you may remember the actual quote is in the preface). He went on to say that the lack of understanding of this relationship was undermining medicine, healing and health and here we are over two thousand years later still making the same mistakes.

When we consider that the body is approximately 70% water and most body parts are largely composed of water (e.g. blood plasma is over 90% water, tissues, 70-80%, the brain and intestines are approximately 75%, even the bones contain 25%), then it is not surprising that its role is central to our health, given that water is implicated in all our physiological processes. All of the approximately sixty trillion cells that make up the human body are carrying out their biological activities within the intracellular fluid (found within the body's cells, also known as cytoplasm) and extracellular fluids (which occupy the spaces between cells and tissues). These fluids also carry nutrients (vitamins and minerals) into the cells that are vital for life and are also responsible for removing the waste products, which as we've already established is critical in order to keep both the cell and the body healthy.

The average adult body contains about forty litres of water (seventy pints). Every day, water is lost from the body in the form of urine, sweat, water vapour from the lungs and faeces. To maintain a healthy balance of fluids, we need to drink at least two litres (three and half pints) of water per day because we lose around two and a half litres of water just in maintaining the health of all of our systems.

The implications of inadequate amounts of water for cognitive functioning are equally significant. A 1-2% reduction in the normal water volume of the body is considered to be the point at which we become mildly dehydrated and it is at this point that there is an increase in irritability, loss of concentration and reduced mental functioning.

Two studies conducted by Armstrong and Ganio in 2011, looking at how mild dehydration affects mood in healthy young women and men, carried out in near identical conditions, concluded that dehydration affects everyone, whether they are working at a computer all day or are marathon runners. What these studies indicated is that the critical figure is the percentage of body weight loss due to dehydration. This figure was calculated to be on average 1.36% for women and 1.59% for men. At this point of reduction in water volume, there are measureable changes in mood and temperament.

In both these studies mild dehydration didn't appear at these levels to significantly impair cognitive function but did negatively impact on mood states and created adverse changes leading to increased headaches, poor concentration, impairment of working memory, some anxiety, loss of vigour and fatigue. There was some difference between male and female participants but this was considered to be largely attributable to their size and varying levels of aerobic fitness.

Other studies in the same area (see the work of Walsh, Wilson and Morley) found that a 5% reduction in water can lead to at least a 30% reduction in cognitive ability. At this point perception, personality and performance are all undermined to some degree. If the brain, which we've established is 75% water, experiences a reduction in what is its most vital nutrient, other than oxygen, then is it a surprise that both mood and cognitive functions are impaired? What we're seeing from the research in this area is that it only takes a small reduction in water to create significant and substantial limitations to our ability to function optimally right across the spectrum of human functioning.

So without sufficient water flowing through our bodies we not only become safe havens for viruses, unhealthy bacteria and diseases of all kinds, we also are unable to operate from a position of good mental health. Once perception is distorted, our personalities are unable to reflect the best in us and with that it naturally follows that our performance also falls away.

Optimal functioning of both mind and body is heavily dependent on hydration. We are 'vertical rivers'. This is not to say water is a miracle cure and that it alone can solve all our ills, because it cannot, but it is certainly critical to creating well-being.

Drinking water is arguably the greatest physical therapy of all. Isn't it tragic that most of us in the 'civilized' world have water in abundance and yet take it for granted and the so-called third world has so little of it and yet treats it as the precious commodity that it is. If we were simply drinking enough water, all the functions I've listed would take place effortlessly, allowing for little or no congestion and build up of toxins in the system. All major diseases are caused and preceded by some form of dehydration and obstruction. For example:

i. an obstruction in the liver is most likely due to gall stones in the bile ducts. They affect the nutrient supply, metabolism and energy distribution throughout the body.

ii. a kidney stone can lead to the retention of urine and raise the pressure of the blood against the arteries, causing hypertension.

iii. a constipated colon causes the 'back flushing' of waste which leads to the body being flooded with toxins, which is like going to the toilet inside yourself rather than in the bowl. Can you imagine the damage that does?

iv. any lymphatic blockage can lead to heart congestion, obesity, arthritis, lymph oedema, cancer, in fact almost every chronic illness. And the list goes on….

In fact, if any one part of the body is sick, the entire body is sick. It is impossible to divide the body, as is done in allopathic medicine, into categories such as cardiovascular, lymphatic, nervous and immune system etc. They are inextricably linked and hopefully by now you are beginning to see if a blockage or obstruction exists in any part of the system, all other parts of the system will pay sooner or later.

So without a continuous flow of water running through our bodies we become like stagnant ponds; foul smelling, dirty and struggling to sustain life. Stop the stagnation. Try to drink three or four pints of water from today and every day, and you will experience the many wonders of water.

For those of you interested in looking into this subject more deeply take a look at the work of Batmanghelidj, Emoto and Harbottle who have helped to put the role and importance of water on the agenda of nutrition and medicine and increasingly into the public psyche.

Remember we cannot encourage the mind and spirit to pursue the highest ideals if we do not persuade the body to be part of that process too.

The role of intention

The other 'persons' in this equation, as already outlined, are the mind and the spirit. The primary tug of war exists between mind and body, and the spirit is influenced by what takes place between the two. But, because the relationship between mind and body is little understood, what happens is that one is left with mere hopes, dreams and ambitions instead of real potential and purpose. When mind and body are in harmony the spirit is uplifted. There is joy in the heart and the individual believes in her own talents and abilities and strides confidently towards her potential and purpose.

Biological processes are driven and shaped by what we do, not by our intentions. In modern parlance this is currently described as cell intelligence or body memory. Cell intelligence, or body memory holds the incontrovertible evidence of our actions (not our thoughts or intentions) and this 'record keeper', the cell, in turn influences the patterns and processes within the body.

It's that recorded evidence that unravels our genetic potential. In other words, how your genetic material will play itself out in your life is determined not by what you 'intended' but by what you have actually 'done'. As awesome as the mind is, to try and pull it in the opposite direction against the evidence that the body has collected, takes Herculean determination. It's not that it can't be done but the price that you pay in order to achieve it is often far too great. The task is made unquestionably easier if what you think and say is actually what you do. This creates a state of co-operation between mind and body. If intention consistently becomes action, the body's processes and patterns will be like a gale force wind blowing at your back and will push you up any mountain towards your solution. Equally, when intention falls by the wayside and is simply further evidence of a mind that holds high ideals and a mouth that speaks fine words, but where nothing is ever actualized, then the gale force wind of the body will continually blow you off course making that mountain climb almost impossible.

Once this deep, subtle relationship is understood the opening statement of this chapter makes perfect sense because the first 'person' you actually need to persuade is indeed your body. The reason why your mind falters, struggles and more often than not loses its way, is because the body does not trust it. The body hears the mind thinking fine thoughts and producing wonderful promises but because nothing materializes the body is left confused. The evidence says that the mind thinks one thing and may even say it, but doesn't always translate those ambitions into action, yet this is the only thing the body understands and respects. The body doesn't have the ability to sift through your thoughts to see which of your intentions are genuine. Actions are the only thing your body records. The body does not have conscious thoughts, it is driven by experience and until you say what you mean and mean what you say the body will continue to mistrust the mind's intentions, which will bring the spirit to its knees. It's time to persuade the body that you are telling the truth by translating your intentions into actions.

Mind over matter... or is it really matter over mind?

Persuading the body is about winning the heart of matter. Mind over matter is not simply a case of imposing the power of the mind on the body, although that is a legitimate interpretation. Another way that the mind is able to manipulate matter according to its will is through the power of persuasion. As explained, the body (matter) responds to the 'evidence' of our actions, so if we start making our intentions visible in our actions, the mind will no longer be fighting an on-going battle with the body. By understanding how matter responds and applying your will in a different way, you can win its co-operation without intense labour. This is not to be mistaken for an easy option because it still requires structure, application and discipline.

Once the relationship between mind and body is better understood it becomes clear that winning the trust and respect of matter is an approach well worth pursuing as it offers a life of greater harmony and contentment.

The constant battling with one's mind to fulfil one's dreams is energy-sapping and time consuming and bears meagre fruits. Therefore, doesn't it make more sense to work with the mechanics of matter (the laws of nature) to engineer our heart's desires? We need to understand that even though our bodies do not have consciousness (the power to think and decide their own destiny) they do have a form of intelligence. Remember, the way that this intelligence works is to simply draw on the evidence of our experience (which is better described as body memory) and in turn that experience influences how the cells, tissues, organs etc. in our bodies behave. The main storage area for experience is the brain, unquestionably the most sophisticated part of our bodies. Advancements in cognitive neuroscience have enabled us to understand how stress, anxiety and trauma leave powerful impressions on the right hemisphere of the brain (the side associated with emotional experiences). However, the impact is not limited to that area alone. We also know that the frontal lobes (which are responsible for thinking and speaking) are impaired and the amygdala (also bound up with our instinctive emotional responses) is thrown into disarray. Once the brain absorbs our inconsistencies its overwhelming influence on the rest of the organism begins and the cycle of biological and psychological dysfunction is set in motion. The gut is known as the 'second brain' because all the emotional material that our brains process generates electro-chemical responses in this sensitive area. These responses go on to affect how the body behaves and ultimately the biological consequences will in turn impact on our psychological position (moods, attitudes and perceptions).

The physical heart is also now being described as a key player in how emotional experiences are registered within our anatomy. This is a vast subject that also has a bearing on this story but how we influence the body to move in the right direction is not altered by the data that is being rapidly gathered in this area. For those interested in finding out more about the heart's pivotal role in the emotional dynamic, look at the work undertaken at the Institute of HeartMath.

Persuading the body, which might have seemed beyond your grasp, can be attained by simply respecting the power of your body - and then forming a new relationship with it. So, start today by making pledges you can keep. Start with small, realistic goals. Gather around you as many positive habits as you can and with practice, consistency and heartfelt resolve the green shoots of self-respect and self-worth will emerge. You are not going to achieve all you want immediately but with practice, patience and perseverance miracles will begin to unfold.

Also remember, the journey is just as important as the destination, so try not to see your endeavours as a set of chores to be endured, but as important acts of love and self-respect. Understanding this, the body will work with you when you have consistently laid down these new patterns. These are the non-negotiables I referred to earlier.

This gentle, patient, persuasive approach will, if you become consistent, win the heart of matter, which in turn will heal your own heart and mind.

Epigenetics – the subtle dialogue with matter

This fascinating and rapidly emerging science is changing our understanding and potentially our relationship with matter and this is once again best demonstrated in our bodies. By now it should be clear that if we are truly to be 'masters of matter', moulding her beauty to our intentions, we also have to learn how to serve her. This is not a one-way street in which we continue to take, and manipulate the outcomes to suit our selfish intentions; because we can see that simply does not work. Both our bodies and the wider environment (nature) are shouting that message back at us. Look at the state of the planet; we are slowly (in many cases not slowly at all) eroding away our children's inheritance with the pollution we've caused, the thinning of the ozone layer, the loss of vital minerals from our soils through over-farming and inadequate replenishment and de-forestation, and the list goes on….

As for our bodies, the story there is no different. We are asked to celebrate the fact that we are living longer but the truth is we are suffering longer. A longer life does not mean a better life; it's really quality of life we should be pursuing. During the last one hundred years of so-called progress in which many medical advances have been made there has been a proliferation of diseases. Old enemies like TB, polio, Addison's disease, syphilis, dysentery, scurvy, beri beri, gangrene, trench mouth, have seemingly passed away and new ones just as devastating and in some instances much more profound, have emerged, for example, M.N.D., M.S., Alzheimer's, many more ferocious forms of cancer, H.I.V. and A.I.D.S. There is also a whole new family of autoimmune diseases and many more besides. So have we really progressed or simply changed the face of our challenges?

The Story of Health will not go away; it keeps reminding us that if we don't tend to our needs in all four areas (spirit, mind, body and environment), our problem never does go away. It simply turns up in our lives looking different, having undergone a metamorphosis, the same enemy in a different disguise. Progress has not brought the improvements we boast about, it has brought about a different set of challenges and our bodies and health are sending us this message loud and clear. The planet sends it too.

Epigenetics offers us an opportunity for a better dialogue with matter because of a better understanding of our relationship with her. It has illuminated the truth that the ancient masters of India and China knew i.e. to be masters of anything you have to serve it too. The concept that we are more than our genes simply isn't new. It is a message, which has echoed loudly down the corridors of the past, but we simply haven't been listening. However, now that scientific data is emerging we are beginning to understand that everything that affects matter affects the mind and that whatever affects the mind affects matter too. They are intimately intertwined.

This knowledge offers us the opportunity to be free of the predestination of our genetic inheritances by choosing a consciousness and life-style that does not simply heed the past conditioning. We can either allow pollution, poor nutrition, inadequate hydration, negative thinking etc. to shape our destiny, which will merely activate (switch on) the genetic inheritance of our forebears and 'live down' to those predispositions. Or we can choose cleaner ways of living, proper hydration, optimal nutrition and positive thinking and 'live up' to our as yet untapped potential.

Where the mind goes the molecule will follow

Another rapidly developing field of research known as psychoneuro-immunology (PNI) has been uncovering ways in which the brain and immune system interact to influence our susceptibility to diseases.

Many studies have established the numerous connections between the immune system and the central nervous system - such as the nerve endings, which exist in the thymus, lymph nodes, spleen and bone marrow, suggesting the existence of a complex communicative and interactive network between the brain and immunity.

In addition, the cells of the immune system seem to respond to chemical signals from the central nervous system via neuroendocrines, neurohormones and neurotransmitters, including growth hormone, insulin, histamine, vasopressin, dopamine, adrenalin, noradrenalin, prolactin, testosterone and prostaglandins.

Given these complex connections and subtle interactions between the brain and immunity there is now no doubt that psychosocial factors play a decisive role in the development of illness as well as in the restoration of health.

Most basic clinical experimental trials show clearly that stress suppresses the immune system function. Chronic stress in particular can result in immunosuppression by acting through the HPA, the hypothalamic-pituitary-adrenal pathway. Under stress the hypothalamus produces a corticotropin-releasing factor that triggers the secretion of an adrenocorticotropic hormone by the pituitary, which stimulates the adrenals to secrete corticosteroids; these are known to suppress the production of antibodies, reduce the size of lymph nodes as well as reduce both the number and responsiveness of lymphocytes. Several studies have reported the direct relationship between a stress response and a decreased immune system function.

For example, Kiecolt-Glaser reported a decreased lymphocyte proliferation among medical students on the first day of final exams. And Bartrop found a significantly depressed T-lymphocyte function in recently bereaved spouses. Schleifer found a diminished lymphocyte proliferation after bereavement in husbands of women who had terminal breast cancer.

When considering immuno-enhancement, Keicolt-Glaser also found that elderly people who were taught progressive relaxation and guided imagery techniques showed, compared to controls, a significant increase in their natural killer cell activity, as well as a decrease in antibodies to herpes simplex virus, which means improved control of the virus by the immune function.

There is also mounting evidence that psychosocial factors can affect or moderate the stress-immune response even before and certainly after a stressful event occurs. These studies indicate that any behavioural intervention, whether in the form of counselling, meditation and relaxation techniques, hypnosis etc, can be just as effective in both prevention and treatment of ill health.

It is important to understand that the functioning of the immune system is the end result of an extremely complex and intricate interaction between a multiplicity of factors which, besides psychosocial factors, include genetics, age, sex, environment, sleep, exercise, drugs, bacteria, viruses etc. The rapidly evolving science of PNI has helped us to understand how powerful our thoughts are in shaping our biology. In fact, every thought has a consequence. Where the mind goes the molecule will literally follow.

This is why teaching individuals how to enhance and improve their 'inner world' is vital to health. Not only must we concentrate on what we put in our mouths, we must also take care of what we feed our minds. This is why The Reach Approach brings together many seemingly unrelated disciplines with the potential to improve your personal welfare and the welfare of those around you. Remember you are the major shareholder in your destiny. It's time to exercise that power.

There are many possibilities

In this chapter I've begun to piece together many of the components that are pivotal to the 'eternal dance of life'. We've come to understand that if we are to alter and re-shape things at the macro level, we must begin by making those changes at the micro level; after all what we see in the bigger picture is merely a duplication of what takes place further down, all the way to the level of the most subtle dynamics, the quantum level.

Nowhere is this more true than at the cellular level. As I've previously stated, the body is made up of approximately sixty trillion cells; each cell is like a little person with its own brain, digestive system, circulatory system, immune function etc. operating as part of its wider community. When those cells are well and are functioning healthily we have what can be called 'quantum coherence' (biological harmony at every level), which equates to health and well-being. When the individual cells are not functioning as they should for whatever reason (such as a lack of oxygen, pollution, poor nutrition, excess stress, dehydration, emotional and psychological issues etc.) one experiences 'quantum dissonance' (biological discord at every level). This is experienced as ill health or disease.

The way that quantum dissonance manifests in each person depends in turn on genetic predisposition, but as we've already discovered, genetic predisposition is not set in stone. There are many variables that impact on the genetic story, none more so than thought. What we think really matters. This is why we must not fall foul of the old premise of the primacy of DNA, which falls a long way short of explaining human potential. We have thirty thousand genes performing over four billion activities every second (and these are only the ones we know of). Therefore the infinite possibilities, that the mind-body system is able to manifest goes way beyond genetics. These infinite possibilities have been described as pleomorphism/polymorphism (there are many possibilities), which relates to how one's genetic story unfolds, which is dependent on the relationship between latent predispositions and environment. In other words, you may have cancer, heart failure, diabetes, M.S., dementia or other such latent conditions (encoded in your DNA) as possibilities. However, whether they are 'switched on' or not does depend on the 'data' coming in from the environment. There are no certainties, only potentials and possibilities, and as we've come to understand, the role of 'I' is central to this equation. We can either 'opt in' or 'opt out' of life's dance. This is where our free will and resolve really count for something as we can, through our choices, influence outcomes. This is another subject that I will bring you back to as I explore the rapidly moving developments in this area.

When the cell is well, all is well

As I discussed in Antiquity Comes Full Circle, what was intuitively understood and practised by our ancestors, particularly those from the East, is now re-emerging as 'new' information. It's fascinating to watch the cutting-edge science of the West slowly confirming the spirituality and ancient wisdom of the East. The closer we look at the new science, the clearer it becomes that there are five crucial factors which most influence the quality of our lives. Our thoughts and feelings are first and foremost amongst these. Their influence is arguably as much as between 60% and 80% in terms of the impact on the cell's behaviour, activities and proper functioning.

You may remember in Chapter 1, I made reference to Candace Pert's pioneering work in relation to the 'molecules of emotion' - her work has been developed further by Bruce Lipton and others. Dawson Church (see his book Genie in your Genes) has made a valuable contribution by helping us to understand, with his exploration and research of the IEGs (immediate early/experience genes), that nothing impacts on the story of the cell more than our thoughts and our feelings.

Also the work of Dr. Sondra Barrett in her fascinating and thought provoking book, Secrets of your Cells, has added some more valuable data and telling insights, with her research into the architecture, functions and intelligence of the cells. She has, drawing from past healing traditions, cutting-edge biology and energy medicine, concluded that our cells are not a haphazard or fortuitous arrangement of chemicals 'mindlessly' keeping us alive, they are a community of trillions of sentient entities working to create a sanctuary for the human soul/spirit/being. Through her work she invites us to take the 'journey within' - the journey of inspiration, hope, transformation and healing.

The second critical factor in this group of five is diet and nutrition. It has long been understood that we are what we eat. Yet this relationship between food and mood is still being played down even though it is pivotal to how we think and feel. If the body is laden with toxins how are we meant to keep a stream of pure positive thoughts flowing? Surely a toxic state simply sets up further tensions within the system.

Next in line is a life of meaning and purpose. Those who have no sense of who they are and where they're going are arguably the most afflicted, having the worst strains of anxiety, fear, depression and self-loathing. A lack of meaning and purpose accounts for many mental health issues and this may explain why mental ill health is one of the fastest growing problems that the developed world faces. Address this essential need and much of what afflicts the human spirit will be healed.

The other key player in the health of the cell is our relationships. A life of meaning and purpose addresses our relationship with ourselves but as we are social beings we also need relationships with others. These relationships require integrity, intimacy, respect, warmth and love, if they are to sustain both parties. Sadly, so often the relationships of the modern world sacrifice quality for quantity, which means that also all too often we don't make the necessary investments in these areas. Relationships that lack these core elements put stress and strain on the spirit and so one's sense of self and the quality of one's well-being are dramatically reduced.

Last but not least amongst this primary group of five is the environment. We cannot divorce our well-being from our environment. For those who doubt the truth of that statement, what is happening to our planet currently should be ample evidence. The mirror of reality is being uncomfortably placed in front of us, reflecting back the consequences of our actions. There are always consequences for the choices we make and the actions we perform. The sooner we acknowledge this and apply this truth to our lives the sooner we can initiate the changes we want to see. The environment is constantly impacting on our genetic make-up. Our genes are not playing out a predetermined pattern. They are in fact telling the story of our relationship with the environment. This relationship as I outlined earlier has been described as polymorphism. In other words, there are many possibilities and so the outcome is not certain. What is certain is that, if we do nothing, negativity, uncertainty and further demise will manifest in our lives.

This is a brief summary of the five critical factors, which are shaping our lives minute by minute. This is why I say, when the cell is well - all is well. What happens at a microcosmic level, i.e. at the cellular level, will and does shape what happens body-wide (macro). When you understand this, you are able to appreciate the power that you have over your own destiny. If you're able to see the extent to which thoughts and feelings are shaping the way that your life is unfolding, along with the other factors discussed, then you can see that any efforts to bring about improvements in these areas will have an incredible effect on your growth and your life.

In this book I do not aim to write about everything that is relevant to the evolution of the human spirit. This simply wouldn't be possible. What I do hope to achieve is to help you and those you might speak to about this book to think more laterally about physical, emotional, psychological and spiritual health. Far too often, human understanding is being compartmentalized in such a way that these different areas are dealt with as if they were somehow separate. Unless we start joining up the dots we are destined to keep making the same mistakes.

Some excellent work has already been done in the area of food, water, nutrition and supplementation. For those who want to delve deeper, see among others the work of, Dr. Joel Fuhrman, Patrick Holford, Dr. Paul Clayton, Dr. Udo Erasmus, Dr. Masaru Emoto, Andreas Moritz, and Dr. Linus Pauling. A staggering amount of research has already been done in the area of human health and nutrition. It's time to look deeper and with an open mind, if we are to persuade the body to join us in this highest of all endeavours.

Ten life-changing principles

Listed below are ten powerful ways that can persuade the body to work with you rather than against you. Apply them for at least three months (six months would be better) and you will be surprised by the wonders you can create.

Nothing in the body works properly without water. Every message, process and function in the body depends on it. How can you expect the body to perform miracles if the primary fuel for optimal function is missing? It is imperative to become consistent in this area, as only then will the body respond to your requests. You are a vertical river, so ensure your river never runs dry. Remember, the latest research is showing that less than a 2% reduction in water begins affecting cognitive functions. In other words, you cannot be at your best if you are dehydrated, which if you stop and think about it, makes perfect sense. After all, the brain is made out of water and fat, so if there is insufficient water to maintain its innumerable functions, how can we be expected to focus, concentrate and perform optimally?

In order for the body to deliver its full potential, waste in all its guises must be removed. This is why it is essential to embark on a detoxifying way of life. This is not about following protocols for detoxification as and when the body has reached a point of crisis. This is about understanding that prevention is better than cure. Therefore, exercise regularly because the lymphatic system (which is responsible for detoxification) struggles to do its job without sufficient cardiovascular input. Also, as a preventative measure, consider such activities as colonic irrigation, feet detoxes, massage, more sensible eating regimes etc. all of which will help the body lower the toxic loads accumulated from waste products.

Structure governs function. The internal organs cannot operate effectively and efficiently if the body's structure is in any way misaligned. In the art of persuading the body it is really important to make sure that your structure is right. To this end one should seriously consider seeing an appropriately qualified and experienced osteopath, chiropractor, biomechanics practitioner or someone specializing in the Bowen Technique. These are all disciplines that can address any structural or alignment issues.

Develop respect for your body. This of course starts with what you put in your mouth but remember it's not just what you eat that determines health, it's what you absorb from what you eat. So ensure that you chew your food thoroughly, otherwise the process of absorption will be stifled before it even begins. Also avoid drinking fluids whilst eating otherwise the priceless enzyme function that ensures proper breakdown of foods and drives all bodily functions will be compromised and a substantial percentage of what you eat will actually pass through the system without delivering its true nutritional value.

The art of persuading the body would be incomplete without adequate amounts of sleep. Sleep is invaluable. About 85% of the body's housework (vital renewal functions, repairing and replacing of cells, ensuring the vitality and effectiveness of all the primary systems etc.) takes place whilst we are asleep. Although the amount of sleep is important, (between five and eight hours is what most people need), it is not actually the quantity that is critical for health, it's the quality. Without the deep restorative sleep, which accounts for about 20%-25% of the time you're in bed, the critical household chores that the body undertakes simply are never completed, leaving the individual in a cycle of chronic fatigue.

So, do all you can to ensure that your sleeping patterns are healthy. Nature has a wonderful pharmacy from which you can draw help e.g. magnesium, avena sativa, passiflora, valerian, tryptophan and melatonin, to name a few. There is also a range of essential oils that will help greatly in this area. But before self-medicating always take advice from your doctor or an experienced health practitioner.

Find time to do something regularly that says to your body 'I respect and value you'. For example, tai chi, yoga, pilates, massage, reflexology, aromatherapy etc. are activities that could be undertaken daily/weekly subject to your lifestyle. Be sure to choose something you enjoy because you're more likely to maintain it. Build your chosen activity into your self-care regime, and this will deliver a strong message to your body that self-nurturing is really important. The body will internalize this message and will offer its support and respect in return. In time such pampering will not be pampering at all, it will be an essential part of your life, helping you to maintain strength, poise and balance.

'Me time' is vital. This is not a selfish activity, nor is it to be mistaken for self-indulgence. It is essential. Just as the in-breath would have no value without the out-breath, a life without 'me time' is no life at all. If all that you do is externally focused, with no true internal attention on your own needs, what message do you think you are giving your body? To breathe in is to draw in life; to exhale is to sustain it. To have a life rich with social contact, meaningful relationships, a feeling of purpose and satisfaction, is wonderful (like breathing in), but without the balance of silence, contemplation and quiet reflection (breathing out) the demands of such a life will sap you of all that you have. So pursue a path of balance and remember not to hold your breath!

Create new memories. Because your body collects the evidence of your actions and your biological and ultimately your emotional processes are influenced and driven by that, then it's critical to start by thinking about how you are going to begin each day. For example, where can you create moments for reflection and appreciation? How can you maintain a positive mental attitude with the push and pull of everyday life? What are you going to give your body as fuel to meet the challenges of the day? Living a more mindful life where you consider what you are doing and are proactive rather than reactive is essential if you don't merely want to be a victim to the past. There is no need for an elaborate strategy because simple is best, but there's no doubt structure builds discipline, discipline generates momentum and momentum brings success. So devise a plan today.

How you think affects the nervous and immune systems and also what are called your 'natural killer cells'. The sciences of psychoneuroimmunology (PNI) and epigenetics have helped illuminate the role and the power of thoughts in achieving well-being and in causing disease. As I said earlier, quantum physics now largely supports the principles long expounded by the spiritual masters, "where the mind goes the molecule will follow". This chapter has hopefully shown you how this relationship has in part broken down and failed to deliver because our minds are distracted and confused, leaving our bodies unsure what instructions to follow.

If we are to turn this relationship around we need to practise focused thinking. There are a number of activities that can help with this, such as positive affirmations, creative visualization, personal prayer, mindfulness etc. When we consistently focus the mind in a positive direction, therefore ending the body's confusion, the central nervous system, immune system, in fact all the body's processes, stand in a co-operative line ready to engineer health and well-being.

Think kindly thoughts. As I've just stated, 'where the mind goes the molecule will follow'. The research in kindness is a very good example of this principle. As we learned, anyone being kind, receiving kindness or observing it, receives the wonderful gift of oxytocin. When the body is challenged, and it will be, given the nature of the world we live in, it is important that you respond with the right mindset. If the mind is constantly dripping kind, compassionate thoughts and feelings into the reservoir of the body, the body will be stimulated in line with those thoughts to seek out the best solution for whatever is challenging your health.

It would be folly to think, given the pollution of the planet and the state of the environment, that any of us is totally immune to ill health. All we can do is adopt a preventative lifestyle, living as consciously as we can and thinking in a way that enriches our lives and the lives of others. This will persuade the body to come with us. If we lead in the 'right' way, the body will follow.

Dearest body

Below is a dialogue that I would encourage you to set up with your own body. Don't treat it as a script to be followed verbatim, it's a template that you can use to create your own conversation with your body. You'll find it invaluable, not only to change your relationship with the body but to persuade the body to work with you rather than in its own interest. Remember when the body does not have clear instruction, it moves into a survival mode, as it seeks to protect itself against our neglect. Here, you will be invited to ask the body to move out of a state of panic and self-interest into a position of growth where it can flourish.

It's worth reminding you at this stage that everything about the body can be summarized in two words, growth and protection. When the body is growing, evolving, rejuvenating, metabolizing effectively, breathing optimally, detoxifying fully etc. - all of which can be described as growth - the mind and spirit are able to flourish. However, when these activities are compromised and the body is doing just enough to survive, this position is called protection. It is under these conditions that the mind and spirit plummet.

The protective state is where the body is withering and its primary functions are stifled. This leads to, amongst other things, a state called endotoxicity, where the body reabsorbs its own waste as everything closes down. You may remember that it's under such conditions that blockages occur as the system becomes sluggish and stagnant and disease is able to run rampant.

Try the following and you'll see that you can genuinely influence the direction body takes. The key is the 'quality of sincerity'. The more you can speak from the heart, the more potent the results.

Sit comfortably away from any distraction and become the observer of yourself. Watch yourself and listen to yourself breathing. Every time you breathe in and out, thank your body for the preciousness of your life. Recite in your own words something along the lines of…

"Dearest body

With each breath you oxygenate my cells and that oxygen carries nutrients into the nucleus of each cell, where energy is produced for life. That energy makes everything possible, from digestion to the beating of my heart, to my liver cleansing; even these thoughts that I'm having right now are supported by the gift of each breath. Your skills do not end there because after the combustion of nutrients that take place in each cell, you then, with great humility, remove all the waste via the many pathways of detoxification, colon, kidneys, liver, lungs and skin. All this takes place under your amazing stewardship and all you ask of me is to co-operate and co-operate I will.

Thank you for the countless miracles you perform each day in my name. You're so amazing. If it were not for you, I would not have the opportunity to learn, understand and grow from my experiences. I'm in awe of your infinite skills and talents. The way that you keep breathing, digesting, producing energy, detoxifying and so much more, all at the same time, makes you the greatest wonder of all. I am honoured and privileged to be in such an intimate relationship with you. Sadly, I have not always given you the love, respect and appreciation that you deserve, but from today I promise my heart will sing your praise. No longer will I overlook your greatness and wonder. Thank you.

What I have come to understand is that you never work against me. You're always giving me the best chance of survival. Despite my neglect and complacency you use all your experience and wisdom to find the best routes for health. You are truly the most loyal friend and ally that I could have, no matter what I do, you're always striving for the best outcomes. You're so forgiving of my misdemeanours, great or small. How can I ever repay you? This friendship has been so one-sided in so many ways. I have not thanked you enough for the gifts that you serve up each day. Starting from today, starting from right now, I thank you. I will learn to fully appreciate you and your kind, magical ways…"

Let these thoughts resonate for a while.

As you sit listening to and being aware of your breathing, and appreciating the wonderful processes supported by this one act, make a promise to your body right now, a promise you will do everything in your power to fulfill.

"Dearest Body, I promise to give you all the raw materials you need. I will ensure you are properly hydrated, I will eat as diversely as I can to ensure you get the necessary vitamins, essential fats, amino acids and minerals that you need. I promise to be consistent with supplementation, so that any deficiencies in my diet will be bridged. I will not allow you to struggle when you constantly fight for my survival and well-being. I will strive for the rest of my life, not only to take on board the right foods and fluids, but also to generate the right thoughts…

I've come to understand that my negative thoughts and feelings hurt you the most. For that I'm sorry. I will endeavour to keep my mind thankful, kind and forgiving because these are the thoughts you love most of all. These thoughts and feelings are natural healers that work with you, not against you."

Communicate in this way with your body on a regular basis and it will help you immensely, especially at times when you're physically or mentally struggling. No challenge will then feel too great.

> *"We are what we repeatedly do. Excellence then is not an act but a habit."*
> Aristotle (384 BC – 322 BC)

CHAPTER 5: ENVIRONMENT REALLY MATTERS

"When the personal life is cultivated, the family will be regulated; when the family is regulated, the state will be in order; and when the state is in order there will be peace throughout the world! All must regard cultivation of their personal life as the root or foundation of peace and order."

Confucius (551 BC - 479 BC)

Persuading the spirit, mind and body will prove a futile task if we don't also form meaningful alliances with the powerful forces of the environment, for its influences are many and it literally touches every aspect of our lives. In figure 1 (see The Story of Health in Chapter 1) the environment is depicted as a circle interfacing with the triangle, which represents the spirit, mind and body. You can see from the diagram that the environment impacts on all three and in this chapter I will attempt to show you how far-reaching its effects are and more importantly what can be done to ensure that you don't remain a slave to the many environmental forces shaping our lives. To illustrate the relationship we have with the environment and why we should treat it with greater respect, let's begin by looking at some examples that demonstrate its powerful effects on spirit, mind and body.

The spirit always pays the price

As you know, the spirit needs a life of meaning and purpose. Without this it is rudderless and like a ship will almost certainly run aground. The spirit, as I previously explained, also needs to find forgiveness if it is to be free and live a life of gratitude and joy. Benevolence and altruism also ensure that the spirit is able to blossom and prosper in all that it does. Yet to achieve and sustain these things without understanding the role of the environment is almost impossible.

We saw in Chapter 1 that when the mind and body are caught up in a tug of war, battling tenaciously in order to get their own needs met, it is the spirit that actually pays the price. Its sense of value and worth can quickly plummet as it desperately seeks clarity, direction and certainty. The environment can have a similar effect on the spirit, forcing its power to swiftly drain away. This is because the spirit needs a sanctuary, a sacred space of some kind, which it can retreat to, if it is to prosper. This space doesn't need to be elaborate, it simply needs to be clean, ordered and where possible, airy and light. It also helps immensely if this space is quiet, as the spirit awakens in an atmosphere of silence, an atmosphere which is conducive to reflection and contemplation.

Sadly the pace of modern life increasingly divorces us from ourselves; we are so busy meeting its requests and demands that self-neglect is now commonplace. Worse than that, the need for introspection and quiet time is considered by many a luxury that they simply cannot afford if they are to fulfill life's many demands. The irony here is that quiet reflection and introspection would actually lead to a mind more capable of dealing with the demands of modernity. But what is it that prevents us from making the time to connect with the 'truth' about ourselves? Experience has taught me that this is due to a lack of self-awareness. We're so busy being consumed by the 'external', that our 'internal' needs are easily overlooked.

So I would invite you to ask yourself whether the objectives that you are relentlessly pursuing are even yours? Are you in fact even living your 'own' life or one that has been mapped out for you? Are you simply following a script that you've been given, which when you look around, is the same one as those around you? Pause now and consider; have you ever really pondered and reflected long enough on who you are and where you're really going - because if not, this is a very good place to start, if you are not to be a victim of the environmental forces.

Try creating a sanctuary of some sort, where you can make the space and take time to reflect on these pivotal questions. Making time regularly for 'conscious contact' with yourself, will present you with clarity and many insights.

The ghost in the machine?

Could it be that the 'ghost in the machine' that Descartes referred to, the soul, a spiritual force that transcends matter and yet brings its presence to bear on the way human atoms and molecules behave, actually exists? This is a question that epigenetics does not provide conclusive answers to, but it certainly invites us to look at what is really going on in the universe at a much more subtle and invisible level. It is helping us to break free of the notion that our DNA, (our genetics), is responsible for all of human life.

I do believe in the 'ghost in the machine', a soul, a higher self, that is responsible for the countless miracles that take place within our brains and our bodies each day and is also responsible for our countless thoughts, feelings and imaginings. I believe it's the most formidable force in human life, whether it's moving in a positive or a negative direction.

The amazingness of the mind-body system points to a consciousness greater than matter. Despite the miracle of the body (matter) there is 'something' that influences and directs it. Who is it that creates the thought that instructs the brain to produce the neuropeptide (the molecule of emotion)? What is the catalyst for the millions of activities taking place simultaneously in the body? What is the wisdom that can enable a multitude of activities to happen unconsciously whilst you're asleep or engaged in quiet, thoughtful reflection? The magnificence of life is driven by something powerful, a consciousness and it seems to me that when there is any degree of self-mastery, life is magical and wonderful and when there is not, one can become a victim to a lottery of nightmares.

I believe you are the ghost in the machine, the one who is reading, interpreting and understanding these words, the one behind the eyes, listening through the ears, speaking through the mouth. The one who sits in the heart of the brain, juggling the colossal energy and phenomenal information that makes life possible at all levels. I'm not suggesting that you accept this proposition because my belief is that we should not accept any doctrine that we've not tested in the laboratory of own lives. But before you dismiss this notion, why not try connecting with your ghost? That intangible presence that appears to be beyond reach yet is always there. In other words start listening to your heart, start honouring your truth and you may in fact discover it's not a ghost at all - it is in fact you.

My experience is the more we try to make conscious contact the more we discover we are much more than our genes, in fact we are separate and distinct from our bodies – spiritual beings having a human experience.

Me-time

In the course of running a very busy practice - UK wide and with many overseas projects and initiatives - what has become clear to me is that very few people live mindfully. Most people's lives are being 'driven' by events and they are not actually sitting in the driving seat at all. Circumstances, people and events largely dictate the pace and pattern of their lives – most remain busy complaining but do very little to change it. It's not that they don't want it to change, but they feel bullied by their fears, or imprisoned by doubt, guilt or some false sense of duty. Or maybe they are stuck in the mud of complacency and ignorance. There are many reasons for the inertia that I see every day. The ones I've listed are actually secondary reasons but often appear to be primary ones. However, the main reason for a lack of positive change is quite simply insufficient 'me-time'.

The lack of a sanctuary or a sacred space, which I spoke of earlier, denies the individual the stillness and silence that would create the opportunity for the clarity and insight that comes from regular reflection. Silence has a language of her own, but in order to learn that language you need to spend time immersed in her.

Not being still and not connecting with our inner world has left many of us spiritually bankrupt - we wouldn't know the truth if it were staring back at us because we've stopped communicating with our hearts. Although it's important for us to decide with our heads this should only be after we've listened to our hearts, otherwise we are in danger of making lop-sided - or more precisely 'lobe-sided'- decisions (operating from one bit of the brain, whilst ignoring the virtues of the other). For the sake of balance I should interject and say, deciding with the heart without consulting the head is also folly, and will lead you down many a cul-de-sac.

The neuroscience revolution I referred to in Chapters 1 and 2 is rapidly unravelling the sophistication of the brain in such a way that it is increasingly clear that we in fact have two brains! And if it were not for the corpus callosum with its two hundred and fifty million axonal fibres, which connect the left and the right hemispheres, we would all be busy living as split personalities with the two hemispheres going about their separate tasks. (I will say more about this neuroscience revolution in Chapters 11 and 12 where I'll also explore more fully the relationship between science and spirituality).

In my work, what I've observed is that most people I interact with are 'leaning' either more to the left, or more to the right. In other words, either their logical drives (left hemisphere) or emotional drives (right hemisphere) are dominating the way they interact with the world. Very few are 'whole brain' thinkers - using left and right hemispheres appropriately and harmoniously.

There is definitely a gender dynamic to this, in that in men the logical drivers are often stronger and in women there's a predominance of the emotional drivers. But this is not an absolute position; it's more complex than this and it's unhelpful to oversimplify the issue along gender lines. What are often more powerful than the gender dynamics are the social/environmental factors that have influenced the individual's development, i.e. their 'leaning'. These external factors mould the brain, influencing perceptions, which lead to the 'lobe-sided' decisions.

Whether one is 'camped' in the left or the right hemisphere, has much more to do with what one has been exposed to in one's formative years and how one's brain has been wired, on the back of those influences. This is so important to understand, because even gender forces are manipulated by these environmental factors. In other words, boys go on to do what boys do because they are told what boys do, or they are exposed to those messages that exacerbate those latent predispositions. This is of course equally true for girls. So discussing gender issues without examining environmental politics doesn't provide us with accurate data to draw satisfactory conclusions.

Later in the book we will look more closely at the anatomy of the brain, because it is over simplifying things just to talk about the two hemispheres. But for now it's important to understand that camping out in one bit of the brain and making choices and decisions from there without consulting the other part of the brain does not offer us the best outcomes - both are equally needed to excel at being human. The question we should really be asking is why does this happen? Surely being whole brain thinkers is what optimal health requires.

The reason however that we become dethroned from the 'whole-brain' position has a lot to do with our formative years and whether we were in receipt of the Three As. If we did not get adequate amounts of Attention, Affection and Affirmation, patterns of dysfunction are set up in us and we adapt our personalities in accordance with the environments we are in. In other words our sense of self is surrendered as we attempt to 'fit in'. This is because the need to be loved and belong is such a powerful drive that when the Three As are absent or insufficient, we find other ways, which are not always healthy, to get our needs met.

This is why our recovery depends on The Story of Health. Until all four areas of one's life are tended to with equal priority, the sense of self continues to be skewed and the self-destructive patterns undermine our sense of well-being. Therefore to become whole-brain thinkers, the four legs of our table (spirit, mind, body, and environment) have to be positioned correctly i.e. each given the respect it is due.

Once this has been achieved neither logic nor emotion dominates; instead these two engage in what becomes a divine dance, where the 'right' energy leads at the 'right' time. There are undoubtedly times when the emotional position offers the greater insight, but there are equally those times when it obscures our vision. The same is true of logic: it can be clear, accurate and so precise in its assessment but in the next moment its rigidity and certainty can get in our way. So to re-establish harmony in the brain, we must do those things that elevate consciousness and a wonderful starting point for the spirit is to provide it with a sanctuary. The benefit of a sacred space and 'me time' cannot be overstated. Find space and time and watch your spirit soar.

Nocebos and placebos

Having looked at some examples of the environment's capacity to affect and undermine the spirit, let's look at its incredible ability to both enhance and diminish the mind. The environmental factors that have the greatest impact on the mind are your thoughts and beliefs; they would not ordinarily be classified in this way but they are the orchestrators of your whole experience – they do determine your reality.

Mahatma Ghandi said 'Your beliefs become your thoughts, your thoughts become your words, your words become your actions, your actions become your habits, your habits become your values and your values become your destiny.' Stop and think about this before reading any further and you'll see the truth encased in these words.

You may remember my earlier reference to John Haygarth and Émile Coué who began the pioneering work in the area of placebos. More latterly an enormous amount of research has been done around placebos, particularly in the area of depression. Professor Irving Kirsch, in 2002, found that 80% of the effect of anti-depressants could be attributed to the placebo effect. In more than half of the clinical trials, the six leading anti-depressants did not out-perform placebo sugar pills at all. The placebo effect is considered to be so real that some have proposed placebo pills be the first treatment for patients with mild or moderate depression. What placebos have helped us to understand is that when the mind believes something it unquestionably affects our biology. It is not all in our heads. The placebo effect affects the body too.

Nocebos are negative beliefs. Our perception dictates how our biological processes act out. If you believe something to be true even if it isn't, you produce the corresponding neurotransmitter and neuropeptide. So let's assume that 'something' makes you feel anxious. The pharmacy of the brain is then busy producing 'anxiety molecules', which in fact are proteins but these proteins are toxic. Countless toxic proteins now flood your body and these neuropeptides attach to the receptor sites on the cell membranes and literally have intercourse with those cells. The emotion of anxiety is now locked into your cells, influencing their behaviour and destiny. You subsequently discover the thing that made you anxious was no threat at all but by this time your perception has already taken you on a biological rollercoaster of negative consequences. Here is an example of the nocebo effect in action. What you 'believed' to be the case has dictated your experience whilst the truth has actually passed you by. So we can see how the messages taken in from the environment are significantly impacting on the mind and it's behaviour and the environmental triggers in this context are the thoughts you are generating, based on your beliefs.

When the mind, through positive suggestion, improves its health or its position, it is referred to as a placebo effect. Conversely when the mind is engaged in negative suggestions that can damage its health or diminish its position - this is known as the nocebo effect. Hopefully, what is becoming clear is that we are in danger if we don't sit in the seat of consciousness in the boardroom of the mind, of being subject to a 'take over' by the nocebo effect.. The nocebo effect, if left unchallenged, leaves us driven by perceptions often not our own, that are incredibly self-limiting. It's time to call an Extraordinary General Meeting in order to reclaim your position as Chair.

Change starts by making a plan, so make a promise to yourself to do that today.

Your beliefs are the key to your transformation. Start believing in the miracle that is you and you'll be able to perform many miracles, and you'll stop taking for granted arguably your greatest skill, which is your power to influence the direction of your thinking.

Order creates peace

I explained in Chapter 3 the intimate connection between mind and spirit and hopefully you were able to see how there is an on-going dialogue between the two. This conversation does not merely apply to spirit and mind. If you recall, we saw that the mind and body connection is equally powerful. However, the difference between the mind-spirit connection and the mind-body connection is that the mind-spirit relationship has significant areas of overlap; it's how they express the things they have in common that best exhibits their differences.

I want to explore something here that's pivotal to the mind and how it functions whilst also leaving its mark on the spirit i.e. how one feels. The mind loves order because within the structure of order it is able to find clarity and peace. There appears, from my observations, to be a modern myth that would have us believe that structure, order, routine, discipline and their allies are somehow the enemies of a life of fun, laughter and pleasure. This is in fact the 'propaganda' of those who have never ventured into the loving arms of order and its companions. Those who've experienced order, discipline etc. never stray far from their wonderful embrace, because they know to do so means they cannot ascend to their own highest point. They realize that order, in fact, creates peace.

Before we venture further on this part of the journey, please contemplate the following…

This sequence is an easy formula to remember. Used regularly, it will help you to create a consciousness in which positive thoughts and feelings can steadily grow in your life. Try and learn this formula and recite it often and watch what happens to your inner dialogue:

Order creates peace…

Peace creates love…

Love creates abundance…

Abundance creates success…

Success creates confidence...

Confidence creates courage...

There is no doubt that when you create order in your life it generates peace of mind. The reason so few of us experience the friendship of peace is because our lives are so full and cluttered. We have traded simplicity and clarity for a life that is too busy and crowded with demands. Our pursuit of kudos and materialism has deceived us into believing that the more we have, the happier we will be! With such beliefs, a mind is rarely at peace. A mind that is at peace with itself is at peace with others and is able to find love within its depths. A loving mind is rich and generous, overflowing, wanting to share what it has. This is abundance. One who is abundant gives lovingly and freely and finds that the world responds in kind and so success is born. A life endowed with success is a life filled with contentment and confidence. Success breeds belief in oneself, one's talents, one's ambitions and experiences. This is not a confidence that seeks or needs approval from outside. It is a confidence sustained by the inner reservoir of self-belief. An individual with this kind of self-belief lives a self-fulfilling prophecy, whatever he/she focuses on and puts energy into comes to fruition. Confident individuals have the courage of their convictions. They are not afraid to honour their hearts. They pursue their dreams with love, kindness and integrity. It seems that no matter what cards life deals them, they have that extra something that enables them to shine and remain true to their values.

Look closely at your life. When events seem to be flowing against you, a loss of perspective often follows and chaos ensues. Your mind becomes disturbed and confused, maybe even distressed. There is certainly a lack of peace. The absence of peace initially makes you more impatient and judgmental, which turns into a dislike of the self and finding fault in others. Left unattended, this becomes self-loathing. One who does not love him/herself cannot taste the sweet fruits of success. True success is contentment and those who live in that place of contentment grow in confidence and self-belief; it's that confidence and self-belief that give them the courage to be true to their hearts. Those who are true to their hearts, love and respect order. So you can see the circle is complete because in the end order will always create peace.

Find some time each day to sit quietly and think about this formula. Don't simply recite the words, but contemplate the meaning of each bit of the sequence. The more you delve into the significance of each phrase, the more its depths will become clear. There is so much wisdom housed in each part of this mantra and incredible power to be found in its synergy. Although each bit can stand alone, it's the interdependency of this sequence that will serve up the strength for the change that you seek.

What has all this got to do with the environment? Everything! If the mind lives in chaos it will imbibe it. The mind is unlike any sponge you've ever used; it absorbs everything. It's like a perfect magnet that leaves no iron filings 'un-clung'. Its power of attraction and ability to absorb are second to none. This is its greatest strength and also what makes it vulnerable to external forces. So if it's not switched to the correct frequency it will absorb negativity, at such a rate and to such a degree that it can easily lose its identity and sense of purpose. This is how so many of us lose our way, as the mind as a result of chaos, is not 'tuned in' in a way that would attract what it needs to prosper. This is where the environment has a lot to answer for because it can quickly help us to generate either clarity or confusion if we allow it to. Hence, we need to form a constructive and creative relationship with it if we are not to become its slaves.

Rice and mice!

It is worth saying at this point that everything is in some way under the influence of the environment. For example, the genes in your body are telling the story of their relationship with the environment. Much has been written about the role of genes and their ability to impose their will on the way our lives unfold. Nowhere is this more true than in the debate about disease and illness. Every day there is another gene that is held responsible for one medical condition or another. If we are to believe the populist scientific 'proof' served up in the media there is a gene for every pattern, function, characteristic and behaviour and yet the Genome Project (1990-2003) presented a verdict that clearly demonstrates that this could not be the case given how few genes we actually have – a mere twenty five to thirty thousand! So how can so few genes, the same number as those of mice, and interestingly, a grain of rice, be capable of the countless wondrous things that our incredible bodies and brains produce every second and minute of every day? Current estimates of the body's amazing range of tasks performed from moment to moment, keeping us alive, are around four billion per second - simply unimaginable. So the idea of the gene-driven organism defined by its biology has to be a myth. We are far more complex than that and I will try to prove it to you beyond reasonable doubt.

So what is it that drives this organism? What is it that drives and shapes our genetic expression? Given that genes have a set of predispositions and characteristics that lend themselves to certain outcomes, how can we have a say in that? Is it possible for me to be an architect designing my own reality or am I a victim to circumstances and fate? These mind-blowing questions can only be answered by understanding the power of the relationship between spirit, mind, body and environment. Our genetic story is influenced most of all by our environment. Environment here means, our thoughts, our diet and nutrition, as well as the dynamics of the planet and our relationships. The awesome power of the environment and its ability to affect body, mind and spirit is hopefully increasingly becoming clear.

We can no longer hide behind the explanations provided by genetic determinism because it is clear that even our thoughts, and not just physical energies influence the behaviour of genes. In other words, we are in part responsible for our life's unfolding and given the role and power of thoughts in that equation, we are indeed able to engineer incredible transformation. You may remember my reference to the IEGs (immediate early/experience genes) in Chapter 4, which are heavily influenced by our thoughts and feelings. Within less than three seconds they are able to change the destiny of our cells, tissues and organs. This can certainly be called mind over matter. Here we see thoughts, via the medium of the brain, making an impact body wide. This is why the mind's ability to both positively and negatively affect matter is increasingly becoming difficult to dispute.

The power of the mind can be maximized to such an extent that we can transform the internal biological landscape. But we need to understand the opposite is also true. If we are not exercising our power to be the spiritual engineers of our destiny then we become victims of circumstance. This is why so many of us stand on the shores of infinite possibility but without a boat. So instead of taking the exciting voyage into new and unchartered territory we find ourselves stranded, victims of whatever the sea of circumstance brings to our shore. It's time for change but you need to realize that change begins with you.

We can now see that the environment has many forms and plays many roles in our lives. It's not something that is merely about the physical dynamics of life, something you can easily manipulate by moving objects around in your personal space. Your environment also refers to the food you eat, which when broken down, goes coursing through your veins, touching and influencing every part of your anatomy. Could there be a more intimate relationship than that? Your environment as we have seen also refers to the metaphysical 'stuff' of thoughts, that invisible yet probably most powerful of all energies that switches genes on and off according to our moods and attitudes.

We also have to contend with the pollutants whizzing around in the atmosphere affecting the air, soil, rivers and foodstuffs. As our bodies imbibe a plethora of toxic compounds our very biochemistry is being altered and affected in ways that have still not been fully investigated and understood. What we can say is our immune systems, both the acquired and the innate, are under constant attack and we are struggling to cope, hence the rise in chronic infections and the conditions that flow from those biological events. To understand more about the importance of immunity and what can be done to support it, see the work of Dr. Paul Clayton and Dr. Joel Fuhrman – Eat to Live.

Before you go and find a dark room to sit in and ask 'what is the point?' I want to bring you back to why the mind craves order, structure, routine and discipline. The answer is, they all set the mind free, they offer healthy control over one's self and one's environment. Order and its allies take us from victimhood to a place of self-realization and self-mastery. We are able to influence life's events if we pursue positive choices. This is where free will and destiny meet. In every moment of every day there is the choice to be a victim or a master of circumstances. So why not exercise the power of choice? Choose order over chaos and watch your mind find clarity and make wise decisions about the way forward.

Soil meets soul

Before concluding this chapter we need to look at the last piece of the jigsaw, the environment's deep and profound relationship with the body. This has many layers, the most obvious one being the fact that the physical components of the body are made up of the same material as our physical world. We live in a world of matter and even more accurately the world of matter wraps its arms around us in the form of these incredible biological wonders, our bodies. The five elements that make up our world (earth, air, fire, water and ether) are the very substances that offer our bodies life and on-going support. In other words, we are literally entwined with the physical world. So to abuse the planet is to abuse ourselves, as our very existence depends on nature's wonder. It is our incredible ignorance about something so glaringly obvious that maintains our destructive habits and on-going decline. We simply haven't really made the connection between what we are doing to the planet and what the planet is in turn doing to us. We literally are reaping what we sow.

Consider this; in the 1930s one could easily find in excess of seventy minerals in the soil just about anywhere but due to a lack of crop rotation, overuse of nitrates damaging the soil through poor farming methods, various political influences and subsidies, we've now created a situation where minerals are often found at levels below twenty and in some cases now even in single figures. What do you imagine the effect of that is on our bodies? The body needs ninety nutrients a day - this is a minimal figure for good health - sixty minerals, sixteen vitamins, eleven amino acids and three essential fatty acids (EFAs). A whole host of other nutrients and their co-factors are needed in addition to this to ensure proper biological and metabolic function. So imagine if over two thirds of those minerals are missing, not to mention the vitamins, amino acids and EFAs, all of which are compromised too. How can our bodies do their jobs properly? They simply cannot. What is the price we are paying for this? Living below our biological potential, which of course, given the laws and principles of synergy, means we are living below our emotional, mental, spiritual and social potential too. Most of us are shadows of our true selves. We've probably never met him or her and would be shocked if we did. This book will offer you the opportunity to truly meet with yourself but first you must understand what needs to be done.

If we don't respect our environment and work with it at all the different levels we will remain out of 'sync' with ourselves, the planet and our destiny. If you are to find your purpose and live according to it, you must meet the body's needs, you must align it to the environment. If you do not provide the body with the basic nutrients it needs, nothing in you can work optimally. These biological nutrients that are essential to the body also affect brain function and once the brain is affected so are the three Ps, perception, personality and performance. There are another three Ps I will also discuss much later on and they are, patience, practice and perseverance. These relate to the attitude and approach one needs to develop to achieve success in life.

Perception, personality and performance

For now, let's return to perception, personality and performance. Your whole life is shaped by these three aspects. Perceptions come first in this sequence, but what shapes perceptions? Of course there are our past experiences, upbringing and other social and cultural influences, which are enormous, but added to this is our nutrient and micro nutrient profile and pH (acid-alkaline) balance and our hydration levels which are also absolutely essential to this equation. These biological factors alter our brain chemistry - either enhancing our perception, awareness and understanding, or diminishing it. A lack of water alone is able to undermine the production of every hormone, neuropeptide and the countless neurotransmitters being produced by the brain. As these chemical agents are compromised, so is our outlook. A lack of vitamins and minerals equally has a devastating effect on how we see ourselves, and the world. Orthomolecular medicine, (the science of having the 'right molecule' to ensure optimal mental and physical functioning) has demonstrated over the last fifty to sixty years that what we put in our mouths unquestionably affects our minds – I will say much more about this later on.

Again we can see that what the body needs from its environment is critical to the construction of our perception. Perception defines our reality. We are all living in the worlds that our perceptions have shaped for us. Unless we challenge the limitations of those perceptions we remain trapped in the narrow corridors of our opinions and the need to be right.

Our perceptions then drive our personalities. Subject to how we see the world, we 'act out' in ways that we 'believe' will help us to belong, to be liked, to be valued. We unconsciously construct narratives and roles that allow us to get our needs met in all the different contexts and settings in which we interact with others. Unless we are living conscious, aware lives, we are mostly driven by the fear of rejection and the need to be loved.

If you look closely at your own life and perform an honest audit you will see that much of what you do is because of fear of something or the need to be liked, to fit in, to be loved. To be free of these drives requires courage and application, the courage to be honest about what binds you and then also the burning desire to change it. Even these positive urges are influenced by our diet, hydration and nutrition.

So of course performance will be impeded if these essential factors are insufficient. How could it be any other way? Once perception is distorted our personality 'acts out' in accordance with those perceptions and one's performance is automatically diminished. We simply can't give the best of ourselves because the necessary ingredients are not in place. This is why it is imperative to give the body what it needs. We must also ensure that we respect the environment and understand its crucial role in moulding the body and its responses - if the two are not appropriately aligned then that imbalance can just as easily dismantle the body's health.

There is much more to say about the environment because I've not yet fully explored the role of relationships in this equation, which we'll look at as we go further, and these too are critical to the evolution of the self, peace of mind and happiness. Also deeply connected to that is a social conscience, which brings us back to living responsibly on this planet, for we have the honour of being its custodians. All of this and more will be carefully examined.

Are we in control?

What we have established so far is that you are the major shareholder in your life. Genes play a part but in fact it's how our genetic information interfaces with our environment that is pivotal. In other words, the choices that we make determine how our genetic story unfolds. Our choices really matter. The chief factors that define how nature and nurture relate to one another are thoughts and beliefs, food and nutrition, hydration, relationships, pollution and environmental influences, upbringing and social contact, a life of meaning and purpose. The outdated debate about whether it's nature or nurture is well and truly arrested by the expansion of our understanding through epigenetics and cognitive neuroscience.

A more accurate description would be nature plus nurture. We come with a set of predispositions but according to our relationship with the environment (which includes those in it) our predispositions are either diluted or accentuated. It is time to acknowledge what the latest evidence is telling us and make the necessary changes in our lives. We are not victims unless we choose to be. You are the chairperson of your own board. Exercise the power and the rights that come with that position. Make the choices that will set you on a better course.

In the work of Candace Pert, her research clearly demonstrates how, through 'active awareness', the mind can, via the brain, generate molecules that calm and heal the system, overriding negative patterns and impulses. In other words, proper use of consciousness can bring health to an ailing mind and body. Her work shows that where self-awareness is absent the molecules of emotion (neuropeptides) that are produced simply create dis-ease through the mind and disease in the body. We can actively choose, by increasing self-awareness, to respond differently to environmental signals. The conscious mind's capacity to override the subconscious mind's pre-programmed behaviours is the foundation of free will.

However, the big problem in achieving this is that so much of our programming tells us we are not worthy, we are not good enough, and because of such beliefs we are driven down destructive pathways. Unfortunately our subconscious mind does not have discrimination - it is driven by the 'evidence' of our past experiences. So because perception (what we believe about ourselves) controls biology, it follows that when we are handicapped by mistaken perceptions, these then have the power to drive us away from our potential and purpose. It is imperative that we change this, which is one the primary reasons for writing this book – to encourage you to reclaim your poise, purpose and your power.

The whole and the hole

Now The Story of Health has been outlined to a depth where you can hopefully see the futility of a one-dimensional approach to health and healing, the rest of this life-changing story can follow.

As I said in the opening pages in Chapter 1 The Story of Health is the centre-piece of this unique approach, but it's only in fact the beginning. Interestingly, by the time you've got to the end of this book you'll see it is also the end point. You will come to understand that health is actually a circle, which is why healing and recovery can't take place without addressing the 'whole' person. This is also true if we drop the 'w' and change whole to hole. Although the whole person does need to be focused upon, in order to do that successfully the 'hole in the soul' also needs to be addressed as the two are inextricably linked. The whole cannot be completed without addressing the hole. It is through the hole, in many cases holes, which exist in the inner world that the individual's power is lost and with that their courage, confidence, self-esteem, faith, joy and much more. This is why we must concern ourselves with both the hole and the whole, for it is impossible to find peace of mind without turning our attention and energy to both…

This is the next step in our journey. How do we find the hole, or holes, through which our power drains away? For it is almost certainly these holes which prevent you from rising up to and reaching the pinnacle of your potential.

We've seen what needs to be done to persuade spirit, mind and body and how the environment needs to be respected and managed to support those changes, so how do we prevent our power from evaporating in order that our best efforts are not in vain? It's time to explore N.O.S.E. a clear and effective way of addressing the hole in order that we might become whole again.

"The greater danger for most of us lies not in setting our aim too high and falling short; but in setting our aim too low, and achieving our mark.
Michelangelo (1475 – 1564)

CHAPTER 6: N.O.S.E.

"You can avoid reality, but you cannot avoid the consequences of avoiding reality."
Ayn Rand (1905-1982)

A unique way forward

The Reach Approach has been built upon two and a half thousand years of philosophy, medieval science, religious thought and spirituality. It has also been constructed on a deep and subtle understanding of social and cultural forces, psychology (past and present), and modern-day science in all its new technical brilliance, but most of all The Reach Approach has been built on client experience, the hundreds of thousands of hours spent sitting in a room with individuals, couples, families and groups from every background imaginable, working tirelessly to improve the mindscape of those seeking positive solutions. This marriage between knowledge in all its various forms and human experience has helped us to craft something so wonderfully simple, deep and interconnected that our methodology and approach is seamless and crystal clear.

The more you explore the model, the more you will see that it is underpinned by a desire and ambition for co-operation, where 'ego' and individuality has been dissolved, leaving in its place a model of unity, balance and harmony. At the heart of this approach is the indisputable truth that, "the whole is greater than the sum of its parts". Truth is an egoless pursuit. The moment it turns its focus on personality or becomes a case of 'my point of view is better than your point of view' truth is lost to us all.

It is within this simple observation that the concept of N.O.S.E. was born as I gradually wedded the ancient truths from many sources to the modern-day schools of thought because it became clear that the answers were not to be found in one place and the problem with progress is that it tends to believe that it always knows best. Experience has taught me this is often not the case.

Antiquity has taught us that what we haven't resolved continues to define us and drives us down familiar paths, whether we are aware of it or not. This is because unresolved issues are such powerful subconscious drivers; they simply don't relent until we heed their cries. Therefore it is in facing our deepest fears, traumas and experiences that we can best find the resolution our hearts need.

Modernity has presented us with various ways to 'repair' the individual; these have somewhat clouded the picture. Psychology, in all of its many forms, from person-centred to psychodynamic approaches, has also complicated the picture, each school of thought offering us a slightly different take. On the one hand there is the point of view which says that the person seeking help is the 'expert' and wherever she leads, we therapists follow, and as long as the therapeutic conditions are right, the individual will naturally move towards her own solution. So very little outside intervention is required, as the power for change simply resides in the humanity of being present, non-judgmental, offering unconditional positive regard, empathy and congruence. It is in the gift of these 'core conditions' that healing and recovery is said to take place. This approach is described as non-directive.

At the other end of the spectrum is the passionate belief that when clients are disconnected from themselves by their emotional and psychological difficulties, they are unable to see what they need. Furthermore, even if they could see what was required, they simply don't have the skills to facilitate the changes they may then seek; hence a professional (expert) with the necessary skills is required for therapeutic movement and healing to take place. This approach is often described as directive. There are many different permutations and degrees both in directive and non-directive approaches but in practice the differences between the many schools of therapy are often less significant than at first they might appear. The primary differences between the directive and non–directive approaches are that the former is driven by the idea that the therapist is the 'expert' and the latter believes the client to be their own expert. The directive approach intervenes with what it believes to be effective often 'proven' strategies to steer the boat of consciousness towards health and recovery, whilst the non-directive approach 'gets out of the way' and trusts that through the support offered via the relationship, the client will find her way, as she has all the resources she needs dwelling somewhere inside herself.

I believe the tug-of-war between these different schools (which in some limited cases is changing) continues to miss the point, that is, both aspects are needed. In fact, both things are true. The client is her own expert and at a certain point in her evolution (which she will both see and feel and therefore 'know') she can navigate the boat of consciousness herself. However, it is equally true that when there has been a 'disconnect' within the self for whatever reason then someone is often needed to help re-build the bridge back to the self. That doesn't have to be a therapist, it could be anyone you trust, but it does need to be someone who is warm, non-shaming, thoughtful, sensitive and who has the necessary insight, clarity and skills to help. So don't get caught up in the idea it has to be one thing at the expense of the other - person-centred ideology (non-directive) or something from the psychodynamic tradition (directive) – we need the 'push-pull' of both to help create the conditions for recovery and sustainable well-being.

N.O.S.E: both a directive and a non-directive approach

What does the acronym N.O.S.E. stand for? Name it, Own it, Surrender it and Empowerment. I dare to suggest that these four stages house literally all you need to know about achieving positive change. The premise is simple; until you name and own your stuff, you cannot be free of it. The reason most of us remain stuck in our negative patterns, going around the same loops over and over again, is that we are busy denying, justifying and defending our opinions, drives and patterns as if our lives depended on it. This is why positive change eludes so many of us. N.O.S.E. directs us to the starting point for change, which is 'naming' and 'owning'. Only then can we find our way out of our mental enslavement and behavioural immaturity. What follows is a summary of N.O.S.E. and then I will explain each of the four stages in more detail.

It is difficult to take the vast subject of personal transformation and conceptualize it into small manageable parcels. However, within the acronym N.O.S.E., I have attempted to do just that. There is no greater propeller for personal progress than being given the ability to see clearly the point of the journey ahead and how the destination can be reached. N.O.S.E. offers the clarity most people are looking for in an attempt to find their own solution. So, let me define exactly what N.O.S.E. means.

A summary of the four stages

Name 'it': The journey of personal transformation is unlikely to be successful until one has defined what it is that is blocking one's path. Until you have named your demons, your shortcomings, your sickness, they will continue to have power over you. In fact, the reason why most people are unable to break out of their negative loop is because they have not yet named what ails them. For example, if you think your problem is anger when in fact it is fear, whatever interventions are made to overturn your anger may well deliver short-term benefits but are unlikely to offer a sustainable solution. In other words, if you do not trace your anger back to its previous incarnations (which for many requires help) you will simply be treating the symptom and not the cause, leaving your fear to continue transmuting and deceiving you under its different guises. So, the first step along the path of positive change is to name 'it', i.e. give your problems/feelings a name... your pain, hurt, anger, fear, shame etc.

Own 'it': Having named your ailment, the next critical step is to own it (embrace it). Far too many of us engage in non-ownership activities, such as justification, denial, pretence and blame. All these activities allow us to continue deceiving ourselves. In other words we do not take responsibility for who we are or where we find ourselves, which in turn means we are denied a solution. To own your 'stuff' in whatever shape or form it exists is an extremely courageous act. This is why the dividends are enormous. Once you own your pain, fear, anger etc. the realizations, the 'awakening', is life-changing. Instead of drowning in feelings of blame, shame and guilt etc. you are able to see, probably for the first time, beyond your sickness and to witness your true beauty and worth and with that you discover the possibility of a better tomorrow.

Surrender 'it': To truly surrender something, which in this context means letting go, is only really possible when you've accurately named it and fully owned it. These two processes will give you real power over your ailments, issues and concerns. The naming and owning ceremonies make it possible for you to cut the negative ties that you have with your 'stuff'. To surrender means to disassociate yourself from attitudes, behaviour and moods that no longer reflect who you are and what you aspire to. It is a conscious detachment from those things that burden your spirit. This is achieved primarily through the practice of forgiveness and gratitude both of which are difficult to carry out with success until the 'truth' about your condition has been honestly faced. When the 'non-ownership' activities have been put to one side and the 'truth' has been embraced, surrender becomes easy.

Empowerment: To surrender unblocks the pathways in the mind. Disease is a state where the organism (the body and/or the mind) is unable to express its energy freely. This leads to disharmony and malfunction. Health, on the other hand, is the state where the organism's energy flows without restriction, expressing its power and potential in an optimal way. This is what happens when we let go. The mind is able to fully express its boundless energy and enthusiasm for life. Empowerment is not something we have to strive for, it's the natural consequence of surrender. Once your blockages are removed your true value, meaning and purpose become clear. With naming, owning and surrendering you are automatically empowered which means you're able to fully embrace life and express your truth.

Now that you have an outline of the four stages, what follows is a more comprehensive explanation of each stage. This I believe will enable you to see clearly how you can best generate positive change in your life.

Name 'it' expanded

I believe that until you name 'it' (your pain, hurt, fear, doubt, in fact whatever is wrong) you will be unable to break the negative cycles that enslave you. In fact, I would go even further than this, until you accurately name your 'stuff' your capacity for peace of mind, contentment, stability and happiness is significantly reduced. Many people are busy living the lie that they're ok when in fact if they looked beneath the surface what they would see is panic, fear and insecurity lurking deep within. It's within these murky waters that the stench of dissatisfaction, repeated disappointment and periods of delusion and even depression can be found. All of this exists because the individual has not truly identified what is wrong.

Do any of these questions sound familiar? "Why can't I break free from these patterns I despise?" "Why don't I have the courage to be true to my beliefs?" "Why do I busy myself fitting in when I don't even respect what I am a part of?" "I'm tired of pretending and yet find I don't know how to do anything else". Can you see yourself in these internal chantings? If so you have not named what is limiting you. How do you name 'it'?

Naming your 'stuff' is not as easy as it might first appear. It requires excruciating honesty, quiet reflection and a fearlessness that enables you to look into the dark recesses of your mind. If you take a close look at yourself through your moods, attitudes, ways of being, interactions and most intimate relationships, you will be able to see the multifaceted personality that you've constructed over the course of your life. And in this mirror, if you look closely and with the piercing eyes of honesty and the courage to face the truth, you will see those things that are less desirable about you. This is where the process begins.

Once you've gathered your list of 'undesirables', the next phase is to take a closer look - and this requires stillness and silence. Under the microscope of quiet reflection you are able to understand the 'viral-like' nature of emotions and their incredible ability to transmute. Just like a virus constantly seeks to re-invent itself within the cell in order to ensure its own survival, in the same way emotions are very protective of themselves and once under scrutiny or threat of attack, they find a way to metamorphose in order to maintain their existence. This instinct is common to all life force/energy. This is why naming 'it' can be such a challenge and without a deep desire to see the truth one does remain prey to this 'viral-like' activity.

So, in order to trace the previous incarnations of your emotions, look at yourself closely in the mirror of your moods, attitudes, interactions and relationships. Regularly sit in silence and listen to the songs that your heart sings and the origins of your present day activity will become clear, if you are willing to listen. Realize that what currently stands in front of you is unlikely to be the whole truth, so don't be afraid to take a closer look because whatever you find, even though you may at first be afraid of it, offers the keys to your mental emancipation. You may find in addition to your own regular silent reflection that you need the help of someone you can trust to completely unveil your previously unnamed issues.

Own 'it' expanded

To own your 'stuff' takes enormous courage. For many it will involve ending a long career of blaming others and pointing the finger of responsibility elsewhere whilst sitting comfortably on the seat of self-righteousness, wearing the crown of 'not guilty'. Without naming your demons and shortcomings, you can't begin to identify and own your issues. To own it means facing the truth about your attitude, your approach to life and your actions, and taking responsibility for all three. Through the naming process one learns about familial inheritances and how these have shaped the person you are today, and by understanding how your past has defined you, you gain access to many wonderful insights. However, the point of the exercise is not to apportion blame to those who may well have failed you. The real point is to understand how the past has made you the person you are today and to illuminate what you can do to change those things you wish to change.

Shame has been described throughout the ages as the emotion that most binds the spirit and I've discovered through my work that nothing quite holds the individual hostage like the emotion of shame. Shame is the feeling that 'I am not good enough', it's the fear of being 'found out'. Guilt is the emotion we feel when we've made a mistake. Shame is the feeling 'I am the mistake'.

In our attempt to conceal our shame we bend and twist ourselves out of shape to such an extent that our true identities become camouflaged and in some cases lost, as we become what our environment needs or demands of us and our true natures are subjugated. If we can face our shame there is an incredible journey of awareness and insight that awaits us.

The journey of shame is where the person, probably for the first time, not only sees what the world has done to them, but can also see his/her negative contributions to the world. Without understanding both sides of this equation the individual is unlikely to be emotionally and psychologically balanced. How can we be balanced if our view of the world is based on the idea that we have played no part in getting where we are today?

Whenever we stand in the place of victimhood i.e. not taking responsibility for our actions, we deny ourselves the truth and beauty of personhood. Personhood is the recognition that " I am the major shareholder in my life and if I do not exercise that authority I give my power and destiny away". Shame-work can be extremely difficult because the ugliness of some of the attitudes and behaviours that are unveiled is such that the individual would rather not take a closer look at the undesirable aspects of the self. This is why for many of us owning rarely takes place. Think about it, if we find it too difficult to look into those dark and less desirable aspects of our being, how can we see what's there and what needs to be changed? However, if you are able to look your shame in the eyes, as difficult as that might be, you can retrieve the power that your shame continually leaches away from you. Your shame is like a parasite, it lives off you, its willing host. What is more, it persuades you never to truly face it for fear of being led to your decline. In fact the opposite is true. By not facing your shame your demise is almost certainly guaranteed.

So owning 'it' takes nothing from you, in fact it gives back the power you have long lost. Every time you have concealed, denied or justified some aspect of your behaviour, you have simply strengthened the parasitical nature of shame and in turn weakened yourself.

Now turn and face your shame, guilt, anger, fear, pain etc., and you will be able to reclaim the power that has been lost. Although this journey can be taken alone, for most the challenge of 'owning' their stuff is best undertaken with another because the mirror of feedback is important in this revelatory process, as some of the challenging and, at times, painful discoveries that will unfold are easier to make sense of with the aid of feedback. However, you need to take this journey with someone who understands the challenges of this courageous undertaking and who can offer the compassion and support required. It is only with the balance of constructive feedback and kindness that you will be able to see yourself clearly. It is my experience that when you have the courage to embrace the whole truth about yourself, rather than disliking yourself even more, you are able to discover how beautiful you really are, so do not fear what you consider to be ugly about yourself because even that has something really beautiful to offer you.

Living in the now?

As I've explained the thing that most binds us is our shame. It is a fear like no other. It literally nails us to the spot. So we become tied to the illusion that we are free and living in the now when in fact we're often in bondage, tied to a past that keeps being re-cycled, a past we're living and re-living over and over again.

There is a lot of talk in the personal development movement about 'living in the now' - but the single biggest obstacle to that is shame. The reason most people are unable to celebrate the present moment is that the past anger, traumas, hurts and experiences that need to be resolved keep the individual tied to his history. What is history anyway? 'His-story'. Whilst we remain entangled in the story thus far, we cannot be part of the story yet to be told.

There is a magical journey of possibilities bound up in each moment but if we remain tied to history or 'her-story' we cannot be part of that unlimited expedition. It is the fear of being found out, of not being good enough, the fear of not belonging that keeps propelling us down the many pointless paths of the past. That fear is shame.

Shame is so pivotal to our liberation that I want to try and help you to better understand it because without transcending shame, the S and E (surrender and empowerment) of N.O.S.E., are simply not possible. So let's continue our excursion into the anatomy of shame.

How does shame begin?

Shame is the primary by-product of emotional neglect, poor communication, family dysfunction, all of which lead to a loss of self-importance. It begins (usually in childhood) with an absence of positive mirroring (responses), positive affirmations and intimacy and is fed further and nurtured by a range of mixed messages, which pollutes the child's sense of worth. This in turn confuses the child and sets up a state of internal conflict. It is in the midst of this conflict that shame carves away at our 'core self' and our authenticity.

We all come into this world with amazing beauty and potential but if we are not affirmed and helped to feel good about ourselves we never make real contact with our essence, our real purpose and nature. This leads us to believe that what does lie inside of us is inadequate and not good enough - one's true nature is then gradually substituted by various false selves. These false selves are largely created by the child's inability to make sense of the mixed messages that it is being fed, by the central characters in its life.

There are many overt and covert demands, expectations and conditions imposed on the child, which are often tied to the child getting its emotional needs met. Thus the child learns to act in accordance with both the spoken and unspoken conditions and expectations to get what it needs. Repeated exposure to this conditional environment perpetuates an internal culture of confusion and the child unknowingly substitutes her 'real' self for a self her world seems to prefer.

Once these 'conditional characters' (sub-personalities) have been conceived, we then begin to lose ourselves, and also a sense of our own intrinsic value. These sub-personalities are actually distorted images of our real nature, which help to hide, and at the beginning, even protect who we really are. They are also the means by which we get many of our emotional needs met.

We then over time become further entangled in a web of pretence, denial and falsehood, created by these sub-personalities and unfortunately we learn to dance to their tune. We become convinced that our true self is something to be ashamed of. So, the many faces and voices of shame begin their diverse and varied career with vigilance and dedication. Each face and voice ensuring that who we really are is never 'found out' or discovered, not even by ourselves - all of this because of our need to belong, our need to be loved.

As I said earlier, guilt is, "I have made a mistake". Shame is, "I am a mistake". Guilt gives us hope that we might be able to make amends and put things right. Shame denies us this possibility and keeps us trapped within the feelings of inadequacy and low self-importance. Much of the negative dialogue that has been set in motion inside of us resonates in our minds and is propelled by the feeling of shame. It says to us with unhealthy frequency, "you are flawed", "something is wrong with you", "you will be found out", "you could never achieve that goal" and continually goes on churning out negative self-talk which becomes integrated into our belief system and shapes our perception.

These voices (our negative self-talk) create many sides and various shades to our personalities, which in fact make us very different people in a range of situations. These voices help to emerge the faces of jealousy, irritability, stubbornness, prejudice, hypocrisy, as well as a network of denials and elaborate defence mechanisms, all of these having been created and then sustained by us continuing to dance hypnotically to the out-dated rhythms of our sub-personalities.

Understanding the anatomy of shame offers us some of the solutions to our mental divisions and the continuing disintegration of ourselves. It allows us to begin to make the distinction between the 'acquired self' (what we've become) and the 'authentic self' (who we really are). If we are to re-establish a connection with the authentic self we need to disentangle ourselves from the many faces and voices of shame, and the best way to do this is with understanding, kindness and compassion.

Embracing your shame

Healthy shame is being in touch with our 'human-ness', it reminds us of our limitations and boundaries. It breeds humility. Healthy shame prevents us from becoming stuck in the "I know it all" state of being, where we are unable to benefit from our experiences. Healthy shame does not leave us standing on unstable ground as we try to maintain the pretence of being that which we are not. Healthy shame does not limit or entrap us, in fact it frees us and allows us a state of continued development, ever-enthused by the magic and the mystery of life. Healthy shame is an acceptance of our nature, feelings, instincts, drives, needs and sexuality. When we deny our nature and cut off from our primary emotions we then convert healthy shame into toxic shame. It is this pollution of our real nature that we must address.

By clearly understanding our condition we come to realize we need to embrace our shame, to re-connect with the frightened, untrusting and emotionally deprived bits of ourselves in order that we can heal. There will be some who in addition to this, also need to grieve for their lost childhood, which is also healing.

The social and cultural structures we conform to often view grief as a negative and at times undesirable process, yet we are unable to fully understand and accept events until we have truly grieved. It is our unresolved grief that keeps many parts of us locked and shut down and feeds our negative behaviour patterns. Grief is not unhealthy, it enables us to heal, it allows us to feel what is real inside us and in doing so truly address it. We cannot heal what we cannot feel. Until we feel it we do not know that it even exists within us, so it is able to masquerade as some other emotion and continue to wreak havoc. This is why it is imperative to make contact with what we really feel (naming and owning) so that the healing process can begin.

Being able to recognize our emotional disabilities may initially bring some painful realizations, fears and anxiety with it. However, it also brings with it the capacity to liberate ourselves and transcend that which limits us. This liberation offers our true identity back to us and with it all the potential, ability and talent that we have either only had a taste of or, in most cases not yet discovered.

It is time to relinquish the shackles of the past and our fears and doubts about the future by using what we know, in order to empower ourselves in the present. We've come to understand how our sense of self-worth is constructed and from where much of the dialogue we have inside us originates. We also have an understanding of how the illusions about ourselves are kept nourished and alive. We recognize why, out of a need to feel that we 'matter' as well as a need to survive, we have established certain patterns of behaviour and particular roles, which we are now sub-consciously locked into most of the time. We can also see why there is a need to lovingly embrace our own vulnerabilities and shortcomings so that we can be whole again. So, how do we use all these realizations for personal empowerment? This is the next step on the road to becoming whole.

Where to now?

Having successfully 'named' and 'owned' your stuff, you will almost certainly have met your own 'oracle' along the way - your sage or 'sagess', the latent wisdom that has been speaking to you for years, but has been ignored through a lack of introspection and communion with the self. It's interesting to note that out of the honesty and courage required to face your demons, you discover a depth to you that you just didn't know was there – the therapeutic experience my colleagues and I have amassed tells me this is true.

Naming and owning introduces you to different levels of consciousness. This is why we place so much emphasis on both. However, to achieve this state of insight and wonderment, the non-directive 'core conditions' I spoke of earlier are needed - unconditional positive regard, a mind-set that suspends judgment or more accurately judges what it sees kindly and with compassion and in addition warmth, congruence and sensitivity are needed.

My approach in my work with clients is to trust the creative intelligence of the individual to face her demons and then to support her in those ways that are constructive and healthy. However, my approach goes much further than that. In fact, where it is obvious that the creative intelligence is malfunctioning or is unable to see its 'blind spot', at that point I act on the trust and the power that has accrued in the relationship and combine that with the relevant knowledge and experience I've gained to help engineer positive change. In other words, the process of N.O.S.E. both 'directs' when needed and 'gets out of the way' when appropriate. This is achieved through genuine empathy and rapport.

With the state of clarity that naming and owning brings, and the insights that emerge from that clarity, it's now possible to engage in surrender. Surrender is the ability to let go, but letting go is only really do-able once there is resolution.

Resolution creates time, space and energy

Resolution of past issues is critical to growth because the negative experiences gathered through our lives literally occupy precious space within the self. It is as though we are occupied by an oppressive regime of negative experiences.

Whilst these experiences remain unchallenged, the areas under siege cannot be used in constructive and creative ways. Like an occupying army, these negative energies deplete us, but when the issues are resolved the occupied territories can once again be returned intact to the self. A helpful way to conceptualize this is to think of a square. The square represents the self. Let us say for the sake of this illustration that 25% of the square is shaded, and that this shaded area represents all the pain, hurt, sadness, unresolved anger and trauma gathered over the course of one's life. This then leaves 75% of the square unshaded, representing what potential is left within the self. In other words, this individual can only ever achieve 75% of his/her potential because the remaining 25% is shut down and therefore unavailable. Bound up in a negative way it remains inaccessible in that form. By facing up to and doing what is needed to resolve the dysfunction in that 25%, the space can be reclaimed, allowing the person to become complete, therefore able to fulfill his/her potential.

This fairly simple illustration contains the essence of self-transformation. If we were to really understand that the negative occupation by past events and hurts denies us the space and the energy to move forward, we would focus intensely on resolving those things that hold us back. Just think how much energy and time is wasted re-living events that you can do nothing about, where you crucify yourself over and over for your past mistakes. Think how much time you waste holding grudges, thinking unfavourably of others and wasting the opportunity to improve and change relationships. Just think how much time you waste justifying your own behaviour and motivations and laying the blame at the doors of others rather than taking responsibility for your own actions. All this time, energy and mental space given over to this type of thinking is terribly wasteful, but worse still are the countless missed opportunities to create positive change and establish a new beginning.

Every minute of every day is an opportunity for a fresh start, it is your chance to leave the past where it belongs, behind you, and to slip into the now and experience the joy of being you. If you take an honest look at yourself you will often see you are living beneath the ceiling of your potential. Every moment is another chance to change that. All you need to do is grasp the nettle of personal responsibility and make a pledge to resolve and release the past. Then you can create the space, time and energy to be all you are capable of being.

Hopefully you can use the metaphor of the square to invoke your determination. Once you finish reading this section, make time to sit down by yourself and think of all those people and events that still hold you hostage, that negatively bind you and through a simple mental role-play, talk to the people in question in such a way that all that needs to be said is said. Speak from your heart without apology because it is only when you truly express your feelings in a healthy way that you can be free of them. Unhealthy expression breeds even more negative consequences. Healthy expression brings resolution and the opportunity for a new beginning. So, systematically over the coming weeks and even months if necessary, speak in your mind to those individuals where you need to address outstanding issues/concerns and in time the negative feelings will ease and eventually evaporate and you will be able to make peace with those things that once troubled you. This is one of a number of ways to bring about resolution. However, you will need to do these exercises several times before you achieve the desired outcome. But you can be sure of one thing, if you do repeatedly address these issues in your mind in this way, you will become free of them and be able to fully reclaim yourself.

Of course you could go and speak to the person(s) in question but you need to be aware that they may not be ready for such a discussion and so great care should be taken if this is the route that you choose because if they are not ready, you may do more harm than good (see The Three Gatekeepers in Chapter 7).

Furthermore, it should be said that it's not always necessary to resolve something with another person because in most cases the issue needs resolving in one's own mind. That's the place most of us are imprisoned. Our minds can either be the Garden of Eden, a paradise, or a torturous space, hell, where we revisit time and again issues that have long passed us by.

Letting go

There is a beautiful Hindu story that talks about the bird that is struggling to fly but hasn't realized that he is still firmly holding onto the branch, so even though he's flapping his wings frantically he's unable to go anywhere! Sound familiar? Many of us are exactly like this bird. Even worse than that, we are irritated, impatient and at times cruel to ourselves. Time and again we are tortured by these questions, "Why me?", "Why can't I ever move forward?", "Everything I do seems pointless and futile", "I'm tired and fed up of going round in circles." And so the inner narrator produces a script of quiet condemnation, self-doubt and lack of hope. This is the equivalent to the bird holding onto the branch. In order to be free, you must let go of those thoughts and beliefs that hold you back. In fact, you need to go further than that and put the old script in the bin of waste thoughts. It has no value anymore. It's time to 'surrender it'.

Try this self-talk script. Read it allowing the dots to act as pauses in which you contemplate each phrase. You'll find it not only slows down your thinking but it will provide you with a useful template for letting go.

The more I hold onto the past and those things that remain unresolved the more I live a life defined by yesterday... There's no chance of living in the now, embracing the infinite possibility of each moment, whilst yesterday's script is influencing my thoughts, moods and perceptions... I need to resolve anything that is still occupying space in my mind... The things that haunt and possess me that I have not made peace with continue to shape the present moment... I must face and embrace those things that I continue to deny, those things that I run away from, hoping they won't be there tomorrow... Unless I do this, my mind will continue to be held hostage to the past... I choose in this moment to turn and face those things I need to resolve... I look honestly into the eyes of my issues, hurts and fears and as I do so I feel a growing sense of relief... I realize that my biggest obstacle is not facing my issues but running away... The more I run away the more power I give away... When I face and embrace my unresolved 'stuff' the flame of courage inside me begins to flicker and I realize I have more to fear from my re-cycled past than from what awaits me... The future is not my enemy, nor does it wait to greet me with hostility... In fact, it offers me the hand of friendship... All I need do is to stretch out my hand to meet it... And I am best able to do that by letting go of the past and resolving those things that bind me to yesterday... It's time to live in the now and open my arms to greet the future, my friend... I'm no longer afraid to face what I need to... I'm no longer afraid of today... I'm no longer afraid of tomorrow... I'm free to live a happy and fulfilling life... And so I do...

Surrender 'it'

When you honestly face the 'truth' about your condition, as described in the guided commentary, you will be able to let go of the obstructions and limitations to your growth. Surrendering can only happen after the naming and owning ceremonies have taken place. You will by now have understood that sustainable transformation becomes possible once you're honest about what needs to change and once you have stopped making excuses for why you act and behave in certain ways. To surrender is easy in principle and yet in practice it can be a huge challenge. It's like the bird I spoke of earlier holding onto the branch really tightly, flapping its wings with all the energy it can muster and yet asking the question "why can't I fly?" Of course the answer is the bird cannot fly because it is not letting go of the branch. The branch represents all those things that we hold onto out of fear. Fear that the world would not like or love us were we to own up to our 'stuff'. Fear that we will be rejected and abandoned. Fear we won't be good enough and will be found wanting. Because of our fear, which is entwined with shame, we hold onto the branch as if our lives depended on it, flapping our wings desperately at the same time because we ache to be free. The wings represent honesty and courage. Without these two qualities we have little chance of being free. Honesty and courage will lead you towards authenticity (your true nature), which in turn disables the 'acquired selves' (what you've become) and make it possible for them to fall away.

So, in order to appreciate the beautiful feeling which surrender evokes within the spirit, simply let go of the branch! Naming and owning begin the transformational process and the honesty and courage that both these activities require make it possible to experience the beauty and power of surrender. Surrender is not an intellectual journey - it is a journey of the heart. To surrender 'it' is to truly feel your feelings and your emotional and psychological blockages are removed as the pain and the hurt of the past fade. There are many ways to do this and I will explore them with you as this journey unfolds. The journey of forgiveness and gratitude can then begin in earnest. Facing what holds you hostage with sincerity and compassion enables you to let go and to fly freely. Surrender is about both letting go and then developing a different conversation with yourself.

Change your self-talk

Please make time to undergo the journey of forgiveness. I explored this in some depth in Chapter 2. Even at a sprint this is an activity which is likely to take some two to three months. Forgiveness deals with any residual emotional rubbish that remains and makes room for a better today and tomorrow. Forgiveness is like the air beneath your wings. It will ease your transition and maintain your flight. The more you forgive yourself the more you will have the capacity to forgive others. Then in time forgiveness becomes a way of being, a way of life.

Gratitude, its loyal companion, will equally keep you soaring like a bird in the sky, flying way above all the things that bring you down. Gratitude is not something to start today with a view to stopping at some time in the future. Gratitude is a lifelong appreciation of things that you take for granted, especially the gift of your own life. The more things you find to be appreciative of, the more your heart will sing. To surrender is to have found your beauty and to promise never to let it go. This is achieved by remaining true to yourself, true to your beliefs and principles. It's based on a life of forgiving yourself for your mistakes and affording others that compassion too. Surrender is to live within the 'generosity of gratitude' and by doing this you will no longer be that bird flapping its wings, yet unable through fear to let go of the branch.

Try another self-talk exercise, designed to cut the negatives ties to your past. You'll find it helps greatly the more you practise it.

My head and my heart hurt as a consequence of my unresolved issues, thoughts and feelings... At times it feels so difficult to let go of those things that have hurt me and in many cases changed my life... And yet the more I hold on to those pains, sadness, regrets, anger and trauma the more I hurt and the less able I am to move on... Where is the benefit in holding on to that which hurts?... Is there really any value in remaining in this place?... My lack of forgiveness hurts me more than anyone else... Have I not suffered enough already?... It's time to move on, to look forward and to take what lessons life has offered me on my journey... Forgiveness sets me free... It's not a position of weakness, it is in fact a position of courage and strength... It's much harder to let go than to hold on... As I come to realize that my past hurts imprison me and keep me tied to the past, I also realize that I am being punished all over again and I choose not to do this to myself... There is literally no future in the past... It's time for me to move on and I do... I set myself free by asking for forgiveness for my own mistakes and forgiving those who've trespassed against me... As I do this I feel the burden of the past hurts and regrets slowly lifting and my spirit is able to fly free... At last I'm free and I can look forward to a better tomorrow... And I do...

Forgiveness is such a beautiful feeling, a sublime and exquisite state of mind, free of bondage. The mind feels light and as a result easily transcends the limitations of circumstances and challenge. It is from this wonderful vantage point that self-realization and personal empowerment are able to be experienced. The activities that make surrender possible are many and as this story continues to be told I shall introduce you to several more.

It is as a result of this surrender that the 'E' in N.O.S.E. is achieved – E for empowerment.

What is empowerment?

Empowerment is a self-realized state, it is where the individual embraces her potential and creativity and then expresses them in their highest forms. It is a self-loving, kind and compassionate state that acts for the good of the whole.

The whole point of personal-transformation is to reach for the 'jewel within'. Empowerment *is* the jewel. It is a place of true freedom, where the mind is no longer shackled by doubt, fear, shame, anger and regrets but truly cherishes itself. Empowerment is a proper and just reward for those who have had the courage and the honesty to look deep within. The empowered state recognizes that negative thoughts simply sap one's energy, strength and sense of perspective. The empowered person is like the flowering plant searching for the light of the sun, intuitively knowing that this is the source of its enrichment. In other words, s/he looks only to the 'light' of quiet reflection, positive thinking and meaningful relationships because it is from here that the individual finds further learning, and the constant opportunity for growth and happiness.

For those seeking sustainable solutions, the concept of N.O.S.E. helps clarify a way forward that is clear, simple and concise. There are now so many models, methods and strategies showing the way to the 'promised land'. The problem is that the current plethora of information is leaving those seeking solutions for their issues often more confused about what to do and how to find their way out of the maze. N.O.S.E. simply states 'to be free of what ails you, you first need to name 'it'. How can you heal what you don't recognize or understand, or even realize is there? Once named, you need to own 'it', then you can unshackle yourself from whatever 'it' is by taking responsibility for 'it'. Whilst caught up in a culture of blame and victimhood, one can never find the solution. Having embraced your stuff, the endeavour of surrender then becomes a real proposition. How can you let go of pain, anxiety and fear when you don't even realize how *you* contribute to these negative patterns? Surrender then sets you free. It is at this point that those dams that have been blocking the pathways in your mind begin to disintegrate. It starts with a trickle of water finding its way through the cracks and, as that water gathers momentum, its force widens those cracks, destabilizing the dam and reaching the point where its structural integrity is compromised. What began as a trickle eventually completely demolishes the dam. In the same way, the moment the person begins naming their stuff, the first cracks appear in those blockages within the mind and in the act of surrender (actually letting go of their personal limitations) the energy of the self is once again flowing freely.

The above analogy is a very powerful way of visually relating to the journey you are actually taking. It helps you to understand that empowerment is not something you create, it is something that is always there, all you're really doing is creating the conditions to enable you to access it and then express it. We are all empowered beings and our dysfunctions exist because of the negative experiences we have collected along the way. Some of our experiences are affirming, liberating and uplifting, whilst others shut the door on our potential, confuse us about our purpose and keep us enslaved to ideas and illusions that do not mirror what's in our hearts.

Empowerment is the point where one is no longer living a life of apology. It is where the energy, enthusiasm and joy for life are abundantly visible and are constantly seeking a means of positive expression. To live in such a place is to live in a consciousness of creativity, contentment and joy and it is my invitation to you to truly name your stuff, embrace it and then let it go. Once this is done, being true to yourself will be your primary objective in life and this will encourage others to do the same. Don't think this is a journey that others are more qualified and better equipped to make than you. This is a journey that anyone who has the awareness, courage and the honesty to look into their own abyss can take. Empowerment doesn't belong to someone else. It belongs to you. So why not claim it today?

Empowerment is the beginning

The whole point of the journey offered by N.O.S.E. is to achieve empowerment. Empowerment is the prize. But what should we do with it once we have it? Empowerment is the beginning not the end. Those who are fortunate enough to reach this destination and experience its abundance, quickly realize they are at the beginning of their journey and have to re-evaluate their positioning in the world. Who am I? What am I doing? What's really important? Am I doing what I am meant to be doing, given my gifts and experiences?

These questions and many more will need to be answered as an empowered consciousness is a position of individual and social responsibility. Charity undoubtedly begins at home but it has no boundary. In other words, it goes much further than where one is standing. It starts with self, family and friends and moves towards one's community, society, the world and indeed the planet. The empowered mind has the capacity to serve on all these levels. However because it respects the laws of entropy and realizes that we can't give what we haven't got, it never fails to replenish itself. Empowerment does not become complacent or arrogant, it knows its gifts can easily be lost without proper care and nurture and so this is the charity it gives to itself. Through self-care it also protects the self from 'compassion fatigue' and 'spiritual exhaustion'.

And so although empowerment is a state of celebration and joy, it is also the point at which the 'I' becomes more connected to the 'whole' and so it carries with it a universal responsibility. The beauty of this position is that the empowered individual is always equal to the task because having named, owned and surrendered his stuff he is able to move towards his potential and find his purpose with less effort, as little or no internal opposition or resistance remains.

The 'stuff' of the here and now that threatens his continued evolution is treated with 'loving kindness', with an attitude of compassion, forgiveness and gratitude and so he is not burdened by the habit of accumulating mistakes nor is he persuaded by the inner narrator to criticize and condemn any further. Instead he sees his mistakes as invaluable tutors. His challenges become opportunities to learn and life becomes a blessing, perpetually offering growth and self-improvement. The empowered mind becomes a steward, a custodian not only for herself, but for others and the world. Her benevolent mind nurtures the good in herself and seeks that out in others. This is why empowerment is the goal we should all be pursuing and N.O.S.E. is a simple and elegant way to achieve it. All you will need is courage and honesty - a kind, patient disposition will also certainly help.

"My religion is very simple. My religion is kindness."
The Dalai Lama (1935 – present)

CHAPTER 7: THE THREE ASPECTS OF CONSCIOUSNESS

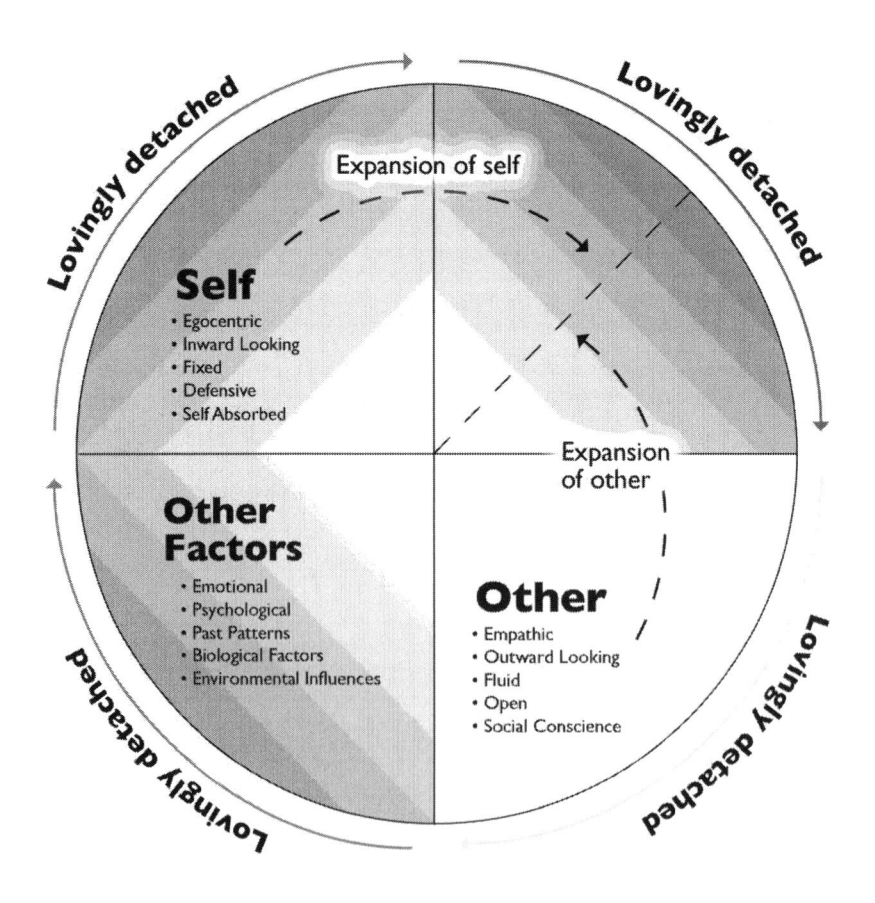

Figure 2: The Three Aspects of Consciousness

"That a man can change himself… and master his own destiny is the conclusion of every mind who is wide awake to the power of right thought."
Christian D. Larson (1866-1954)

Making the unknown known?

This is a vast subject and I hope that my synopsis will do it justice. Please don't make the mistake of thinking once you have read this you will have fully understood this topic. You'll almost certainly have to revisit it several times to extract all its meaning. My hope is that you will understand the different aspects of consciousness sufficiently and thus be able to place yourself more accurately on the map of awareness, and as a result have the opportunity to choose where you want to be. A great many of us are not driving our lives in the direction of our choice, but are being driven, by our past, by out-dated patterns, circumstances and most of all by our fear and shame. It is time to take the wheel…

Self

The first of the three aspects of consciousness is Self. This is quite a complex level of awareness and embodies many subtleties and intricacies, but the following commentary will hopefully provide a useful introduction to this aspect.

Most people are 'locked in' to Self, which is easily done, as it takes no real effort. It is, after all, the position we all start from. We enter the world with little definition, becoming increasingly defined by our environment, particularly by the relationships closest to us. It is through that social contact and feedback that the sense of self is constructed. There is a debate to be had around whether this sense of self bears any resemblance to one's Self at all. Given that the Self is moulded by a largely conditional environment and given that we are so desperate to be loved and to belong, we would do just about anything to fit in, and in the main we do.

So can a version of the Self, constructed under those conditions, be trusted to be a true reflection? I would say not. The sense of Self we have acquired is the identity most of us are busy protecting at any cost. The position of Self, when skewed and out of balance, is one that is largely fixed, defensive, blinkered, aloof, shackled by prejudice, easy to anger and lost in its own point of view. It believes that the way it sees the world is how the world is and this arrogance (to which it is blind) obscures the way forward. As a result of this position the Self gets caught up in self-defeating cycles and victimhood. It blames everyone and everything for its demise, never taking responsibility for its own actions and circumstances. For the sake of accuracy it should be said that when the Self is balanced, whole, and in harmony, it is filled with humility and wisdom and transcends the illusions generated by the ego. I will address this more fully later.

Other

The second of the three aspects of consciousness is Other. Here, the position of Other means stepping away from Self and looking at Self and reality from the other person's position. This is a position which recognises that reality cannot be viewed or fully understood by standing in one place. It is a standpoint, which recognizes that the position of Self offers us inconclusive 'evidence'. Quantum physics has helped us to understand that just by observing something we affect it, so how can we hope to see the complete story without looking at what else is shaping the moment we call now? The position of Other is a place of empathy. There is greater discrimination and humility applied from this position as our humanity begins assessing reality with care and consideration. Greater vision, warmth, sincerity and insight inherent in this position offer valuable wisdom to the position of Self. Other, at its most noble, is kind and regal in its concern for Self, others and the planet; it values all life and all things. However when it loses its way it can also lose itself. It can become so preoccupied with Other, that it neglects the importance of the Self. This often looks like kindness, benevolence and care, which it can be, but it is a dangerous place too, one of self-neglect. This can lead to a systematic dismantling of one's esteem, respect and regard for Self. Sound familiar? Good mental health is found in being able to move between the two positions, not locked in to either. Only then can there be true stability, strength and clarity. One neither becomes lost in the delusion of ego nor in the potential for self-neglect.

Lovingly detached

This is the highest of the three positions. It is an awareness that completes the circle of reality. We know a circle has 360°. The position of Self occupies approximately 90° of the circle of awareness - this can be extended through the practice of silent reflection and positively affirming activities. The position of

Other is also about 90° and it too can be extended as we increase our empathy, acts of kindness and balance between personal and social responsibility. However even with the potential for extending each position of awareness we would still only cover a maximum of 270° and that is a rare achievement indeed, as such a maximising of consciousness requires determined and single-minded endeavour over a significant period of time. So for most, the view of reality ranges between 90° and 180° (see Figure 2) depending on whether we are locked in to one position or not. If we are not locked in we have access to the rest of the picture, but as I stated earlier, to acquire such a position, can only be achieved through diligent practice. However, in order to practise effectively and then extend one's awareness, the three aspects of consciousness must first be understood.

To be Lovingly Detached grants an amazing vantage point of love and pure kindness, where there's no negative criticism. This does not mean it lacks judgement and discernment. On the contrary it has no shortage of either; it simply chooses kindness and love when 'looking in' because it knows the alternative is without benefit.

This is a position of total benevolence and clarity, standing outside both positions of Self and Other, with the ability to assess clearly and honestly, without hidden agenda. It is also able to see all the other factors that impact on any given moment of time, such as fear, past conditioning, social forces, self-image, ignorance, the list goes on and on. The Lovingly Detached position sees it all as it is, not blinkered by prejudice. Instead, its view is protected by the filters of kindness and love. This beautiful pairing immunises the spirit against any of the harshness and limitations of the other positions and gains the advantage by seeing what is missing from them.

This position has been described by great cultures of the past as the sixth sense or the third eye, the eye that sees what the other two cannot. I think both descriptions are accurate because one who is Lovingly Detached transcends the limitations of both logic and the senses. This is a point of view that recognises that logic and the senses can only take us so far down the road of truth and true awareness. So how is such a position achieved? How can we become those who view reality from a 360° perspective? Is it even possible? The answer is yes it is possible, but only through practice.

The practice we have to undertake is to regularly step away from only seeing things through our own eyes. We cannot possibly see and understand reality from that limited vantage point. We must strive to see the other's point of view. Whatever relationships you are exposed to, mother, daughter, father, boss, colleague, carer, lover, friend etc., practise seeing the world through the other person's eyes. This takes regular effort, it is not a fleeting activity – if you try, really try, you will, over time, develop an empathy that will become advanced. This is the first step. Practise moving between the two positions and each will inform the other, as they share their gifts and insights. It is only when you have truly mastered this that the third position will start to come more easily and naturally.

You can then practise adopting a more transcendental consciousness, which involves stepping away from Self *and* Other and beginning to 'look in' from the outside. Theoretically, this may not appear to be a great challenge, but to really step away and look in is not as easy as it may seem. It will take time and patience but it's certainly worth the effort because it introduces you to a reality and awareness that will almost certainly leave you awe struck and genuinely grateful, as you are able to fully appreciate life's rich tapestry.

So start by stepping away from Self and looking kindly at others. Once this is done it gets easier to truly respect and look after the Self and to value others. This practice of self-nurture and social care moves one ever closer to the kind wisdom of the Lovingly Detached position. At every opportunity, experiment with seeing things from your position, but then be willing to surrender that and step into the other person's point of view. You will find this very enriching and illuminating. And you'll discover how many times when you thought you were right, you were in fact wrong. There is a great lesson for us all in humility here. The more proficient you become at this, the easier it will be to move into the Lovingly Detached consciousness.

So start practising this today and enjoying the results.

The paradoxes of consciousness

I referred to the enormity of this subject in the introduction and hope you are developing a working understanding of the subtleties surrounding awareness and how they relate to consciousness. I tried to illustrate how your awareness is always determined by the consciousness you are bound to in any given moment - whether that be Self, Other or Lovingly Detached. One's view of reality is governed by one of these positions, each offering a different perspective and awareness. Good mental health starts with being able to move between Self and Other according to the need and context of the moment. It is not healthy to be fixed or locked in to either Self or Other because we are denied understanding of the wider picture.

Optimum mental health is being able to move easily between all three positions. One who is able to occupy the right position at the right time lives in true harmony with life. Their sense of self is in sync with the biorhythms that drive life's countless processes and patterns. Such individuals live within the natural laws because they realize we are all part of nature's dance and to be outside of that symphony is to be at odds with what works. In fact we are co-creators and have a responsibility to stay within the natural laws for only then do the laws of the universe co-operate with our highest intentions.

What I hope to deal with in this section are some of the paradoxes of consciousness, because consciousness, like truth, is not simply black and white. There are many shades of grey too.

Let us begin with the Self. I spoke previously of this position, largely in a way that shows how the Self becomes an obstacle to personal growth. However, as I indicated before, the position of Self is also magnificent when in balance. The ego dominates the landscape of the Self when it is out of balance and so a rigidity of perspective and arrogance take over. However, when one is self-loving and full of self-respect there is order and peace. The Self becomes selfless, which doesn't mean a loss of Self, on the contrary, one maintains a healthy relationship with the Self. This 'healthy attachment' means one lives in a conscience driven way, meeting one's own needs but never consciously at the expense of others. It is largely fear and our emotional inheritance that denies us this position of well-being. One who is locked into Self has bought into the idea that their needs are best met by focusing on themselves. They do not see the limitation of the locked in position as they are so busy defending their truth and sadly cannot see the bigger picture. Conversely, a life of self-nurture gives us access to an awakened Self that is in harmony and balance.

The paradox of Other is also very interesting because the one who can move from Self to Other has access to amazing empathy and can see some of the unseen. It is not a position of total clarity but it allows for a more bountiful view of the world than the position of Self alone, and with time and practice the social aspect of conscience is further developed.

However, as I touched on previously, if the individual gets trapped in Other, what looks like selflessness does in fact lead to loss of Self, as the person moves to a place in which they over identify with the needs of others and thus becomes consumed by others' needs and issues. So what begins as kindness and empathy becomes self-harm, even self-abuse. This is a trap that many fall into because of their desire to help. This is often made worse by the fact that if they have not been adequately affirmed over the course of their own lives this 'helping' may be the primary way that they get their own need for affirmation met and so such activities can become addictive. This is a classic pattern, which ties so many to the unhelpful aspect of Other.

Other, in its full glory, is where genuine psychological and emotional contact is made with another person. From this position one is able to surrender one's own views in the name of truth, while never surrendering the beauty of the Self in that gesture, for the deep recognition of one's own value is never compromised. This is the version of Other which we need to pursue. Interestingly, the more we do, the more the position of Self expands. Remember, 180° is the most that those in the position of Self and Other can see of the 'circle of awareness' (reality). However, when one practises travelling between the two, the 'collective consciousness' of 'me' and 'we' (Self and Other) can expand up to 270° of that circle of awareness, leaving only 90° beyond view. This expansion of consciousness takes daily practice and involves stepping away from Self and moving into Other, so that 'me' becomes 'we'. From here reality looks very different indeed.

The Lovingly Detached position also has its own paradox because although this is the truly divine aspect of consciousness, without the 'lovingly' bit all that we are left with is detachment. And detachment alone tells a very different story. The power of the Lovingly Detached position is the wedding of love and kindness to the ability to stand outside the circle of awareness, looking in without prejudice. If this were detachment alone, the position of being a witness to life's events could in fact be a rather cold, clinical and aloof perspective, one that even becomes arrogant in its assessment. This sense of superiority could overthrow the humility and wisdom which form an integral part of this transcendental place, so that, instead of floating above a situation or issue with a benevolent eye, one would see it without warmth and compassion. It would become purely a 'fact-finding' observational out-post, divorced from kindness and humanity.

Detachment alone can also lead to a sense of persecution, paranoia, fear and panic as the lens of clarity becomes distorted by the absence of love and kindness. This is why kindness is detachment's eternal life partner. Separate the two, and everything goes awry. The Lovingly Detached person never loses her warmth, humanity and spirit of kindness. The lens of clarity always remains clear, which is why she is not deceived by the limitations of logic or of the senses. This position recognises that although logic and the senses are invaluable windows onto the world, the view they offer is incomplete and it is only intuition (the sixth sense or third eye), validated by experience, which completes the circle. Intuition here does not refer to those gut feelings we all get, which are often right but are also sometimes wrong. It is a more sophisticated aspect of consciousness than gut feelings alone. To be more precise, those who set up a genuine and consistent inner dialogue develop a relationship with their gut feelings. This listening-in allows them to hear the voice within and a relationship of trust ensues. This new-found, intimate relationship, then takes them into the world of insight. This also takes time and practice, because without practice these insights never become yours.

Those who choose to tread this path of loving detachment come to realize that this is 'the road least travelled', where one is able to see the unseen and hear the unsaid. It is a place that through its kindness is able to both embrace and see beyond Self and Other and to also detect and decipher all the other relevant bits of information contained within the moment called 'now'. Loving detachment offers a life beyond limitations. It is a joyous, wise and humble position that neither seeks nor needs any recognition as it basks quietly in its own state of bliss.

Hopefully by now the depth and complexity of this subject has been made a little more transparent. The paradox of each position can at first appear to muddy the waters but on closer inspection it is possible to see that how each aspect of consciousness behaves is entirely dependent on whether there is order, balance and harmony. Each position depends on its relationship to the other positions - they are truly interdependent.

Optimum mental health is the smooth and fluid movement between the three positions, never getting locked in to any one position because to do so threatens the overall balance and harmony of one's own reality. So make the effort from now, in your very next interaction, to step away from Self and engage with Other. Unless of course it is a transaction where to remain anchored to the Self is what is essential. If you're really paying attention, you can feel which position is most beneficial in any given moment. Practise this again and again, until you are good at it, and you will be!

Then try practising being in the Lovingly Detached pose. This will take more effort and time. In truth this requires the underpinning of other practices as well, but trying to stand outside a situation you are a part of, and looking in on it, which includes observing yourself, is actually quite an interesting and challenging pastime, well worth the effort. You will come to enjoy it. Really looking with kindness at yourself and others will open up your heart and mind and rapid healing and recovery will follow.

Lovingly detached and empowerment

As the Three Aspects of Consciousness comes increasingly into focus, it is clear that the Lovingly Detached vantage point is undoubtedly the best place to be and would appear to be the 'pinnacle of consciousness'. This begs the question, is it any different from the empowered mind referred to in N.O.S.E.? Are these separate destinations and is one expected to pursue both? Thankfully the answer is no.

Empowerment offers access to the Lovingly Detached position. You may remember in the Story of Health that until all four legs of the table (spirit, mind, body and environment) are equal in size and strength and properly positioned, the table can neither support itself nor what's placed on it (life and its various demands and challenges). However, the point of the table (the Self) being stable wasn't so it could simply endure life, but so it can reach up for and claim its full potential. This just isn't possible until the table of the Self is stable. N.O.S.E. is how that can be achieved.

Empowerment is then the prize, and as explained previously, this is where the journey really begins - it's not the end. She who reaches empowerment then aspires to be Lovingly Detached in her dealings because the alternative - entrapment in Self or Other - simply deceives the mind and takes the individual away from the authentic self and the truth.

The Lovingly Detached position on the other hand loves the truth above all else and so chooses to see the world from beyond just Self and Other. There are many that would say that such a position is unattainable as we can only ever bring subjectivity to any discussions about consciousness and truth, but this is only the case for the uninitiated and unpractised mind. You can go beyond the limitations of the intellect, the emotions, your sensory experience, conditioning, education, upbringing etc. But it takes resolve and discipline. Nevertheless, it's a position that we can claim.

Empowerment is the position of positive choice and the empowered individual gravitates to the Lovingly Detached consciousness. So, these are two states of being which are intimately entwined.

To assist you on this journey, you'll find that there are three allies that will really help you in your endeavour to master the subtleties of awareness. I think they are best described as The Three Gatekeepers and the more you align yourself to them, the more they will illuminate the path and protect you on this journey. I've found them incredibly valuable for myself as I continue to walk the road of self-improvement. And thousands of clients and those who use our materials across the world have attested to their supportive power and effectiveness. Let me provide you with an overview and you can judge for yourself whether you would like to make them your companions too.

The three gatekeepers

"Speech is silver but silence is golden". Most people are only familiar with the second part of this ancient phrase, silence is golden and on hearing the first half are both surprised and a little bemused. What does it mean, 'speech is silver' and why should silence be compared to something as precious as gold? In fact, to separate this phrase is to diminish and devalue its meaning. I believe it's worth us taking a closer look at the relationship between the two. It is clear we are being told that however much importance we place on speech, its value does not compare with that of silence. There are several interpretations of The Three Gatekeepers found in the corridors of time, but the one I think is most relevant and useful in everyday life is the one I'm going to go on to explain here. The three main characters are Truth, Kindness and Benevolence. Let's explore each of them in greater detail.

Truth

To apply the 'silence is golden' rule to everyday interaction we need to ask three important questions, the first one being, "is my position one of truth?" When you are in any interaction, situation or experiencing 'something' whatever that may be, before reacting ask yourself the question, "is my reaction true, is it the right response to the individual, circumstance or event?" If the answer is yes, then you can proceed to the next Gatekeeper but if the answer is no, the 'silence is golden' rule then applies, because at this point it is better to say nothing than to react. Far too many of our actions are merely reactions which are ill conceived and lack proper consideration. This is why we unconsciously and sometimes consciously hurt the hearts of others. A simple pause before reacting and asking yourself this question, "is my position one of truth?", would make a world of difference. How many times have you paused and fully considered the ramifications of your words or actions? I would dare to suggest not often enough. Next time you find yourself about to react, why not check in with the Gatekeeper of Truth and see if your thoughts stand up to this first test.

Kindness

Once your thought processes have passed through the gate of truth, the next keeper of right action and good conduct that you need to persuade is Kindness. The question you have to pose to yourself at this point is, "is what I'm about to do or say truly kind and compassionate?" If it isn't, you should swiftly retreat from speech into the sanctuary of silence. It is at this point that you should again choose gold over silver. It is better to say nothing than to cause harm. To be unkind to another is to be unkind to oneself. Ask yourself, "why should I treat another in a way that I would not wish to be treated myself?" Kindness and compassion are now the subjects of many scientific studies. It seems that we have become so beguiled by scientific endeavour that unless we can see the 'evidence' under the microscope or in a laboratory it somehow does not exist, even though it is glaringly obvious that kindness and compassion are intrinsically good and therefore should be applied in our lives wherever possible. Isn't it time we also applied the principles of common sense? If what you are about to say or do can walk through the gate of Kindness then you can proceed to the third Gatekeeper.

Benevolence

The final gate through which our thoughts have to pass before coming into speech is Benevolence. The question to ask yourself at this point is, "is what I'm about to say genuinely necessary and useful?" Be sure before embarking on your chosen path that what you are about to do benefits others and yourself, because far too often we pursue our own needs and become trapped in our own opinions to such an extent that we do not consider the real value of what we are about to say or do. We are literally driven by impulse and unhelpful habits, which compel us to speak and act. Discrimination has been overthrown as we pursue the need to be right and to defend our position. Self-interest now reigns supreme because we are not concerned with the rightness of what we are doing or saying. It is at this point that the greatest harm is often done as we say and do things that hurt others and even though we may not be aware of it, these actions hurt us as well.

Our actions not only damage us psychologically, they damage our bodies too. The more we understand the mind-body interface, the more we realize that anything that is negative affects both mind and body (as discussed in Chapter 1 – The Story of Health). It is folly to think that we are immune to what we do to others or ourselves. This is why I would encourage you to make The Three Gatekeepers your friends and allies. The more you practise aligning yourself to these positions the more you are freed from negative consequences. This does not mean your life will be free from challenges because challenges are often where our most important lessons are learnt. It does mean, however, that you will always have the resources you need to rise up and meet those challenges.

I'm sure you can now see the wisdom of this ancient mantra - silence truly is superior to speech - as it enables you to apply the appropriate discrimination to your thoughts, words and your actions. Silence teaches us all the art of responding rather than reacting.

Reaction tends to be immature and short-sighted and is overly concerned with winning, as it equates winning with being right. To truly win we simply have to do the right thing and how can we do that when we have not taken time to consider all the options? Responding, on the other hand, takes its time to deliver its message. It understands that 'patience is the mother of wisdom'. All things come to one who can wait. Practise slowing yourself down and remember that other great adage, "more haste, less speed".

The practice of The Three Gatekeepers will only add seconds and at most minutes to our decisions and responses. However the time added is more than repaid in the many positive outcomes that will follow. You will find that you begin to leave a positive trail and the fragrance of good feeling wherever you go. You will also add value to every situation and find that you can extract benefit from all your interactions. At this point you really begin to understand that how you see the world does indeed shape your reality.

The Three Gatekeepers will free you from the slavery of being a victim as you move away from a culture of blame into the healthy mindset of personal responsibility. This is what good mental health looks like and feels like and it's yours for the taking. None of us are denied the gifts of Truth, Kindness and Benevolence. However, an attitude of determination and quiet resolve is required. These changes are unlikely to occur where the individual is not fiercely intent on transformation. It is important to note that there is no force in nature equal to the determined mind.

Make a pledge today to acquaint yourself with Truth, Kindness and Benevolence. Promise yourself you will at least try to make them your companions. The more you practise implementing them in your day-to-day life the more peace and contentment you will find. Your heart and mind will naturally move away from conflict and you will seek out creative responses and solutions. Each moment will either offer joy or benefit, in some cases both. Remember the three questions are; "is my position one of truth or am I trapped in my own point of view?"; "is what I am about to do or say kind or am I simply being driven by the force of habit and the need to be right?" and finally; "is there really any benefit in the position I'm taking, or would it be wiser to maintain silence?" By asking yourself these questions again and again, you will eventually acquire the habit of honouring the wisdom of The Three Gatekeepers.

"Kindness is more important than wisdom, and the recognition of this is the beginning of wisdom."

Theodore Isaac Rubin (1923 – present)

CHAPTER 8: THE DISCIPLINE DILEMMA

"In theory, there is no difference between theory and practice. But in practice, there is."
Yogi Berra (1925 - present)

Is discipline our friend?

Without order there is chaos, without structure there is instability, without discipline there is a lack of personal growth. Discipline is frequently perceived as negative, a means of containing and controlling, usually someone's behaviour, and is often associated with stern, harsh images. This is partly why we do not recognise its immensely liberating value. Discipline does not get in our way, it opens the way; without discipline our words and intentions only have potential and lack realization. Without discipline we have ambitions and dreams that remain elusive and unattainable and we remain frustrated by our inability to achieve our goals.

Effort alone cannot take us to our destination. Effort is like having an engine but no vehicle to propel converting that potential into a useful and constructive force. So, simply applying ourselves energetically to the task of self-improvement is not enough -we need something that helps us to harness that energy and create momentum, we need a vehicle. That vehicle is discipline. Discipline gathers up our endeavour, and converts it into personal power. Discipline offers us structure and order; creates personal growth, which it achieves through a quiet resolve and consistency. Once there is consistency, momentum is gained and momentum is more than half of what is needed in order to reach our destination. Effort without consistency feels as though we have done a lot yet there is nothing really to show for our expenditure and so the fruits of fatigue and futility are conceived.

The law of application is simple, put anything positive into practice consistently and we are guaranteed success. However we must apply patience and perseverance to this process otherwise we will expect results before we have earned them. Impatience trips most of us up, often at the first hurdle, and so we prevent ourselves from walking the path of progress whilst blaming other things for our lack of movement.

Discipline is a curious creature because most would say it is hard to put something consistently into practice (which can be true) and yet the moment we pass the first phase of resistance and engage in really trying, it becomes relatively easy. This is due to the power of momentum. The momentum of our actions establishes a habit and we are all familiar with how easy it is for a habit to take control of our lives. This is exactly what is needed - we have to put beneficial, enabling and empowering activities into practice to such an extent that they become healthy habits propelled by their own momentum. Through discipline we can establish a framework, which enables us to wholeheartedly pursue our aspirations. Then momentum will do most of the work.

Once we have established and have begun to harness the momentum, our discipline needs to shift its focus. Our initial cultivation of discipline is about creating positive change but once our creation is in place our discipline has to become a force for sustenance - because any improvements we have made cannot sustain themselves. This is why we have to be aware of complacency and arrogance. Having acquired a momentum sufficient to keep us moving we may think the job is done, when it has only just begun.

If we hope to hold on to the success offered to us through discipline and application then it is important to realize the changes we have engineered are lifestyle changes which need to be maintained if they are to become permanent fixtures in our lives. Then stability, peace of mind and meaningful growth will always be available to us whatever life presents us with.

Once the dilemma that discipline poses is understood, the role of The Three Ps (Patience, Practice, Perseverance) becomes pivotal because the power that discipline generates is one of the most formidable forces in nature – but without The Three Ps discipline can and almost certainly will wane.

Remember, discipline frees us, it doesn't imprison. So you need to pursue it as if your life depends on it, because in reality it does.

The three Ps

These are the other Three Ps, I mentioned in Chapter 5 - Patience, Practice and Perseverance - The Three Ps need to be your companions on any journey of personal growth. In fact, they need to become life-long companions. The more you travel with them, the greater your successes.

Patience

Patience has been described through the ages as the Mother of all virtues. I've come to refer to it in my work, as the Mother of wisdom. When challenges come, she who is able to wait, knowing that the calm and reflective mind will always win through, remains in the loving embrace of wisdom. Wisdom is happy to wait because it has learnt through experience that waiting provides the sweetest fruits and the gift of certainty. It recognizes that impatience generates peacelessness and causes the mind to lose clarity and perspective and so where's the benefit in that?

For most, Patience feels like a chore. We are easily fatigued by its request to keep waiting and yet, if we learn to wait, the vastness and the beauty of its promise offers incredible insights and joy. Patience is not a 'tapping your fingers' kind of waiting but an understanding that the outcome you seek is assured when you have faith. So she who has really embraced Patience busies herself doing the 'right thing', acting in accordance with her conscience and simply allowing the outcome to take care of itself.

Practice

We are all familiar with the saying 'practice makes perfect', however, we casually use the phrase without truly grasping what it means. Yet if we look carefully at our own experience we will discover how true this saying really is. She who practises finds what once seemed difficult, even impossible, not only becomes attainable but can often become easy. This is the promise of Practice. The more we repeat an endeavour or activity the more neuronal pathways we create in the brain. This connecting of neurons in the brain is what forms the patterns, which eventually become habits and personality traits. In other words, we can think, speak and act our way into just about any mental position or desired activity and we can also think, speak and act our way out of those habits and patterns we want to remove (see The Journey of Becoming – Chapter 10). This is why it's not enough to simply understand the myriad of self-help concepts, many of which do in fact work - one has to repeatedly put them into practice - this is the key.

Perseverance

We've all heard the saying 'if at first you don't succeed, try and try again'. Why on earth should we? The reason is simple - the one who keeps knocking on the door of greater understanding, personal growth and happiness will find that this door eventually opens. The only reason it remains closed at all is our lack of Patience, Practice and Perseverance. The door always opens for the one who refuses to give up. The path of progress is one of peaks and troughs and so it's important to understand the nature of relapse. Whilst we are striving to reach a destination relapses are inevitable. However, relapses are not the enemy. They are often our best teachers. Whenever you find yourself falling off the path whilst striving to be the best you can be, always ask the question, "what have you (the experience) come to teach me?" You'll be surprised by the answers. What you shouldn't be surprised by is that the answers can sometimes take time to come (our friend Patience again). Remember, all things eventually come to the door of she who waits.

The Three Ps is yet another subject of great depth, which could easily be expanded upon. However, I offer this brief summary in the hope that those who strive to reach their potential and to fulfill their life's purpose will be sufficiently persuaded and driven to align themselves to Patience, Practice and Perseverance and as a result their journey will be made so much easier.

Each of these qualities can be paired with a key word worth remembering. Patience is about waiting, waiting with an inner knowing that all will be well. Practice is about discipline, focusing with determination. Perseverance is about tenacity, the 'never say die' spirit. Keep the Three Ps close and you will not fail in your endeavour.

"I have been impressed with the urgency of doing. Knowing is not enough; we must apply. Being willing is not enough; we must do."
Leonardo da Vinci (1452 – 1519)

Routine is power

Once it has been really understood that it isn't what you *know*, it's what you *do* that counts, then the critical ingredient required for positive change is in place. However this central tenet needs other allies. One of its main allies is routine. As I said earlier, momentum is the engine of success. Without it the individual struggles to find his way and simply reinforces the belief that he is not good enough. One of the main reasons why those pursuing the path of personal development are unable to reach their destination is that the momentum required for progress is never effectively established. This is usually because they fall foul of the habit and the belief that incessantly talking about what they know is a substitute for application. Nothing is a substitute for application!

Discipline and routine are very closely aligned – discipline harnesses our focus and resolve, whilst routine establishes the patterns that then facilitate change. We need to create regular patterns and rhythms around life-enhancing activities, because dipping in and out of things that will help us move forward simply isn't enough. This is why the creation of some sort of timetable will prove invaluable. Arranging specific times where you engage in positive practices on a daily and/or weekly basis really will change the landscape of your life. Making regular appointments with yourself in this way is one of the most important commitments you will ever make.

One way to make routine a feature of your life is to decide to put into practice one or two positive activities a day. There are so many to choose from, for example: reading and listening to positive material; exercises such as, creative visualization and positive affirmations; establishing a personal prayer; developing a mind, body, spirit plan; ensuring that you eat a broad and nutritious diet; drinking copious amounts of water; also embroidering a realistic and effective exercise regime into your life is invaluable; finding moments of stillness in which you can delve into the depths of silence; creating genuine 'me time'; it is also essential to practice giving thanks for those things you take for granted; consciously forgiving yourself and others for mistakes; and the list goes on. So you can see there is no shortage of positive choices to make each day.

Once you've selected at least one thing to put into daily practice, it's important that you establish a time where you can regularly implement your commitment(s) - treat this commitment to yourself as if it were a pledge that you have made to someone you love.

Promise yourself that you will do whatever it is every day and as sure as day follows night, momentum and power will follow. Out of that momentum and power will come a greater sense of your own value and worth, which will breed confidence. Confidence will give rise to an even greater desire to build on the power of practice. The more we practise doing the right things, the greater the rewards.

So start with one thing a day. If you feel you can manage two then better still. However, it's absolutely imperative not to overstretch yourself at the beginning. To take on more than you can manage only serves to disempower you as it confirms the illusion that you are not good enough if you fail. It's time to slay this particular demon with all the other mythological characters that it has created. You are indeed good enough but the way to actually experience this is to do little and often.

Once you've become consistent doing one or two things, then think of how you can add one or two more. A good starting point for many is to write a personal prayer (which you may remember from Chapter 3 is your own mission statement) as it helps focus the mind. Once the mind is focused on where it is going the inclination and desire to take on board the practices that will help you reach your destination will grow. This is where momentum, that wonderful engine of success, kicks in. So if you want to experience the awesome power of routine, begin your journey in this way – by making time in your day to install good, life changing habits. You will then find that courage and faith will grow inside of you as your practice and your endeavour increase. As a result, personal power you never knew you had will fill your heart and mind and breathe life into your dreams.

Where are you on the map of consciousness?

In the previous chapter I introduced you to The Three Aspects of Consciousness to help clarify the subtle relationship between consciousness and awareness. However, one of the things I've repeatedly noted in my work, that prevents individuals from deepening the connection with themselves - is their lack of routine and discipline, which is why I've covered these topics here. I'm now going to show you how you can deepen your relationship with consciousness through the structure of discipline and the power of routine.

Your first task is to find out where you are on this map of consciousness - you need to know this in order to figure out the best strategy for you. So are you trapped in Self, Other or caught between the two? Let's explore...

As previously explained, those trapped in Self are tied to their own opinions, ideas and perspective and so they tend to be unwavering in their point of view. For them the position of Self *is* the world. Rarely do they see beyond their egocentricity. They are stubborn, selfish, opinionated, always right, arrogant, ignorant, often acting without empathy, kindness and conscience. It should also be noted that the position of being trapped in Self is often a fearful one, where the individual, behind their 'wall of certainty', is in fact a quivering, uncertain mess who has bluffed their way to a place where others and even they believe their own hype.

The truth however, is that this individual, although trapped in Self, is actually afraid of the landscape of Self. They avoid the wonderful adventures offered to them through introspection because the known (what they 'think' they know) seems more comfortable than the unknown. They busy themselves in avoidance and distraction, which is why they build elaborate defences that are so unreasonable and largely impermeable. The illusion of certainty offers what they believe to be freedom, when in fact they are imprisoned by the limitations of their position. Their rigidity means they are unable to see much beyond where they stand and this limited world view means that in relationships they are often the takers - unable to see their own shortcomings, as they are busy blaming and criticising everyone else.

As their conscience is largely disengaged, they often don't enter into giving and receiving transactions with a spirit of justice and equality – they are far too busy acting from a position of self-interest. So their self-talk goes something like this: "what's in this for me?"... "does this really serve my cause, goals and ambitions?"... "if not, it's a waste of my time and energy"..."I'm tired of not being recognised and appreciated for all that I do". And so it goes, "I... I", "me... me"; the chatter of Self, drowning out the voice of conscience and empathy.

Those trapped in Self are rarely happy and the happiness they do enjoy is often the gift of ignorance; they are trapped in thinking they have the best view, after all there is no other point of view worthy of more consideration. With such a limited state of mind in place how does one ever break free of the limitations of the Self and experience its true expansiveness?

You'll hopefully remember from the previous chapter that the first practice required to break free of the limitations of Self is practising seeing the world through the other person's eyes – whoever the other person might be. What this does is help to deepen one's empathy and develop one's conscience. Interestingly, this 'looking through the eyes of another' also illuminates what the Self really needs. So the deep, subtle connections between Self and Other start for the first time to become clear and in time are able to be understood.

The way to access the higher aspects of Self and leave its limitations behind is firstly to understand that such a destination is indeed possible. If you don't know the possibilities you're unlikely to reach for them. Once you know this destination is attainable you then need a map. It needs to be clear and simple so you can navigate your way through the emotional, physical and psychological terrain. That map is The Story of Health, which by now you are hopefully becoming more familiar with.

What follows next is a summary of what is needed to become free from the limitations of the Self.

The magic of the right method

The primary purpose of personal growth and self-improvement is to reach the apex of Self-Love, because without reaching that apex the individual is unlikely to fulfill their potential and deliver their promise. You simply cannot be the best you can be, without the sweetness of Self-Love. It is nectar like no other. When it is in place nothing is beyond your reach. Not only is there peace of mind and contentment, but there are also feelings of confidence and well-being - which are like rivers flowing, perpetually nourishing your mindscape. This is what makes it arguably the greatest attainment. But like most things worthy of pursuit and endeavour, effort is required. Having said that, the journey is not as difficult as you might think. The reason that most people do not achieve the prize has nothing to do with who they are or their shortcomings, it's that their method is flawed. Hopefully by the time you have read this section you will understand what is required of you.

There are three steps you need to take in order to reach the apex of Self-Love. What follows is a summary of what's involved…

Self-Care

It is not possible to experience the extraordinary sustenance of Self-Love without Self-Care. In fact the reason most people never progress beyond their frequent self-assassinations is because there is inadequate Self-Care. As the name suggests, this is about looking after *you*. This, however, cannot be a half-hearted contract with yourself; it is a job that must be done properly if you are to extract the dividends. Self-Care means meeting many of the needs I listed in the section about the importance of routine, such as: finding time to relax, doing things that you enjoy, pampering yourself, socializing, pursuing hobbies and interests, eating well, hydrating your body properly and getting the necessary exercise and deep restorative sleep. Sleep is one of the cornerstones of good physical and mental health, and we all know from personal experience we are unable to function properly when we are tired. In fact, to compromise on anything listed so far means you cannot give the best of yourself to the task at hand. This is why Self-Care has to be taken seriously if you want to access and experience the very best in you.

My personal and clinical experience has taught me that it is a lack of Self-Care that most undermines the individual and keeps the experience of Self-Love beyond their grasp. This is why one must become obsessive about caring for one's heart, mind and body.

The next step to achieving Self-Love is…

Self-Nurture

Those who take Self-Care seriously will initially experience the wheels of transformation turning slowly (although in some cases they may turn more quickly). Self-Care delivers a very powerful message to the sub-conscious mind. The message is: "I am worthy and I am valuable… my contribution really matters" and once this feeling is installed, opposing messages begin to wither and fade and the individual begins to like himself. This is when Self-Care naturally becomes Self-Nurture, the point when the habit of caring for the self starts to become non-negotiable. You may remember from Chapter 3 that a non-negotiable is something that an individual literally refuses to compromise over. Knowing that that thing is absolutely essential to their growth and well-being, why would they cast it aside? To cast it aside is to cast oneself aside and one who is committed to Self-Nurture simply would not do that. So, whatever the person has committed themselves to: the daily walk, that regular meeting with friends, setting time aside for study or reading, going to bed earlier etc., whatever it might be, nurture is the point where these things are becoming habits which the individual simply refuses to trade in. The power of this resolve is formidable and will literally crush anything that opposes it. This is why The Three Ps, and the routine that emerges from discipline and application, eventually leads to a more powerful relationship between the subconscious and conscious minds. They then become allies in the cause of self-improvement.

The next step on this wonderful journey is…

Self-Respect

Self-Love is no more than a dream without Self-Respect. How can someone who does not respect himself truly love himself? Internal distaste keeps the individual away from their most precious prize. It is the habit of Self-Nurture that generates Self-Respect. Someone who consistently cares for herself, and is therefore truly self-nurturing, 'proves' to the subconscious mind that they are indeed worthy of respect. Until the inner narrator (that voice from within) is persuaded to read from a new, more positive script it will continue to undermine any attempts we make to be more self-respecting as it holds on, out of habit, to the old and familiar. Once a truly nurturing way has been installed, the positive application of Self-Respect, becomes visible in one's life. Individuals who live this way do not hurt themselves with unkind thoughts and feelings, nor remain bound to dysfunctional habits and patterns. They choose positive lifestyles and relationships and they live in a way that does not hurt them or others.

Furthermore, they're not slain by history. In other words, they do not allow the past to dictate their decisions and choices, nor do they live bound to an uncertain future. They realize the only moment that truly matters is now because it's by being truly present in the moment that they are able to be the architects of their destiny. It is when this level of Self-Respect is in place that the individual can claim the prize.

The prize is…

Self-Love

Those who have understood and taken these three steps can easily claim the prize of Self-Love. The reason most people think of Self-Love as a pipe dream and therefore unattainable, or consider it 'New-Age' mumbo jumbo, is that in the main they have not understood the method to attain it. Hopefully you can see in this overview that nothing can be achieved without Self-Care. So you must make a pledge to find ways to better look after yourself on all levels.

Self-Care is a proper, passionate commitment to yourself - it cannot be entered into half-heartedly, otherwise the negative voices of your past will not be silenced. They continue their loud chanting because the opposition to them is feeble and ineffectual, and so they have no reason to believe you are serious about your new-found endeavours. This is why you must turn Self-Care into Self-Nurture. The momentum of Self-Nurture is so powerful it will eventually crush any negative patterns in its way. That self-nurturing position is like a self-fulfilling prophecy, the more the non-negotiables are pursued the more you become the embodiment of those non-negotiables. It is this unwavering resolve that naturally generates Self-Respect.

The beauty of Self-Respect is that it does not 'need' external validation. If external validation occurs, it will always be valued and appreciated, but if it is absent it makes no material difference. This is because Self-Respect looks to the self for validation. It realizes it is not defined by what others think, it is actually defined by its own inner narrative, and so this is where it focuses its attention. It's the respect for Self that enables the individual to fall into the loving embrace of Self-Love.

Now your journey towards greater love and appreciation of yourself can begin in earnest and if you find yourself losing your way, you now have a very simple guide that can put you back on course. Read this formula more than once and you will be surprised how easily, with patience you can achieve what has been laid out here. Your inner world offers many adventures, but the best of those begin from that self-loving place.

If you don't choose the reality you want for yourself then circumstance will choose for you. I hope if you're trapped or locked into Self in any way that you will now be inspired to care for yourself in kind and supportive ways. Self-Love offers you the Empowerment I spoke of in Chapter 6; it also gives you better access to the Lovingly Detached position (discussed in Chapter 7). Furthermore, it frees you from the bondages of the past and enables you to realize that the only thing that really matters is being 'present' in each moment.

Those who consistently make Self-Care their mantra, always reach their desired destination. It's not a path free of mistakes, without challenges, it is a path however, where self-loathing and a lack of self-respect are replaced with compassion and love.

A closer look at other

When someone gets trapped in Other they spend most of their time trying to 'fit in'; as a result they are capable of mortgaging their soul in order to be seen, valued and to belong - somewhere, anywhere. Although being trapped in Other may look kinder and is arguably less offensive in many ways than being trapped in Self, it's important not to lose sight of the fact that this is still an undesirable, sad, dysfunctional place - where the needs of the Self have largely been lost. The inner narrator as a consequence has lost her own script, such is her disassociation - she remains busy quoting from the scripts of others. The 'acquired self' (what she has become) is now the conductor and she drives the attitudes and behaviours in the direction that offers the most affirmation and recognition.

Someone caught up in this dynamic is a 'people pleaser'. They repeatedly neglect themselves, believing the needs of others are always greater than their own and so they mistake their self-neglect for kindness. In fact their need to be liked and to fit in is so strong that they rarely learn from their own mistakes. They continue giving or supporting even when it becomes obvious that it is counter-productive and unhealthy to do so. Their mind becomes so foggy with countless compromises they believe giving is always good. Nothing could be further from the truth.

The dysfunctional position of Other is just as poisonous and toxic as the 'sickly self' pattern; it's just different. Being locked into Self is a prison bound by the limitations of one's own point of view, whilst being trapped in Other is a prison without a point of view! Self has now been lost and with it the ability to see clearly and to know one's own truth.

So how can one move away from the negative manifestations of Other into its more glorious and splendid forms? The simple answer is through practice. The best of Self and Other can be easily accessed by putting into practice the best each one has to offer.

We know The Story of Health is the map and that the best of Self is accessed through both stepping away from Self to see the world from outside the limitations of one's opinion, and developing Self-Care. To access the best of Other, one also needs the stability offered by The Story of Health. In addition, you need the practice of seeing the world from the position of Self. You need to look at what's missing from your own needs 'quota'. How can you develop the compassion you need for positive change if you never identify and meet your own needs? We discovered that it is empathy that is first required to achieve the best in Self, and the best in Other is initially achieved through compassion for oneself.

Other in its balanced and more enlightened form is benevolent, kind, sensitive, generous, forgiving, nurturing and warm. It's a position that sees the bigger picture and puts service before Self. However, this isn't a position of self-neglect because it understands that for this position to be sustained there will be times when that equation needs to be inverted. In those moments, it has no trouble meeting its obligations to the Self, because self-service is to serve others, just as serving others automatically serves the Self. It is a virtuous cycle, a self-replenishing wheel of good fortune.

The more I meet the needs of the Self, the more I can meet others' needs and the more I meet the needs of others, the more the Self is naturally restored. This beautiful reciprocal relationship helps maintain good mental health. By practising moving between the two positions a beautiful sense of familiarity emerges that will propel you towards 'loving kindness', a position that is deeply charitable, so connected to the whole, yet detached in a way that it can see clearly.

I hope by now you will have noticed that the key, if you are trapped in Other, is actually the same as if you were trapped in Self i.e. it all begins with Self-Care. The starting point for each journey is different because of the nature of the problem, however, what's required in both instances is still a greater awareness and attention on the core needs of the Self.

Caught between the two?

Being trapped in the negative aspects of Self and Other is reasonably clear and easier to detect, but what happens when one gets caught between the two? This is often worse as it can be difficult to diagnose and quantify. One day it looks like one thing and the next day like something else. I'm keen to avoid the labelling of conditions because labels can be as misleading as they are useful. However, to illustrate the ambiguity of this 'in between' position some labels are indeed helpful. Those trapped in between can often display bi-polar tendencies, as they can be hyperactive one moment and flat and depressed the next - becoming exhausted and confused as they move between these two positions. They could quite easily be labelled schizophrenic, because of the competing 'voices' that emerge or because of the 'splitting' of their personalities, which then compete for the different narratives to be acted out.

Another sad and tragic manifestation could be a General Anxiety Disorder (GAD), which means the individual is anxious almost perpetually without even knowing why. Not knowing why then makes the anxiety even worse because there is a sense that there is good reason to be scared and until that reason is discovered one must remain hyper-vigilant. Hyper-vigilance is concerned with covering all options. They become so busy trying to cover both positions, (i.e. out of the fear of being found out or the fear of not being good enough) that they end up discovering it is impossible and something has to give - and that something is usually the Self.

I've cited here extreme examples of the 'in-between' position, to illustrate the point, but in reality most people do not exhibit these extremes. They are much more likely to have moments or episodes of being caught between the two, rather than remaining trapped in a position where they swing relentlessly backwards and forwards.

Those who are trapped in these extremes would unquestionably need professional help. However, the vast majority of individuals could take this journey either by themselves, as part of a support group or with help from family or friends – although in some instances, a degree of psychological assistance may also be needed.

The ambition to move effortlessly between Self and Other is a reflection of a healthy mind, whereas running from one to the other out of fear, caught between the limitations of the two, is extremely unhealthy. When this is the case fear drives you to try and be all things to all people. Fear keeps you away from the Self, fearful of what you might discover. It is fear that denies you the majesty, brilliance and awe of the authentic self and keeps you tied to the scripts of the acquired self. Fear is what leads those caught in between to lose their way. In the end they are so driven by fear that they are eventually overwhelmed.

We know empathy and compassion are needed, which we discovered are the starting points for getting the best out of Self and Other - both are needed here too. In addition, you need to straddle the paradox of acting without self-interest in one moment (altruism) and meeting all your own needs in the next (self-care). The more you can get this balance right, the more you are able to anchor yourself healthily to Self and Other.

Then you can start to become part of the benevolent stream of consciousness. Over time, you will experience the pure delight of the Lovingly Detached position. She who marries the best of Self to Other in this way is elevated to that most beautiful vantage point - a view from the front seat within the cosmos.

Virtues always travel in pairs

What does this mean? And why is it important? Quite simply if a virtue stands alone it will eventually become a vice. Furthermore, understanding this concept and carefully applying it to your life will enable you to arrive at your desired destination.

Here are a few examples to illustrate what I mean. Truth is considered to be one of the most prized virtues, yet if served up with anger or indifference it becomes tainted. The content may still have the 'appearance' of truth but the nature of the delivery has now turned truth into a hurtful weapon and any notion of righteousness is automatically forfeited. So the message is now coloured by anger and indifference and becomes something else - revenge, cruelty, intimidation or even worse. The content, due to the delivery, has in most cases now been lost. Truth can only retain its virtue if it is paired up with other virtues such as empathy, kindness or love. The pairing is determined by the context and the situation.

Let's examine further. Kindness, for many, is the most beautiful of the virtues. Even just observing an act of kindness has been proven to have a measurable, positive impact on the observer, and yet if kindness is repeatedly administered without discrimination it can easily become abusive, manipulative, self-limiting and disempowering. Imagine a situation where someone continues to give, regardless of the circumstances. As a result a culture of expectation and dependency emerges. Those in receipt of that kindness, if they lack awareness or virtue, soon come to expect more of the same even when it's clearly unreasonable to do so. The giver in this situation continues to act with kindness even when they are compromising their own beliefs and giving away their self-respect – as illustrated in my descriptions of Other. Is this kindness? Can there be virtue in a situation where one loses sight of what is right and where another becomes absorbed in their own selfishness?

Neither the giver nor the receiver is acting with virtue. In this example kindness has become weakness. The giver has been shackled either by fear, ignorance or by a need to be liked to such an extent that their original intention of kindness is now spoiling them as well as the other person. Kindness, in this example, needs the clarity of discrimination to ensure it is being applied correctly to the individual or circumstances. Once again we see that context matters. In other situations kindness may be paired with virtues such as humour, sensitivity and warmth, to enable its gift to be received.

Let me offer one more example to demonstrate that a virtue that travels alone will eventually become a vice. Very few things can be achieved without determination. Determination can and does drive people to achieve extraordinary things. We can all think of examples where the impossible has been achieved due to someone's incredible desire to reach a particular goal, but here too, if determination lacks empathy and awareness and loses respect for boundaries, the very force that can create miracles can just as easily lead to demise and destruction. If one applies determination without considering one's relationships and environment, then it is easy for that positive force to cause harm to others by not respecting their boundaries or limitations. Is it right for any of us to pursue a course of action that does not take account of its impact on those around us? Is this not being trapped in Self? – a position we've discovered has little virtue.

Determination can become so ruthless that it pursues its ambition relentlessly and is blind to the consequences of its actions. It becomes thoughtless and unkind, even to those who are most dear. The one who is driven in this way also becomes blind to the fact that their determination has now become something else, such as pride, selfishness or stubbornness. In these circumstances the goal may well be achieved but the virtue has been lost. Is any goal or ambition worth such a compromise? You have to decide for yourself. What I've learned is that a prize gained without virtue is no prize at all.

Through these examples I've hopefully demonstrated that it is a mistake to think truth, kindness, determination or indeed any other virtue can ever deliver its message or its promise when it is unaccompanied. It simply cannot. Try applying humour without thoughtfulness and watch it become a knife. Do the right thing, but deliver your message through bad behaviour and watch your message disappear into the ether. No virtue will ever leave its lasting mark if it doesn't come from a considered consciousness. Virtues can literally change the world. History is full of such examples but history is also full of examples where virtues have become vices due to minds that haven't understood the depth of this principle - virtues always travel in pairs.

One of the themes of this chapter is the importance of practice. You will, in the end, become what you think, say and do. So start making choices that are consistent with the kind of person you want to be, the contribution you want to make to the world and the legacy you wish to leave behind.

Practice makes permanent

Modernity and progress have created a less patient and more demanding world (something I discussed at some length in Science the New God?), a world in which we all expect more for less. Our scientific endeavour and investigation have offered us greater insight about the world we live in and yet we appear to be blinder than before. We understand more about the principles and the laws of the universe and although we apply them to everything around us we behave as if we are immune to their effects. Our greater knowledge has fed our egos in such a way that instead of becoming more humble, kind and wise, we've become more arrogant, selfish and short-sighted. It is these negative attributes and the ignorance they foster that have prevented us from seeing the obvious. The truth is often staring us in the face - it stands in plain sight. It is time to open our eyes but more particularly our ears.

As I've stated previously, but it's worth underlining, the idea that there is a gene for 'this' or for 'that' is flawed as it leads us to believe that any given gene we may have binds us to a single particular outcome. Please do the research for yourself and you will see that even though this is the more prevalent and popular view it simply is not true. Each gene actually has thousands of possibilities and which one materialises is dependent on our relationship with the environment. You'll know by now that by environment I mean our relationships with others; our thoughts and feelings; what we eat and drink; our exposure to pollution and the decisions and choices we make in all these areas. We are only really limited by the shackles of our beliefs and past conditioning. So if you can understand that you are not helplessly tied to a pre-determined genetic destiny you will also come to realize the tremendous influence and power you have over your life. It is time to exercise that power. I hear you asking, how?

Well, start by understanding if you are unhappy with your life you are contributing to your own discord and unhappiness. Until you can accept this, you will continue to blame others or external factors for your situation, which will simply keep you bound to your current position. As I discussed in N.O.S.E., positive change begins with facing the truth about yourself with kindness and compassion. You can't fix something until you accept it is broken. The more we cover up, defend and justify our position, the less change is available to us and so of course the self-limiting idea that there is no way out becomes true.

We are all living, self-fulfilling prophecies; unfortunately some of us are already living in hell, whilst a few live in heaven. Einstein said, "Be careful what you think because whatever you think, you will be right" (paraphrased) and the fields of quantum physics, cognitive neuroscience and transpersonal psychology are all proving this to be true. So start believing in the infinite possibilities that reside in you, and your life will move in your preferred direction. Identify what needs to change in you and proceed to resolve it without fear and with kindness. Identify what support and which interventions are needed and pursue them relentlessly.

The more you think the right thoughts, act in accordance with your humanity and conscience, and treat others as you want to be treated, the more you build a myriad of neuronal pathways and connections in the brain that guarantee to make it easier to move in that direction the next time.

We know that we are driven by our habits and patterns so why not make good habits and patterns that will enable you to fulfil your potential. We have all heard that practice makes perfect, which most of us would not dispute, but I think 'practice makes permanent' comes first. In other words the change you want in your life is there for the taking but you need to earn it, you need to create it. Repetition is the key - so identify the right things and apply them in your life again and again. Stop waiting for a miracle and go and create one.

Every moment of every day offers you the opportunity to co-operate and eventually become the master of The Three Aspects of Consciousness with the assistance of your friend, discipline. Seize your opportunity today and reach for the stars. Practise, practise, practise and before you know it you will be sitting amongst the stars, marvelling over the many wonders of the universe, of which you are one!

"There is no chance, no destiny, no fate that can hinder the firm resolve of a determined soul."
Ella Wheela Wilcox (1850 - 1919)

CHAPTER 9: THE RELATIONSHIP BETWEEN THE MIND AND THE MOUTH

"Let us remember, so far as we can, that every unpleasant thought is a bad thing put in the body."

Prentice Mulford (1834-1891)

You are what you eat?

Hippocrates (one of the founding fathers of medicine) is famed for this simple statement of fact and yet here we are many centuries later still debating its validity. If we look at the evidence it is indisputable. In fact, I would go even further and state that we are 'what we absorb from what we eat'. However, whichever definition you work to, the primary premise remains true. That is, whatever you put into your body will make its presence felt. Is this a really deep or profound notion or simply common sense?

I talked earlier in the book about how what is happening at the cellular level (micro) will impact on the global story of the body (macro). We now know that our cells run on vitamins, minerals, amino acids, phyto-nutrients and fats derived from our food stuffs (vegetable matter, meats, fish, fruit etc.). The enzymes produced in our bodies and also present in some of our foods then breakdown that food via the digestive system, using water as a primary ingredient in the breaking down and distribution process.

The body then uses the vitamins, minerals, essential fats etc., that have been extracted from the three main food groups - proteins, fats and carbohydrates - to carry out the myriad of biological functions that keep us alive. Anything the body doesn't use or need results in waste; in a healthy body most waste will be excreted from the system. However, you may remember that when the body is not doing its job properly, usually because it is over burdened and operating under toxic conditions, then sadly waste is not handled effectively or efficiently. This causes countless problems and is in fact the cause of many chronic conditions.

This negative intoxication within the body is often referred to as endotoxicity and has led me to coining the phrase in my work 'waste weakens'. In fact, I'd go further and say that the secret to health is the removal of waste, which I explained at some length in Chapter 4. Without removing waste from the system, well-being is simply unattainable.

I said at the beginning of this section, that it is what you 'absorb' from your food that really counts. Even when you put the right food into your body, if the body is congested with waste products, which it hasn't been able to excrete adequately, the build-up of waste will undermine the breakdown, absorption, and distribution of the vital nutrients. This will lead to malnourishment even in the face of an abundance of food choices and probably most importantly of all, impact on the acid/alkaline ratios in the body.

Acid alkaline balance

Foods may be classified, in relation to the metabolic process, as either acid or alkaline. Alkalis are soluble salts and acids are corrosive agents, which have trouble combining with other things. A balanced diet contains 35% acid forming foods and 65% alkaline. However, if the body is sick, then to restore health, the diet should really consist of 80% alkaline forming foods and 20% acid forming foods.

Human blood pH should be slightly alkaline (7.35-7.45). Below or above this range will lead to a plethora of symptoms and eventually disease. A pH of 7.0 is neutral. A pH below 7.0 is acidic. A pH above 7.0 is alkaline.

The alkalinity of the blood has to be kept almost constant; even minor variations are dangerous. If the blood lowers to pH 6.95 (which is barely acidic), a coma and even death can result. And if the concentration in the blood changes from 7.4 to 7.7, tetanic convulsions may occur.

An acidic pH can result from an acid forming diet, emotional stress, toxic overload, or any process that deprives the cells of oxygen and other nutrients. The body will try to compensate for acidic pH by using alkaline minerals. If the diet does not contain enough minerals to compensate, a build up of acid in the cells will occur.

Any acidic overload will decrease the body's ability to absorb minerals and other nutrients, decrease the energy production in the cells, decrease it's ability to repair damaged cells, decrease it's ability to detoxify heavy metals, weaken the immune system and allow tumour cells to thrive, and generally make the body more susceptible to fatigue and illness.

The reason acidosis (a dominant acidic position in the body) is more common in our society is mostly due to the typical western diet, which is far too high in acid producing foods like meat and other animal products such as eggs and dairy - and far too low in alkaline producing foods like fresh vegetables, lentils, seeds, nuts and fruits.

Additionally, we eat acid producing processed foods like white flour and sugar and drink acid producing beverages like coffee and soft drinks. We use too many drugs, which are acid forming and we use artificial chemical sweeteners, which are generally poisonous and extremely acid forming. One of the best things we can do to correct an overly acidic body is to clean up our diet and lifestyle.

Please bear in mind that foods cannot be described as absolutely alkaline, or absolutely acidic. This is why you will find some disagreement about where foods are positioned on the acid/alkaline spectrum. The truth is it's difficult to be definitive because some food groups are quite large and some foods in the same group can vary quite widely. The situation is further complicated by how food is cooked. Something that begins alkaline can actually be made acidic through the cooking process.

In addition, and arguably the most relevant factor, yet the least considered, is chewing. How you chew your food, has a bearing on whether it becomes acidic, or is neutralised, or even becomes more alkaline. Something that begins as alkaline when it enters the mouth can be corrupted and made acidic if not chewed sufficiently, which leads to poor digestion. So taking chewing seriously is an important part of this crucial subject.

Generally, alkaline forming foods include, most fruits, green vegetables, peas, beans, lentils, spices, herbs, seasonings, seeds and nuts.

Generally, acid forming foods include, meat, fish, poultry, eggs, grains, dairy products and legumes.

The lists below give some idea of the complexity surrounding the classification of foods.

Highly alkaline
Grasses, Chlorella, Kale, Kelp, Spinach, Parsley, Broccoli, Sproutings, Sea Vegetables (Kelp), Green drinks, Pumpkin Seed, Limes, Sea Salt, Lemons, Lentils, Sweet Potato, Spirulina, Vegetable Juices, Baking Soda, Nectarine, Pineapple, Watermelon, Mineral Water, Raspberry, Tangerine, Onion, Persimmon.

Moderately alkaline
Avocado, Beetroot, Capsicum/Pepper, Cabbage, Celery, Collard/Spring Greens, Endive, Garlic, Ginger, Green Beans, Lettuce, Mustard Greens, Okra, Onion, Radish, Red Onion, Rocket/Arugula, Tomato, Butter Beans, White Haricot Beans, Chia/Salba, Apple, Apricot, Olive, Broccoli, Cashews, Raw Honey, Mango.

Mildly alkaline
Artichoke, Asparagus, Brussels Sprouts, Cauliflower, Carrot, Chives, Courgette/Zucchini, Leek, New Baby Potatoes, Peas, Rhubarb, Swede, Watercress, Grapefruit, Coconut, Quinoa, Spelt, Tofu, Other Beans & Legumes, Goat & Almond Milk, Most Herbs & Spices, Avocado Oil, Coconut Oil, Flax Oil/ Udo's Oil, Wild Rice, Sunflower Seeds, Grapes.

Neutral/mildly acidic
Black Beans, Chickpeas/Garbanzos, Kidney Beans, Seitan, Cantaloupe, Currants, Fresh Dates, Nectarine, Plum, Sweet Cherry, Amaranth, Oats/Oatmeal, Soybean, Soy/Hemp Protein, Freshwater Wild Fish, Rice & Soy Milk, Brazil Nuts, Pecan Nuts, Hazel Nuts, Sunflower Oil, Grapeseed Oil, Buckwheat, Brown Rice, Figs, Dates, Millet, Teff.

Moderately acidic
Ketchup, Mayonnaise, Butter, Apple, Apricot, Banana, Blackberry, Blueberry,

Cranberry, Grape Seed Oil, Mangosteen, Orange, Peach, Papaya, Pineapple, Strawberry, Basmati Rice, Oat Bran, Rye Bread, Wheat, Wholemeal Bread, Wild Rice, Wholemeal Pasta, Ocean Fish, Maize, Various Legumes, Veal, Chicken, Green Peas, Fructose, Peanuts.

Highly acidic

Alcohol, Coffee & Black Tea, Fruit Juice (Sweetened / Concentrated / Packaged), Cocoa, Hazelnuts, Jam, Jelly, Mustard, Miso, Rice Syrup, Soy Sauce, Vinegar, Yeast, Dried Fruit, Beef, Chicken, Eggs, Farmed Fish, Pork, Shellfish, Cheese, Dairy, Artificial Sweeteners, Syrup, White Bread, Poultry, Lobster, Wine, Walnuts, Fried Foods, Brazil Nuts.

Acidosis

Acidity and alkalinity are the two characteristic conditions of blood and cell solution. Any solution is either more acid or more alkaline. Therefore, if acidic characteristics dominate, the solution is acid. An acid solution always contains some alkaline factors, and an alkaline solution always contains some acid factors. Neutrality is an 'ideal' condition in which the value of acid and alkalinity is equal. However, as I previously mentioned, what we eat or drink is never wholly acidic or wholly alkaline.

According to modern biochemistry, it is not the organic matter of foods which leave acid or alkaline residues in the body, it is the inorganic matter (sulphur, phosphorus, potassium, sodium, magnesium and calcium) that determines the acidity or alkalinity of the body fluids. Food comparatively rich in acid forming elements are acid forming foods, those comparatively rich in alkaline forming elements are alkaline forming foods.

Acidosis is not in itself a specific disease; it is a description of the acidic status of the blood. It is also the root of many different diseases such as, chronic bowel conditions, severe migraines, diabetes, high blood pressure, arthritis, cancer, tumours and many more. Many people today have this blood condition without ever knowing it and it almost certainly causes death when not addressed.

Alkalosis is not as common as acidosis. It is a description of the blood where insufficient acid exists in the system, which can also cause a variety of health issues, such as: nausea, numbness, prolonged muscle spasms, muscle twitching, hand tremors etc.

An acidic condition inhibits nerve action, whereas alkalinity stimulates nerve action. Someone whose pH is properly balanced can think clearly, decide and act well. They possess mental composure and calm.

A balanced diet, good hydration and carefully 'targeted' supplementation are a great help in maintaining the pH balance of the blood; however the 'right' regimen will not produce results in a day or two. It takes time to restore balance - weeks or maybe months. So our old friend patience is required.

If the blood becomes too acidic, then our bodies deposit the excess acidic substances in other areas of the body in order that the blood will be able to maintain an alkaline state. If this pattern continues, then these areas increase in acidity and some cells die. These dead cells will, in turn, become acids. However, there are some cells that adapt to the 'toxic' environment. In other words, instead of dying as normal cells do in an acid environment, they actually survive becoming abnormal cells in the process. These abnormal cells are called 'malignant' cells. Malignant cells do not communicate and work co-operatively with our brains, nor with our DNA memory code. Therefore, malignant cells grow independently and without order, operating outside the 'normal' parameters of health and so disease follows.

This process is in fact how many cancers develop in the body - below is a summary of events.

Ingestion of many acid-forming foods, fatty foods, refined foods, carcinogenic substances such as nitrates, and chemically treated foods in general.

Increased constipation often then follows, leading to a reabsorption of waste, causing a build up in the cells, tissues and organs.

Increase of acidity in the blood causes an increase of white cells and a decrease of red cells. The increased acidity also affects the natural killer cells in the body, undermining immunity.

Increase of acidity in the extra cellular fluids.

Increase of acidity into the intracellular fluids.

Birth of malignant cells. This is the stage of cancer called 'initiation'.

The further consumption of acid foods, any chemical and drug treatment, exposure to radiation in any of its many forms can also exacerbate the situation. This stage is called cancer 'promotion'.

Waste weakens

Now the role and importance of the acid/alkaline balance has been better understood, we can see that waste in any form is disruptive to the body's health. This applies as much to the mind as it does to the body.

Let me remind you of that story of waste. Consider the following, if we are producing thirty billion cells of waste each day and are not adequately removing them from the system, by the end of a week we will have produced approximately two hundred and ten billion cells that need to be removed from our bodies. If the pathways of elimination i.e. liver, kidneys, skin, lungs, colon etc. are not maintained in pristine condition or are blocked in any way, these metabolic by-products that are no longer useful to the body will simply build up wherever they are trapped.

Now imagine that, each day, you only get rid of half of the waste that you produce. That would mean at the end of a week, approximately one hundred and five billion cells of waste are left behind. At the end of a month, somewhere between four hundred and twenty and five hundred billion cells of waste will have accumulated. Now consider the impact of that amount of waste on the body. Every organ would be significantly challenged in some way. The organs of elimination in particular would be constantly under pressure. In fact, even sleep would not provide rest as the body frantically strives to maintain its own survival and the quality of our lives.

It doesn't take a degree in science to begin to see that our focus should be on what we get out rather than what we put in. Even if we put in the right things, they have to compete with the poisonous substances in the body. This toxic environment becomes the ideal breeding ground for all pathogens i.e. viruses, bacteria, mould, fungi, parasites etc. This is why it is imperative that we change the ecosystems of our bodies. The more toxic we become the greater the proliferation of pathogens and hence the greater likelihood of us falling victim to their onslaught.

In addition to these obstacles to our health, the body also has to deal with all the other environmental pollutants - herbicides, pesticides, heavy metals, xeno-oestrogens etc. Can you see how amazing this organism is that we take for granted each day? It is constantly trying to create health against all the odds. We owe it our allegiance. It is always fighting for our survival against the background of our ignorance and neglect, which constantly undermine it.

This is why in the current climate where much has been written and continues to be written about what constitutes good nutrition, I'm not so much seeking to add to the debate as to bring another dimension to it. The formula is simple; if we want to give ourselves the best chance of good health, we need to eat fresh, uncontaminated food, from a diversity of sources, as close to what nature intended as we can (unprocessed and not de-natured). But most of all we must seek to keep the pathways of elimination clear and value detoxification above all else.

Having spent some time looking at the biological consequences in this story of the relationship between mouth and mind, let's reflect on the emotional and psychological aspects of this equation.

Our programming really matters

My pre-occupation with the past exists because we are all by-products of our pasts. In some quarters of the psychotherapeutic and personal development movements, the role and relevance of the past is considered to be out-dated and even inconsequential. I would want to stress that looking to the past for its own sake or treating it as a self-indulgent pastime, is not only unhelpful and self-limiting but also potentially destructive.

However, understanding the role the past plays is crucial and the new face of biology is bearing testimony to that. The latest research shows that parents are more than genetic engineers and that this process begins even before conception. In the final stages of egg and sperm maturation, a process called genomic imprinting adjusts the activity of specific groups of genes that will go on to shape the character of the child yet to be conceived. This research suggests that what is going on in the lives of parents during the process of genomic imprinting has a profound influence on the mind and body of their child to be. The latest research in this area has helped state what many of us would consider to be obvious, which is that parents are more effective in their roles when living in a calm and stable environment supported by family and friends and free of addictions.

The developing child receives far more than nutrients from the mother's blood. Along with nutrients the foetus absorbs excess cortisol (a stress hormone) if the mother is chronically stressed. As the stress hormones pass through the placenta, the distribution of blood flow in the foetus alters, which in turn affects the developing child's physiology, for example excess cortisol switches the mother's and the foetus's system from a growth state to a protective one, which at the time of foetal development is psychologically and emotionally restrictive. This puts the foetus in a state of anxiety and hyper-vigilance, hardly a desirable position for an unborn child. The nephron cells, which are involved in regulating body salt and blood pressure, are equally handicapped by excess cortisol. This is just one example of how a biological chemical can affect the growth and development of the child, even before birth. Once the child is born the stakes are raised even further.

The relevance of the past to the present

There has been a lot of research about the impact of the past on the psyche of the child (see the work of Mendizza and Pearce and Gerhardt). This research has largely concluded that children need parents who can playfully foster their curiosity and creativity in order to encourage the 'wonder' that accompanies their children into the world. If we are to bring the best out of our human potential then what we are doing to our children really matters. We are all a result of our nurturing. Mary Carlson, a neurobiologist, famous for the work she did with the Romanian orphans, concluded that the lack of touching and lack of attention severely stunted the children's growth and adversely affected their behaviour. Her research showed that the more stressed a child was the more cortisol was found in the blood and the worse the outcome for the child.

There is an enormous body of evidence underlining the importance of touch and social contact. What we can conclude from the evidence so far is that those subject to such deprivation have abnormal stress profiles and are therefore more likely to become violent sociopaths. So the growing brain of a young child depends heavily on the social and emotional context in which he or she lives. These experiences influence the expression of genes, which in turn determine how neurons in the brain connect to one another and create the neuronal pathways that give rise to our mental tendencies. And so, what happens to us in the past is indeed relevant to the present - understanding this can help us reclaim 'the now'.

Much of what has influenced the way we perceive ourselves has been passed down through various 'filters of perception', often imbibed as the 'truth'. As adults we may choose to scrutinise and analyse our beliefs more thoroughly to see if what was handed down to us does indeed reflect who we are and where we are striving to go. This is what I'm encouraging you to do through the information offered in this book. It's vital to reclaim our self-awareness, so we can become masters of The Three Aspects of Consciousness. Our lives only belong to us when we exercise the gift of choice and free will.

However, as this chapter unfolds we see that we must give equal consideration to what is imbibed through our mouths as well as our minds. Both impact on the way that biology and psychology relate to one another - at each stage try to hold both these factors in your awareness. By wearing these spectacles of awareness we can appreciate that this is in fact a relationship where both constantly impact on each other. It is a mesmerising dance and at its heart it holds the secret to our well-being.

Nature and nurture

Epigenetics, as you may remember, literally means 'control above genetics'. This new science has profoundly changed our understanding of how life is controlled. In the last decade research in this area has established that the DNA blueprints passed down through genes are not set in concrete at birth. This discovery has been described as pleomorphism/polymorphism, which I spoke about in Chapter 4 when we first touched on epigenetics. It loosely translates as, 'there are many possibilities'. In other words genes are not our destiny. They are a factor in the human story but they do not set us on an inevitable course that cannot be changed. Other factors modify the effects of our genes without changing the actual blueprint such as emotions, stress, nutrition and other environmental influences. Arguably, in the earliest phases of our lives it is nurture that most impacts on human development.

Epigenetics is also helping us to understand that we pass on hereditary information through two mechanisms - nature (genes) and nurture (human behaviour). If we only look at one of these we miss the influence and power of the other. For example, we now know that emotions create a myriad of neuropeptides, which influence and can alter the destiny (the behaviour) of the cell. The emotional environments we are exposed to will therefore determine much of how the genetic and cellular stories play out. Food has a similar influence, as I illustrated in the first half of this chapter.

Epigenetics is really the story of how environmental influences and signals (nurture) impact on and control the activity of genes. In other words, an environmental signal firstly goes to a regulatory protein (which directs the activity of genes) and only then does it go to the DNA (which represents the cells' long-term memory) and the RNA (which is the active memory). The end product is another protein (proteins are the driving force of the human organism – our bodies are literally protein machines).

So everything taking place within the body depends on the protein interactions (it takes over a hundred thousand different types of protein to keep us alive). All of this further underlines that we can no longer use genes *alone* to explain why we are at the top of the evolutionary ladder.

You may remember that humans have roughly the same number of genes as rice and mice, as demonstrated by the several genome projects I referred to earlier. It was once expected that something as complex as human physiology needed at least a hundred and twenty thousand genes and yet geneticists found that the entire human genome consists of as little as twenty-five to thirty thousand genes. So clearly, other forces are at play.

Good and bad vibes

You will all be familiar with the idea of good and bad vibes, which really is the story of energy waves. And although this language smacks of 'new ageism', all it is really doing is explaining the truth that every atom has a negative and a positive charge, which, coupled with a spin rate, generates a specific energy signature or vibration. As different energy fields come into contact with one another, they 'interfere' with each other's resonance. Imagine a pebble being dropped into a body of water; as the pebble hits the water, a series of ripples radiate outwards. Now imagine two stones being dropped hitting the water simultaneously. The ripples that they independently create come together causing something described as 'constructive interference' or harmonic resonance. This effect leads to a doubling of energy where the ripples 'interfere' with each other. Now imagine two stones being dropped one after the other. When those ripples come together, they are not in sync and therefore would not be in harmony. This is described as 'destructive interference', which leads to a cancelling out of energy. In destructive interference, you have a situation where some atoms' vibrations cause other atoms to stop spinning.

Put this way, constructive interference and destructive interference could be analogous to us talking about good and bad vibes. Whatever the stimulus might be, good vibes make us feel twice as good because we are in harmony with something or someone and it is the marriage or combination of those vibrations that gives the 'double benefit'. Equally when there is destructive interference or bad vibes there is a cancelling out of energy, which might leave us feeling anything from neutral to awful.

To demonstrate further the phenomenon of constructive interference we could use the example of ultrasound, and non-invasive procedure for the allopathic treatment of kidney stones. Focusing the ultrasound energy beam on the kidney stones causes the atoms within the stones to vibrate to the point of constructive interference, at which time the stones are vibrating at such a high frequency that they shake themselves to pieces, literally exploding in situ, and the resulting fragments either dissolve or can be passed out with the urine without the excruciating pain normally associated with this condition. So here we see the result of 'good vibes' or constructive interference used within a conventional, in this instance, medical arena.

Might this phenomenon also explain hands-on healing, absent healing, reiki, prayer and meditation? These are activities where the power of the mind seeks to establish a 'good' connection either with someone who may not be well, a divine being or a pure goal of some kind and through that connection foster a beneficial outcome. Could it be that the reason these activities have some proven benefit is because they all seek to create constructive interference, which is essentially harmony and it's at the point of harmony that all healing takes place? Certainly a question worth pondering further - and one I will offer a number of insights to as we progress.

The sea of light

Everything you see and even what you can't see with these eyes is made up of light. The universe is a sea of light. Everything at the molecular, atomic and sub-atomic levels tells some part of the story of light. All living and non-living things vibrate at different frequencies. That vibration gives them shape, dimension and form. In fact if you look up right now, whatever you can see is a dance of light.

The smallest particle, the atom, is simply a spark of light and everything is made up of atoms. The atomic story contains yet another drama, that of the sub-atomic particle. At this level most of the mysteries can be explained. Quantum physics, radiology and biophysics are the media that have helped us the most to understand what is taking place at the sub-atomic level. What has become clear through the study of these scientific disciplines is that at the unseen level incredible communication is taking place and driving all of life. In scientific parlance, light is measured in photons and by understanding the frequencies at which organisms resonate, we are better able to comprehend everything, not just within our bodies (i.e health and disease), but also our relationship to each other, animals, nature and the universe.

As the story of light becomes clear, the darkness of ignorance is dispelled. Then so-called mysteries are easily unveiled. For example, each human cell undergoes, on average, one hundred thousand chemical reactions per second, a process that repeats itself simultaneously within every cell in the body. How can such an inconceivable amount of activity take place and then be communicated so instantaneously across the body? This breath-taking phenomenon is actually happening every minute of our lives! The process described as quantum coherence is helping us to understand the amazing feats of the human body. When we take a closer look at the sub-atomic level we see that it is waves of energy (electromagnetic fields), which enable communication to take place at this unfathomable rate. Electromagnetic fields are essentially fields of light. These fields of light are interwoven and linked together in a sophisticated manner enabling them to communicate their findings and share their experiences. It is these fields of light that are responsible for the countless miracles found within nature.

Continuing to look at the microcosmic level makes seeing the detail contained within the bigger picture easier to understand. For example, the light emitting from the sun is imbibed by plants through photosynthesis, we then consume those plants, which we digest and are broken down and converted into many different compounds e.g. carbon dioxide, water, vitamins and other minerals, but essentially we have literally absorbed the photons contained within the plant. Those photons are then stored and infuse the body, acting as the primary source of energy responsible for sustaining our lives.

The light a biological organism emits is referred to as biophoton emissions. These light waves either create harmony in the way that they relate to the body's natural light emissions or disturb and alter the body's biorhythms - remember what we covered earlier about constructive and destructive interference.

Research to date leads us to conclude that light emissions also emerge from the very DNA itself, so when food, a biological organism, comes into contact with another organism, namely the body, health is achieved when there is harmony between the two light emitting organisms. Unfortunately, largely through our interference with the planet (i.e. pollution, deforestation and mismanagement of natural resources), we have literally scrambled many of its frequencies. In other words, we have affected the natural oscillation of these light waves and in doing so have distorted the quantum coherence needed for order, balance and health.

Quantum coherence

We live in an ever-moving sea of light, a sea of ceaseless motion. As things get colder, molecular activity slows down but there is no point at which it stops completely. Even at the point described as absolute zero there is movement and movement equals life and we are all part of that scintillating sea of light. We imbibe photons from food and the environment, which disperse across our entire light spectrum (our bodies) becoming the driving force for all the molecules in the body. This activity takes place on the subtlest of levels and has been linked to our planet's biorhythms. We are in sync with the planet second by second, day by day, season by season, year by year. It is when we are out of sync with these rhythms that we are said to be under the influence of geopathic stress.

Research shows that cancer patients have lost their natural periodic rhythms and so are no longer in harmony with the earth's biorhythms. Their internal coherence (state of order) has gone. So disease can be described as, the point when a biological organism is out of harmony with its environment and internal coherence is lost. Quantum coherence (which I introduced you to in the early chapters) is the point of perfect harmony at the most subtle level between all living things.

With the use of a photomultiplier (which counts photons) quantum physicians have been able to demonstrate that the number of photons emitted from an organism is linked to the complexity of the organism. In some cases, rudimentary animals and plants emitted ten times more light than human beings. It would seem then that the more evolved and complex the organism the lower the intensity of light. It is at this low intensity that the most amazing quantum activity takes place. In fact this is how the many complicated and diverse activities within the body are able to take place and be performed simultaneously.

The healthiest body would have the lowest light emissions and be closest to a zero state. Therefore the most desirable state for us is one of low light emission. In other words, our light, our essence, is being discharged very slowly, and rather than burning like an inferno out of control, we need to burn gently like a candle. The healthiest food is also found to have the lowest and most coherent fields of light, which means it does not cause any disruption to the body. Anything that disturbs an organism or system increases photon production, generating more light than is necessary or useful. Health therefore is a state of perfect subatomic communication and ill health is a state of communication breakdown (quantum dissonance).

The more we understand the story of light the more we are able to make choices that complement our understanding. If we introduce into our lives those things that create peace, balance and harmony then we ensure that our contribution to the sea of light is positive and empowering and we, in return, are touched by its grace.

The most important input we make to this amazing story is with our thoughts. Our thoughts are the most subtle form of energy and are the catalysts for countless actions and interactions taking place within the body. Appreciating the power of your mind in this equation can help you to use your most precious resource (your thoughts) in a more responsible way, adding value, meaning and purpose to your own life and the lives of others.

Hopefully this summary has helped pull together a number of seemingly unrelated topics and given you a better appreciation of how life 'ticks' at the unseen level and how all living things are subtly connected, and though we are not in control of all these miraculous processes, we do have an important say. Far too often we waste our positive influence over these events by not exercising the power of free will and taking up the mantle of personal responsibility. However my hope is that as your understanding becomes more refined you will make better choices and not literally 'burn yourself out'. Remember it is the calm, gentle flame that best represents optimum life, not the raging inferno. So, slow down, reflect and prioritize. Focus your energies in the most important areas and make a positive contribution to the sea of light. The decisions and choices you make and how you live your life really do matter. Don't just be a victim of circumstance - choose choice.

A new contract

As I initially proposed in Chapter 4, the relationship between matter and mind is more complex than it first appears. We've often thought of it as a one-way street, believing that we can exert the will of the mind over matter, and we've done this at times to great effect. However, we've neglected to give matter the respect it deserves, as we haven't understood that it cannot and will not be bullied into submission without us paying a price. This is why we need to pursue the path of persuasion and co-operation and I hope, thus far to have persuaded you of that.

'Mind over matter' has long been one of the drivers of human enquiry and in so many ways we appear to have harnessed and mastered many of matter's versatilities. She has co-operated in helping us create a world of many wonders. We've accomplished amazing things by understanding her laws and manipulating her immense power. The list is endless: airplanes and ships, wonderful buildings and architecture, incredible art using metal, ceramics, glass, paint etc., life-saving advancements in medicine and an almost endless array of beneficial technologies. Sadly on the other side of this creative equation are many destructive achievements: unbelievably powerful weaponry, nuclear bombs, chemical weapons, tanks, missiles, guns etc. We've also used our moulding of matter to interfere with nature's evolution and design in areas such as agriculture (food, animal husbandry, chemical products), genetic engineering (animals and humans), medicine and its associated research as witnessed by the plethora of pharmaceuticals, most of which have as many negative side effects as benefits. For its part, information technology has now led us to a point of information overload and led to so many of us becoming de-skilled in the art of human interaction and communication. The list goes on. We've mastered matter in so many ways but as we can see it has not always been beneficial and in a universe that operates on the basis of cause and consequence there is always a price to pay and if we look around, some of the debts we've accrued are now being called in.

Nowhere is that better exposed than in our own bodies - arguably the most intimate relationship we'll ever have and yet for the majority of us, the one we most take for granted – how tragic. We need to understand not only the depth of this relationship but its importance. It's also time to understand that it's not simply a question of mind over matter but that it also works the other way - matter over mind, so that we can, with humility, apply our new found wisdom to how we live.

The lack of co-operation in this area in particular has brought us to our knees. Look at our relationship with the planet. Is matter not biting back against the arrogance we've displayed, acting as Gods over the material world, retaliating against our ignorance, lack of awareness and insensitivity? If we are to reinstate balance, order and harmony on this planet we must start with ourselves. To that end, our bodies are the first port of call. Only then can we extend our influence positively out into the world. It's time for a spirit of co-operation to prevail - everything else has failed or is failing. It's time for humility.

In summary

All that has been discussed in this chapter is helping us to understand many things at many levels. Could it be that science is now catching up with spirituality? I think it is. The more you are a student of the past the more the discoveries of the present are simply pointing to the fact that modernity is now often reluctantly acknowledging some of the powerful messages of antiquity. It seems to me that in the name of progress we had thrown the baby out with the bathwater and now, rather sheepishly we're trying to put it back in!

Many of the alternative and complementary healing modalities do in fact work. We are beginning to understand that this is in part due to the amazing relationship between thoughts and matter. Understanding the story of light, epigenetics, quantum coherence, our relationship with food and the environment and the importance of detoxification, all end the separation of mind and body and reminds us that there is an on-going subtle relationship where mind and body are constantly communicating and influencing each other.

What we are doing to our bodies, impacts on our minds and what we are thinking in our minds influences our bodies… and of course the spirit pays the price too. So can you now see the deep connection between the mouth and the mind?

"Science without religion is lame, religion without science is blind."
Albert Einstein (1879 – 1955)

CHAPTER 10: THE JOURNEY OF BECOMING

"You create your own universe as you go along."
Winston Churchill (1874-1965)

Knowledge plus application is the key

Hopefully this message has been underlined for you the more that you have read. It's not what you know that really counts, it's what you do with it. This chapter will take you even further in this direction because until you apply all that has been offered so far, this won't be much more than a good read (assuming you've enjoyed it). Let us begin with what I've described in my work as The Journey of Becoming.

THE JOURNEY OF BECOMING...

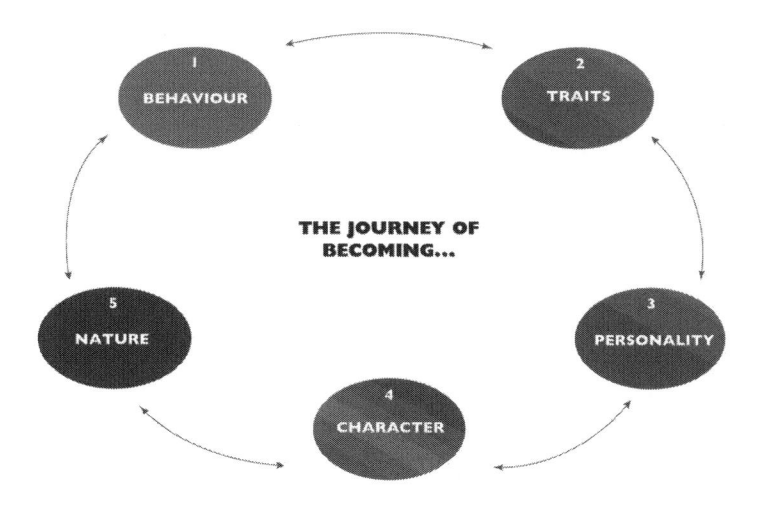

1. BEHAVIOUR
2. TRAITS
3. PERSONALITY
4. CHARACTER
5. NATURE

Figure 3

The journey of becoming

This is a truly fascinating subject because it tells the story of how we become who we are. We are the result of a journey from 'behaviour to nature' – a journey that begins with seemingly innocent and what may appear inconsequential actions and yet ends up creating patterns that become incredible forces of nature (see Figure 3).

As I guide you along this path you will come to understand that your behaviours are like sowing seeds in the fields of infinite potential and your nature is the fruit that those seeds eventually bear. So let us look at not only how you've become who you are today, but more importantly how you can become that which seems beyond your reach. If you believe you are stuck where you are and are unable to change, then that almost certainly will be your reality. However, if you dare to believe that the best is yet to come, then the adventure that awaits you will never cease to amaze you.

Behaviour: this is where our journey begins - with our actions, what we actually do. Of course the precursors to our actions are our thoughts. Before our actions are visible in the world they begin as thoughts and feelings in our minds. If we want to change our behaviour we need to change our thoughts. This is why I've produced so many resources that are geared to achieving that outcome. However, in the end, it's what we do that will bring the greatest changes. Thoughts without actions are simply not enough.

Behaviours, good, bad or neutral, are what we first pour into the moulds that ultimately form our personalities and characters. Those behaviours eventually set up in us virtues or vices, confidence or fear, belief or doubts, peace or anger - in fact everything about who you are today began with those initial behaviours (actions), which then blend and bind together creating those early patterns....

Traits: when our behaviours blend and bind together in this way they create traits. Traits are little pockets of energy, filled with latent propensities and tendencies. It's at this point that our behaviours really begin to make their presence felt. When behaviours begin their journey their influence over us is probably somewhere between 2% and 10%; their power initially is quite weak. However, by the time they have become traits, which occurs as a consequence of repetition, their influence on our way of being is increased to around 25%

and so now they are forces to be reckoned with. At this point in the journey of becoming, traits are influencing our perceptions, moods and attitudes; which means we are more likely to be thinking and at times acting in accordance with those initial behaviours. We still are in control of the pattern being formed, but the seductive dance is beginning to lure us, casting its spell.

If these traits go unchallenged and we don't examine their usefulness and authenticity, then we can quite quickly be overwhelmed by the momentum and the force that they generate. It is at this point that traits develop from just having influence into entities that have real power….

Personality: those seemingly innocent and arguably inconsequential early behaviours are now part of a power struggle going on within the self. When traits find their way into the labyrinth of our personality they begin to have a substantial say on our internal workings - they have real power. At this point the degree of influence over our internal machinations is somewhere around 50%, and so perceptions, moods and attitudes are now becoming beliefs. This is when the force of habit really begins to make its presence felt. Habits start by demanding energy and slowly take control of our self-perception and worldview. This is when most of us find ourselves beginning to lose control of our inner landscape (the mind). We start to feel intimidated and even overwhelmed by the force of habits; our sense of control is slipping away and this instils fear and hopelessness.

It's important to note, for the sake of balance, that if those initial behaviours were positive, then of course we would not be feeling intimidated, overwhelmed and afraid. At this point in the journey we would be growing in self-awareness, confidence and personal power. We'd be reaping the seeds of our positive actions and experiencing the peace and happiness that comes from such activities. We'd then have access to becoming the person we most wish to be.

So it's important to understand that this journey is not one set in stone, it is fluid and changeable because it depends on the decisions and choices we make. So, if the (negative) traits that have unleashed their tendencies on our personalities are not curbed, managed and redirected then we find ourselves in the grip of an even greater force….

Character: once behaviours have become our characters or more accurately helped to create them, then the awesome power of habit dominates the inner landscape. Those early behaviours that were being poured into the mould have now been cast; tendencies and propensities have long gone and we are now at the stage of the journey where we are no longer driving, we are being driven! If positive energy, born of good decisions, good choices and good habits has become part of the fabric of one's character, then this is a force so powerful it can achieve the miraculous. However, if it is negative energy that has found its way to this point then it can create such devastation and destruction it is almost beyond comprehension. It is at this stage of the process that the individual is camped firmly within the fortress of their beliefs and in most cases would happily live or die by those beliefs - some of the greatest achievements in history have been shaped by the sheer force of character. Unfortunately, some of the worst atrocities have been the by-product of its incredible power and ability to manipulate and mould events.

And so you can see, the character is defined by whether our behaviours are positive or negative. Those things that have formed our character also drive our perceptions, beliefs and sense of self and these are not easy to change without a burning desire for positive change. The reason that many people stay 'stuck' with who they 'believe' themselves to be is because they have little or no understanding of this 'cycle of becoming' and coupled with that and maybe because of that, they often have no belief in their own ability to transform. Nothing could be further from the truth….

Nature: by the time behaviours have been moulded into our nature the power and the dominance of the subconscious mind is being completely felt in the conscious world. At this point we are often deceived by thinking that our thoughts are indeed our own! They may feel like our own thoughts, decisions and choices but in fact at this stage in the process we are 'being thought' – things are happening so spontaneously and seemingly naturally that we think we are in control. However, the truth is that the conscious mind is now almost completely in the grip of the subconscious mind and those initial behaviours that became traits, which then became aspects of our personality and moved on to become pillars of our character, have now consumed what sense of self remains. Our patterns, drives and habits dominate the decisions and choices we 'think' we are making. They have formed opinions and beliefs so strong that they no longer listen to reason, as they are busy justifying their own position.

By the time something has become our nature, we are either standing at a point of virtue and divine possibility, or we are holding the key to our own oblivion; it all depends on those initial behaviours, such is the power of our actions to shape our destinies. The idea that we are just being pulled along by the force of circumstances, unable to influence how our lives unfold, is one of the many ways in which we give our power away. The truth is that our actions are influencing the internal machinery of consciousness, which in turn influences the way we relate to each other and the world. Our beliefs, passions, perceptions, relationships, sense of meaning and purpose are all being moulded by what we do or by what we don't do. It's as simple as that. It's now time to take responsibility for our own lives and stop waiting for something else to bring the changes we desperately seek....

The way forward: having taken this journey, which has hopefully illustrated to you how the negative forces born of our behaviour can bring us to our knees, you could be forgiven for wondering where the hope is in this message?

It's become clear that by the time something has become our nature it can be extremely difficult to change and therefore one could be easily disheartened and lose faith. But if this is how you are feeling, then you haven't really seen the tremendous message of hope and the potential for positive change being offered here. This journey of becoming is one where you can literally find the best in yourself by understanding how the worst of yourself has been constructed; it shows you how by having the desire to change and believing in the possibility of that, you can achieve what you'd been too afraid to imagine, you can indeed realize the personal transformation you ache for.

You'll notice in the diagram (see Fig 3) that behaviour (1) and nature (5) have a slightly different relationship with each other - the arrows here are in fact pointing both ways. This is because it is behaviour that started this process and through the power of repetition we have seen how it has transformed itself into the awesome force... nature. The irony here is that it is actually our behaviour that has the power to transform nature into something far more positive, empowering and pleasing.

Now, you need to take the journey from 'knowing to doing' because it is what you actually do that will enable you to change anything that you are dissatisfied with in your life. It's not enough to want it to go away, you actually need to desperately want it to change. Until you cultivate a healthy obsession, a burning desire to change, you're unlikely to do the things that you need to do consistently for personal transformation to take place. Sustainable solutions, as we discovered in Chapter 8, are not found in wishy-washy intentions, followed by lame and inconsistent actions; success does not live in that place. So really grasp the opportunity being offered to you here today and realise that nothing and no one can stop you from fulfilling your potential once you decide that this is what you want. Take the journey of creating new, positive behaviours to transform your nature and you'll soon discover you can really become whatever you choose….

The relationship between time and consciousness

It is difficult to talk about consciousness in any meaningful way without exploring its relationship with time. As human beings our experiences are intimately tied to life's relentless movement forward. Time literally waits for no man. It moves with or without us, ever forward, providing us with endless opportunities for learning and growth. It is however our responsibility to take from those countless opportunities. There are no guarantees in terms of our relationship with time, other than that we have a finite amount of it within which to fulfil our potential.

There are three aspects to time, past, present and future and what follows is a summary of how we can either be a slave to time or a co-operative companion. Consider carefully what's written, because it offers you the opportunity to make your life really count.

"Let him who would enjoy a good future waste none of his present."
Roger Babson (1875 – 1967)

The memoried self

Our relationship with time is central to our relationship with ourselves. Past, present and future are not just descriptions of time's unfolding, they also tell the story of three significant states of consciousness. These could be described as the 'memoried self', the 'experiencing self' and the 'anticipating self'. The experiencing self relates to the present, the anticipating self relates to the future. My focus here is on the memoried self, which relates to the past.

The reason many of us are unable to move out of our unhappiness, hurt, pain and negative patterns, is because we are unhealthily bound up with our pasts. In truth, the past is meant to be our reference library, the place where all of our experiences reside. Everything you've ever thought, said or done lives there. This is what I'm referring to as the memoried self. This aspect of the self has many corridors and rooms, housing all our memories and experiences. When we relate to this part of the self with awareness it positively informs our 'here and now' experience and helps us make the best decisions and choices. Unfortunately far too often this is not the case. As each moment called 'now' unfolds we have the opportunity to learn from what has gone before, to write a new script, move in a new direction or consolidate the positives. If we have no negative attachment to our pasts we choose to find the good in things and the benefit in every experience as our instinct knows this is a far healthier place to live. Sadly, far too often, what actually happens is that the moment called 'now' grabs our attention as it's meant to but instead of us staying with the experience of the present, standing at the door of countless possibilities, we follow that moment as it moves from the 'now' to join the past. Following that moment with all its content we are now looking at reality through the eyes of the memoried self, rather than the experiencing self. Furthermore, when the new moment called 'now' turns up we miss it as our attention is not with the present but with the past.

This happens so frequently for so many of us that we fail to recognize we're no longer living in the 'now'. Most of us would insist that we are, not realizing that we've been seduced by the content of the moment and become busy following the trail back to the past. Then, if that has thrown up any negative reminders of things that have gone before, we find ourselves living a 'recycled past', believing it to be the 'now' because we're not aware of this pattern/habit. The stuff that actually belongs to the 'now' is then missed because we remain emotionally connected to those things that come into the field of our awareness. This is not the healthiest relationship for us to foster with our experiences or indeed with time. Some degree of emotional detachment is needed in order for there to be sufficient objectivity. In that way we can better see the connections between our experiences and life events. When we are too heavily embroiled in the paths we have taken and the experiences we've been exposed to we struggle to let go and so are denied the learning and the opportunities that each new moment presents us with. What we do instead is keep revisiting the experience using our memories as the template for our perception, attitudes, responses and behaviour. All of which is flawed. If you continue to respond to things the same way as you have done in the past, then there's very little capacity for self-improvement and positive change.

It's important to understand that there is a precious relationship that we need to have with the memoried self because we cannot be complete without the evidence contained within it. The encyclopaedic records of the memoried self are not only the building blocks of our personality, character, drives and intuition; they also hold crucial records and points of reference for the use of the experiencing self. Without them, the experiencing self would be compromised in its ability to make the best choices moment to moment and so it's important to recognize that the memoried self is not to be condemned and criticized for the role that it plays, we simply need to form a healthier relationship to it. We need to stop using the past as something with which we beat ourselves or as something best hidden, ignored or denied. Also, when we relate to the memoried self appropriately the past becomes an invaluable tutor.

Hopefully your understanding of the memoried self is becoming clearer (you may need to read this section several times before it is fully understood). As you begin to make the connections, the importance of a healthy relationship between the memoried self, the experiencing self and the anticipating self (past, present and future) will become ever clearer. When all three are appropriately aligned one is able to experience peace, joy and contentment but when misaligned, fear, negativity, hopelessness and despair pull against the best interests of the self.

The script below forms a template of how you might better relate to this aspect of the self in order that the past and present work in the mutual interests of the self. Remember to pause where there are dots, which will enable the sentiments to be better understood and experienced.

I notice each moment as it floats into my awareness…. There is a variety of 'stuff' pulling on my attention…. it has a familiar feel…. things that I recognize from before…. I realize as the familiar comes into my awareness that there is previous learning and experience that can inform how I respond and react…. I can respond and react in the same old way or, in an entirely different way…. where it is beneficial for the response to be the same then I'm happy to respond in the same way…. When my previous responses or reactions have not been beneficial to others or myself, I realize I can choose to relate differently…. and I do…. I do not want to be defined by yesterday anymore…. yesterday has had its day…. this is a new day with new opportunities and I choose to embrace it…. I let go of yesterday and only hold onto those memories and experiences that have relevance to this moment.... I've come to understand that the memoried self is a beautiful ally.... it only wishes to help me make the best decisions.... When it thinks I'm not making best use of what it has to offer it can sometimes panic in its desperate attempt to claim my attention.... In those moments I lose sight of what it is really saying and I then get caught up in the frenzy and subsequent panic.... However, with my new-found awareness, I choose for this not to happen today.... I see, hear and understand how yesterday is relevant to today.... I let go of what is no longer useful.... The memoried self and the experiencing self are now able to be at one.... the conflict has ceased.... they become busy co-operating in the best interests of the self.... Collaboration and co-operation supersede competition and conflict.... I am clear.... free from anxiety.... I am at peace and for that I give thanks.... My awareness is where it belongs.... at one with this moment.... I am at ease.... I am free to choose what is right for me.... and I do.

The experiencing self

The experiencing self could be described as the point where consciousness and time actually meet. It's that point where we are able to positively influence our realities. The experiencing self is the part of us that remains connected to the present moment. It is not deceived by the mirages of the past (the memoried self), nor seduced by the future (the 'anticipating self'). It realizes that the past has gone and cannot be changed and even though it's an invaluable resource, nevertheless it is not meant to define the present moment. The future, on the other hand, may either hold the prize of heaven or the imprisonment of hell, but even that is determined by the experiencing self - by how it responds in the moment, by its decisions and choices. So it is in fact the experiencing self that holds the key to your health, happiness, wellbeing and peace of mind. The more you practise being present the more you will forge a healthy alliance with this aspect of yourself and life's majesty.

As already explained, our different states of consciousness are intimately intertwined with time. Our awareness can either be trapped in the past, driven by the events of yesterday, or bound to a future yet to be created. Unfortunately for many, the future is also being defined by yesterday. The experiencing self understands that whatever has not been resolved continues to steal our awareness, our time and our energy and so it seeks out positive solutions in order to resolve the past so it can properly align itself with the memoried self. The experiencing self also understands the power and the force of yesterday. It realizes that we are all a by-product of the past and if we are not at peace with it, then it will continue to serve up the same patterns, urges, needs, drives and habits that we've always known.... whether they are good, bad or indifferent.

It's important to note that the past does not have a consciousness of its own; it's simply a string of events and experiences that are flowing in the stream of consciousness. When something is resolved the nature of the patterns and drives changes. If issues remain unresolved they can only offer us the 'evidence' of yesterday's experience. All of us are subject to the patterns of the past and unless we relate to them favourably they can only resonate with the same frequency as they always have. In other words there can be no change without change - in terms of consciousness, something cannot be made different if we do not alter the way we relate to it. We can all remember those times where we promised to change and do things differently so as to be free from those things we most dislike about ourselves and yet before we know it we have broken our promise. Such is the force of habit, circumstance and events that we breach the walls of our own integrity, betraying not only ourselves, but also our beliefs in the process. If the experiencing self is not at the helm, marshalling the potency and the power of the past, then as we saw in The Journey of Becoming you are more often than not being driven by habits, circumstances and events that are no longer relevant or true, if indeed they were ever accurate. So my question to you is do you want to change this?

First you need to understand these three states of awareness and how they relate to one another, the past the present and the future. Secondly, you need to understand the role of choice in this. You can either be a victim or you can claim the power inherent in your life. The experiencing self is the part of you that understands you are a miracle waiting to happen. The first miracle is that you are here but the greater miracle is what you decide to do with the gift of your life. If you choose to embrace the countless opportunities offered to you in each moment, then you will be carried along by the current of destiny to your potential. There you will find your meaning and purpose.

Thirdly, you need to forge an alliance with the experiencing self so that you can make best use of the past with all its wonderful insights, but to create this alliance you have to become obsessive about bringing your attention back to the moment. It is really important that you understand that in the end you become what you practise. In fact everything about you today is a reflection of what you have done (practised).

Whether you are conscious of it or not you are practising all the time as your actions lay down the patterns for future behaviour. You can either practise to be the same, better or worse. This will be determined by the decisions and choices you make. So why not practise being at one with your experiencing self and then channel the advantages of that awareness in directions that are favourable to you and to others. This is a treasure you can claim today and every day. All you need to do is to become obsessed about practice and you'll soon discover the dividends are truly enormous… peace, joy, stability, clarity and contentment, to name a few.

Here's an example of how you can develop this practice….

The experiencing self is a place of pure insight, intuition and awareness…. It's that place where my discrimination is best able to see how to use and positively exploit the experiences that come into my consciousness…. As I sit here now I am able to use my past experiences wisely…. I am able to forgive myself and others where necessary so that I'm not merely reacting to events…. as I now understand that forgiveness clears the decks and gives me clarity and so I can respond appropriately to life's flux…. I'm not disturbed by circumstances or events, as I'm able to maintain enough objectivity to see how it would be best to respond…. I realize that habits can be positive or negative…. so I hold onto those that are a positive force in my life and I let go of those that deceive me…. I refuse to get caught in the cycle of blame because it steals my ability to positively influence events and to rise to life's challenges…. Being a responder rather than a reactor takes far less energy and generates better outcomes…. It leaves me feeling more peaceful and clear…. The experiencing self recognizes what it can healthily control…. And what it needs to let go of if it is to maintain balance and poise…. I choose to let go of what is no longer constructive or healthy…. I choose to find the benefit in my experiences…. even when there is pain and difficulty…. Contentment and serenity are not simply freedom from the storm, they are also the ability to find peace within it…. I realize by practising being in this awareness daily that I can claim peace and joy…. even at those times when there appears to be none…..

By practising relating to the experiencing self in this way it will become a lovely habit. You'll come to realize that even though you cannot control the three elements of time, past, present and future, or control all that is happening within the cosmos, you can nevertheless remain anchored to the present and can control how you respond to life's unfolding and events. So why not choose that today?

The anticipating self

By now you will have some appreciation of the memoried self and the experiencing self and how they relate to one another. The anticipating self is the third key character in this trilogy. Like the memoried self it can either enable or hinder, inspire or conspire against you. This is determined by how you relate to this part of the self. The more you are a student of personal growth and examine all the options for self improvement and personal empowerment the more you discover that if there is a secret to achieving your potential then it is indeed synergy, (the whole being greater than the sum of its parts). It is when all three aspects of awareness are intimately intertwined that you are able to get the best out of each moment. This is because the experiencing self is able to positively exploit the assets of the other two. It is neither a slave to the past nor afraid of the future.

The anticipating self, as the name suggests, is that part of us that speculates about what lies ahead. As previously stated, it can anticipate the worst or the best and when our issues have not been addressed or appropriately resolved then it has a propensity to use the past to determine the future. This can of course be positive if there is enough positive material to draw from but in far too many instances this is simply not the case and a negative response is generated. If the anticipating self were acting in accordance with our true nature rather than using the past as its primary reference then we would actually be optimistic, joyous and ecstatic as we marvel at the wonder of life. When we are not properly aligned to the memoried self we downgrade the magnificent into the ordinary. We are blinded in such a way that we are unable to see life's splendour and its bountiful treasures. This is why the mind then anticipates worst-case scenarios. It moves away from peace, contentment and joy and is pulled into conflict, confusion and chaos. It sees the worst in itself and in others and it prepares to compete rather than co-operate. Does any of this sound familiar?

This is the modern day template; a position where we have come to respect competition over co-operation, accepting the negative consequences of competition as a necessary part of progress - consequences worthy of the prize.

This is why for many the anticipating self is not a safe haven, nor a place of hope, aspiration, bliss or rejoicing - it is a place of an underlying, nagging anxiety, a place where fear and doubt cast their many shadows. And so the spirit of competition with all its needs and demands has fostered for many uncertainty, tension and fear, which makes the chance of a better tomorrow seem at best unlikely. This is the pattern we need to break. This mythical position has asserted itself as fact in such a way that it's difficult for most to believe that positive change is actually only ever one thought away.

Claiming the gifts of awareness does not belong to a fortunate few. It is yours to claim today. The need for practice has already been stressed but it cannot be stressed enough. This is not something that's going to fall into your lap. You have to choose to do something about it and once you do you have to regularly dedicate time and energy to this endeavour. The anticipating self is rich with opportunity, bursting with potential. Like the experiencing self, it's a place of infinite possibility. If you're dissatisfied with the way that your life currently is and you feel trapped by feelings of low self worth, crippled by anxiety or panic, doubting that your life can be any different, then by connecting to the experiencing self and using the assets of the anticipating self, you can change your reality…. today.

Change is a process, not an event and so every time you take a step in the right direction you are a little closer to where you want to be. It's unlikely that one single event will bring you the change you want, but if you join up the dots between lots of little positive activities then before you know it you can feel much better about yourself and create a position where hope and wonder sit comfortably side by side.

Here's an example of the alliance you can forge between the experiencing self and the anticipating self.

I become aware of my breathing…. I notice every in-breath and every out-breath… I quietly appreciate that this beautiful, simple act performed thousands of times per day is keeping me alive and offers me the opportunity for greater understanding and continued growth…. How amazing…. it's so easy to take this for granted…. I give thanks for the gift of breathing…. and all that it offers me…. Through the increased awareness of my breathing I become more aware of this moment I'm sitting in…. I notice the many thoughts seeking my attention…. I notice how it feels to be in my body…. I become aware of my relationship to this time and space and my environment…. Right now this moment asks nothing of me and I ask nothing of it.... I'm content with just being.... It's wonderful to just be.... I'm reminded that I can positively influence events by the way that I think and I choose to see an ever-evolving me stepping into a positive and certain future.... a future where my reason for being is ever clearer and I have all that I need to fulfil my meaning and purpose.... I attract the right relationships and resources.... and this support helps me to make the best decisions and choices.... I find myself being ever more open and receptive to life's ups and downs and so am able to make the best of the opportunities that present themselves to me.... My life is filled with kindness, compassion and charity.... It's a life of health, abundance and wellbeing.... I have all that I need.... I've come to understand that if I anticipate the best it won't be very far away.... And so I do.... I choose to be present in this moment and to remain completely open to a life that blossoms, presenting me with advantages, peace and joy.... I am at one with life's wonder and I give thanks for the joy of that.... I now know that my thoughts are the primary architects of my future, so I choose those thoughts that best reflect my highest hopes and aspirations....

The anticipating self is not where we are meant to be but it is inevitable that consciousness will travel both backwards and forwards. In fact, it's necessary if we are to exploit all the benefits of being alive. Consciousness is not a static, stationary force. It ebbs and flows. It's a force of movement and change and we can either be shackled by it or liberated in ways that we couldn't have anticipated. Hopefully, now when your consciousness moves out of this moment into the next it will do so without fear and doubt. It will dare to appreciate that you do have the deciding vote in your life. So why choose to keep going with the old and familiar when you can move towards the new and unchartered? Anticipate the worst and it won't be very far way. Dare to think the best and in time it will be yours. Life is a self-fulfilling prophecy - write the prophecy of your own choosing today.

C.I.A. – the enemies of growth

Complacency, Ignorance and Arrogance are the primary enemies of personal growth. Each one is capable of weaving a sophisticated web of deception, and if you are not aware will prevent you from growing and prospering, as you remain stuck in a time or in events that are no longer relevant. Underestimate them at your peril. Let's take a closer look at these three skillful manifestations of the ego.

Complacency: When the individual does not get her needs adequately met the ego which is the part most focused on survival, will look for those needs to be met elsewhere. This is how a 'false self' is constructed over time. The deep 'aching' for attention, affection and affirmation (The 3 As) drives the individual to embrace anything that might ease the pain when these are absent. The 'authentic self' becomes subjugated as the acquired self busies itself filling the gaps. In fact, the ego will find a way to fill any need that goes unfulfilled because of the survival drive. This is how the authentic self slips slowly away into the abyss and a whole set of contradictions are born.

Where does complacency fit in? Well, complacency is a strange manifestation of the ego because on the one hand it looks like laziness, maybe even a form of procrastination and yet on the other hand it can be a quiet arrogance that believes the prize is already in the bag. Complacency thinks 'tomorrow will do', 'there's no need to worry', 'there's plenty of time'. It is this self-talk and belief that maintains the illusion that all is well, when often the opportunity is in fact slipping away.

Like all manifestations of ego, unless there is some self-awareness, the person under the spell of complacency actually cannot see the deception. Should it be pointed out, often their defence mechanisms simply come rushing to the fore, because they actually see their complacency as 'keeping things in perspective' or simply their 'nature'. Sometimes they have a 'tomorrow will do' attitude or believe 'it's already in the bag', which is the blind spot that prevents them from seeing the bigger picture. This position holds them hostage indefinitely unless of course they wake up and take the journey of self-improvement and self-awareness.

Complacency is a very tight blindfold that inhibits the growth of many. Take a close look and see where you've become complacent and remove your blindfold so that you can reclaim your power.

Ignorance: 'Ignorance is bliss'. We've probably all used this phrase at some time or heard it used to describe the 'joys of not knowing' something. How can it be true that ignorance is a state of bliss? There's no doubt it can serve up an illusion that could be mistaken for bliss, but ignorance is ignorance. It's a position that is blind and yet believes it can see. In some cases it's both blind and uninterested in seeing. It certainly isn't a state of bliss. Bliss is a joy beyond words and even if one were able to achieve that position via the path of ignorance then that state of bliss simply wouldn't be sustainable. The Reach Approach is very much about 'sustainable solutions' and in order to achieve these we must transcend ignorance by increasing our knowledge and awareness.

Ignorance is therefore a blind spot we cannot afford to have as it denies us genuine 'in-sight' (the ability to look clearly within and see the unseen). Ignorance is bound up in its own opinion. Knowledge, facts, truth etc. get in the way of its need to be right. 'Being right' is the ultimate attainment for one caught in the trance of ignorance, for the fear of shame (being seen to be wrong) must be avoided at all costs. The biggest hindrance with ignorance is that there cannot be any adventure outside of one's own perspective. It is a position riddled with prejudice, small-mindedness and sometimes even hatred. It feeds off 'scraps of information' to support its position and 'prove' the rightness of its stance. The primary source of ignorance is fear and it is from the reservoir of fear that it draws its strength. Under the spell of ignorance, it is rare that a person recognizes the fear; they are so busy defending themselves that they cannot hear the truth above the sound of their own denials, justifications and delusions. As with complacency you need to use the powerful lens of introspection and take a close look at where you might be deceiving yourself. I call this the inventory of incongruence. I will explain what I mean by that shortly - in brief it is a simple method for identifying one's inconsistencies and shortcomings and then compassionately seeking to put them right.

Arrogance: In many ways this manifestation of the ego is the most obvious to witness, as it parades its wares with a neon sign for all to see. In fact, it is no more destructive and deceiving than the other two. It's just different. All three are the enemies of personal growth and should be treated with equal caution. To be free of one does not provide immunity to the others either and so hyper vigilance is needed if you are not to fall foul of arrogance.

Arrogance turns up in many forms. It can be quiet and understated, dressed up as humility but in fact ravenously craving the 3 A's (attention, affection and affirmation) and is therefore desperate to be seen. It can often be seen beating its own chest rejoicing in itself, bound up in the belief that 'no one does it better'. For the person entangled in arrogance, their self-importance is the defining principle. Ignorance 'believes' it is right, whilst arrogance 'knows' it is! These are different kinds of 'certainty' both driven by fear but dressed up in different uniforms.

The certainty of arrogance is such that it looks like confidence and may even 'feel' like confidence but the truth is it is an imposter. Unlike confidence it thrives on being noticed, it loves being centre-stage and it doesn't mind how it gets there. It will quite happily make others pay the price for its stardom as it ridicules, mocks and diminishes others so that it may feel better about itself. Real confidence on the other hand is quiet and unassuming; in no way does it seek to be at the centre. On the contrary, it is at its happiest away from the limelight. The only light it seeks is the gentle haze of peace of mind, the sunlight of joy and happiness and the inner illumination of enlightenment, none of which can ever diminish anyone else.

Arrogance also deceives with its pretence that it doesn't seek the light, whilst it remains busy doing the very opposite. Not only does it try to extinguish the light of others, it finds countless subtle ways of promoting itself whilst denying this self-promotion to itself and others. But under closer scrutiny that 'hidden' agenda is unveiled to the awakened mind, as the arrogant posture can't really be hidden, merely masked and overlooked.

So take a look into your soul. Is the C.I.A. anywhere to be found? If so, where? How does it manifest in you? And in the light of this new perspective, what are you going to do about it? Hopefully, take the journey of enough….

The journey of enough

In response to the relentless pace of modern life there is increasing discussion about how we might find peace amidst the frenzy and the chaos. This is why we've seen such a rise in the practice of meditation, in the sales of self-help books, in workshops and retreats of all kinds over the last thirty years, and currently, mindfulness, kindness and compassion being particularly topical. These activities have largely grown out of the desire to calm our minds and soothe our increasingly busy lives; lives in which we have become less 'present', at times even absent. Despite the rise in these more 'mindful' activities, why then are we still no nearer that oasis of peace that our hearts and minds thirst for?

The main reason that the peace, joy and tranquillity we long for still remain beyond our reach is quite simply because we have not done enough. If we are to find the best in ourselves and express that within the world, then we must take the 'journey of enough'. This journey promises us peace and poise amidst the storms. It promises us insight and clarity, health and happiness, as well as the perception and perspective that will ensure we are no longer deceived by our pasts or misguided by our futures. So what is this journey and what does it ask of us?

There are four primary considerations on this path, each one an essential point of retreat and reflection, if we are to really understand how this journey unfolds. They are best summarised in four words: knowledge, understanding, application and realization, and the promise put before us is simple – when there is enough knowledge we are gifted understanding; when there is enough understanding we are compelled to take the journey of action and application; when there is enough application there is the bright dawning of realization. Realization is the point when it can be said that we are truly awake. The whole point of meditation, spiritual retreats, personal development workshops, self-help books, mindfulness programmes etc. is to help us to 'wake up' and be truly present in each moment. So the question you need to answer honestly is, "are you doing enough to be where you want to be and for your life to unfold in the best possible way?"

You may need help to answer this question and if so don't be afraid to seek it, but it's important to ensure that the source of that help also understands this principle of 'doing enough'. We have become caught up with the modern message that there's always a fast-track to wholeness and well-being and so the ancient principle that wisdom, healing and peace of mind often take time and practice, is now less fashionable. We have come to revere speed above all else, as if it were the panacea. In fact, in some quarters, we've reached the point that if it can't be done quickly then there must be some flaw somewhere - we've come to expect everything to come with the promise of immediacy and are not sufficiently concerned about sustainability. What's the point of getting anywhere quickly if you're not there long enough to enjoy it?

This doesn't mean the journey has to be long and hard but it does need to be taken with respect for how the process of change really works. There is no doubt that some change can and does happen quickly but there is equally no doubt that there are times when that just isn't the case and unless we understand this we will keep pushing at those times when we simply need to wait and be patient.

You can, of course, take this journey by yourself, calling on what help you need from time to time but this will require proper planning, self-discipline and maintaining a balance between tenacity and compassion. When we take a journey like this we have to remember to be kind to ourselves especially at those times when we get it wrong - which we will and that's okay. We are not defined by our mistakes but by how we respond to them. Do not be afraid of failure, otherwise you'll fail to find your real meaning and purpose. It is often on the road of mistakes that we discover the best in ourselves and our own paths become clear.

Let me take you back to the four considerations on this path. The first of these is knowledge.

Knowledge: To truly undertake the journey of being the best we can be, knowledge is needed. We cannot get there on knowledge alone, but equally we are unlikely to make it at all without the beauty of knowledge. In this context knowledge is the map. It makes us aware of the terrain and the conditions we will have to face. It enables us to prepare for the journey in the right way to ensure we have the best chance of reaching our destination. The modern face of personal development offers so many solutions, each one more enticing and seductive than the last and so how on earth are we meant to negotiate our way through this?

There is no easy answer to this question, but what you do need to do is start listening with your heart. You have to learn to trust yourself and start by developing a dialogue with yourself. You cannot hope to find your way if you are not consulting your inner world. Consuming all the information available 'out there', whilst ignoring the inner landscape will only help you to further lose your way. You must consult widely, properly researching those things that promise you peace, happiness and fulfilment. But then you must test them using your instincts and intuition and only if they stand up to that interrogation should you move forward in confidence and in faith. When you've done this enough, this will then lead you to the next stage on your journey of becoming….

Understanding: Understanding begins when we have gathered the necessary data from outside and consulted our inner world, listening keenly to the voice within, the voice we so often ignore. Out of the wisdom of that dialogue the concepts offered by the knowledge we have examined, start to be understood. We can then begin to fit the information into the framework of our personal experience from which the countless possibilities, available in each moment, present themselves to us.

The map of knowledge now begins to make more sense and we can see the way(s) we need to go. But the journey is not over at this point, it's really only just beginning. This is the mistake that so many of us make because once we think we have understood, we march forward with a certainty that can often mislead. However, this is a trap we need to be aware of because understanding only introduces us to the possibilities. It's the point of potentiality, where we are able to access those things we haven't even imagined, as well as those we have. But the key word here is potentiality and it mustn't be mistaken for what will actually happen, because that is dependent on what we do - not what we say. In truth, until there's enough understanding there will be no application and application is the key to personal power and positive change....

Application: If you have understood the process so far, you now realize that true understanding actually means to go and take action and that personal transformation and positive change are not possible simply because we appreciate the theoretical concepts. Those who understand this, become busy planning exactly what they are going to do using this newly found awareness. They now appreciate it is only what we do that counts, good intentions simply are not enough. At this point in the journey a healthy obsession for putting what has been learned into practice takes place.

The value of structure, the power of routine and the understanding of the laws that govern change, which we discussed in Chapter 8, are very much at the forefront of the mind. The individual now recognizes the only real power that knowledge has is when it's applied. It's important not to make the mistake of thinking a little application over a short period of time is enough; often what's required at this stage of the process is the 3Ps (practice, patience and perseverance – which I also spoke about in Chapter 8). When we do what's required and patiently wait for the dividends of our endeavours, we are enriched not just by reaching the destination, but also by the journey itself. Doing enough, in terms of application, isn't simply about moving on to the next stage;

it's also about enjoying the beauty and potential of each moment along the way....

Realization: This is the prize, the moment of awakening, the moment when the knowledge that began this process is really understood. No longer are these words inanimate, lying static on a piece of paper, nor do they remain unheard in the heart of the one who owns them. This is the point where innate knowledge of the self and what has been acquired from the world are now clearly understood and become manifest in one's life.

The individual's life is now a testimony to those things that really matter and so their life is a celebration of virtue and truth. This is the point of awareness where what needs to be understood is understood; there is little mystery to such a mind and the knowledge beyond logic and the senses is increasingly unveiled. The journey from this point is full of compassion and love because nothing else makes sense. Realization, as I've said before, is not freedom from the storm; it's finding peace within it. The heart full of peace shares its gifts freely with the world.

It's time to take the journey of enough. There you'll find your true meaning and purpose.

A useful place when setting out on the journey of becoming is to identify your current contradictions. Wherever you are at odds with yourself in terms of your own principles, values and ethics, there you will find the things that are most standing in your way. The 'inventory of incongruence' is a wonderful tool to help individuals free themselves from those patterns and tendencies they wish to leave behind.

An inventory of incongruence

What is incongruence? To be incongruent is to not be true to oneself. It's to say one thing but to do another, to have good intentions but for whatever reason to not carry them out. A congruent human being is transparent and their thoughts, words and deeds are seamlessly woven together. What they say is what they do. Congruence is to be true to you.

Those who have the courage to look at themselves, to look their demon(s) in the eye, are to be applauded. The most difficult journey one is likely to take is the journey of self-examination (as discussed in Chapter 6). Looking into the abyss of the self is not for the faint-hearted because one is not always going to like what one sees. Yet it's within self-examination that the true self is found. On closer inspection we will all find there is a jewel inside waiting to be discovered. It will often be caked in the mud of past, self-limiting beliefs and subconscious conditioning. If we do not have the courage to look into that abyss we're almost certainly bound to remain slaves to these things and never discover the priceless jewel hidden within. However, the thing that blocks us most from our beauty is our own incongruence. Therefore, in order to be free, we need to turn towards it and face it and by acknowledging its existence and embracing it we can begin to turn the tide.

Find some time to sit on your own in quiet reflection and consider where the inconsistencies are in your life. Where are the points of contradiction? Wherever they are is where your power is seeping away. The ancient yogis referred to it as the 'hole in the soul', the point from which the power of the self leaks away. So where are the holes in your soul? Make the time to compose your list. This is probably the most important list you'll ever compile. This is what I mean by an inventory of incongruence.

Once you have compiled this list don't use it to beat yourself with. This list will help you to understand why you're unable to discover the jewel within. It holds the key to why your inner beauty continues to evade you. It is because of these things that doubt, inadequacy and fear continue to undermine who you really are. This list needs to become part of your strategy for self-improvement because once you know where the holes in your soul are, it's important to stop the power seeping away.

This process starts by not hiding your mistakes; it's time to learn from them. Use them as tools for progress. The more honest and honourable you are in your dealings, the quicker you will stop your power from draining away. Try moving through your life with greater humility, striving to leave only positive impressions, making a difference wherever you go. Be more truthful but not unkind. Be more benevolent with your judgment and more forgiving of others and you will find a gentle, soft, yet strong centre that exists in us all.

Transcend your defences - don't reinforce them. Make a pledge now that whenever you see incongruence in yourself you will do all you can to reduce and ultimately remove it. Remember the more contempt you have for yourself and your own actions the more you will need to hide them from yourself and from the world. This is not the way forward. Take this journey of courage and truth but with compassion and you will discover the exquisite beauty of who you are. Before reading to the end of this chapter, just take a moment now to jot down some of the incongruous behavior that you can see in yourself. For many, this is a vital first step towards becoming more whole and fulfilled. Don't use your list to condemn yourself, use it to plan your escape.

Once the enemies of growth have been truly understood, the endeavour to claim mental freedom and personal empowerment becomes real and sustainable. This book is about sustainable solutions and so there is no greater ally to this cause than synergy, which really is the cure for all ills.

Although much more could be said on this topic, I believe enough has been laid out here to ensure you can enjoy a lasting recovery from what ails you. All you have to remember is that knowledge plus application equals personal power and your destiny is then yours to claim. Now that you've finished this chapter, take another look at your inventory of incongruence and formulate a plan for your own transformation.

> *"Be not ashamed of mistakes and thus make them crimes."*
> Confucius (551 BC – 479 BC)

CHAPTER 11: METAPHYSICS – LIFE'S NARRATOR

"We see things not as they are, but as we are."
C.M. Tomlinson (1873 -1958)

Metaphysics is not the property of a few 'new age' fanatics or the pipe dream of those disengaged from reality. Metaphysics is the 'unheard' conversation; it is the language that explains the unexplained. When we listen keenly, it demonstrates to us how everything is connected. It offers great insight and clarity in each moment, if we avail ourselves of its wisdom. Metaphysics is the 'secret' code behind all of life's activities. In order to hear and understand the code we have to look beyond what we think we know and remember the best way to see is with our ears – listening gives us access to that code. We have to let go of our opinions and attachments, only then can we see the seemingly invisible and hear the inaudible.

Metaphysics literally means 'beyond the physical' and as a science - some might say a philosophy - it has a long tradition that goes back to the Upanishads in Ancient India, back to the Ancient Chinese, Egyptians and Greeks. In fact, its heritage has touched all societies and all cultures in some way and yet it is often still talked about as something other-worldly and lacking credibility. I would ask those of you who are interested in truth to look at the depth and breadth of metaphysical thought, reasoning and what has been offered as 'evidence'. Those of you who are unfamiliar with this subject will be staggered at the trail metaphysics has left through history. Sadly it continues to fight for a place at the Table of Truth, and many still question its contribution, even though it has a strong heritage and the latest discoveries in science are reluctantly beckoning it to the table.

However, the reality is that it is only at this level, beyond the physical, that the truth in all its magnificence can be fully experienced and understood. We cannot interpret and understand the world by merely using the senses as our primary point of reference. The width, depth and breadth of reality far exceed the scope of our sensory perceptions, and so if we are to trust only our five senses we will be deceived. The same is true of logic. Logic is often revered as a God-like Colossus that stands towering above us as the ultimate arbiter of truth. We are asked to believe that if logic does not say 'yes' then the information must be flawed; but logic too is able to deceive us.

If you read the first book in this trilogy, Science the New God, you will remember I was able to demonstrate that approximately every forty years science changes its mind. What once stood up to the scrutiny of logic is often rewritten by the next set of discoveries. Logic has both served and failed us and we would be wise to remember that. Neither logic nor the senses can be entirely trusted if truth is our aim.

Let's look more closely at their flaws and see why we must go beyond them both if we want to grow into our potential and experience the unlimited possibilities bound up in every moment.

What can we really see?

Do you remember my reference in Chapter 1 to the four main forces, which combine to create the world as we know it? Let me remind you.... they are electromagnetism, gravity, the strong nuclear force and the weak nuclear force (see the work of Max Planck who is considered by many to be the Father of quantum theory and Albert Einstein whose contribution to the field is second to none). Everything taking place in nature falls into one of these four categories. Electromagnetism accounts for heat, electricity, light, radio waves, TV, X-rays etc. Gravity makes the world go round and holds the planets and stars in place. The strong nuclear force (the most powerful of the four) holds the nucleus together at the heart of the atom. It's the dividing of this nucleus that creates what we refer to as nuclear power, which as we're all aware, is awesome.

The weak nuclear force holds the sub-atomic particles together. This is the most subtle of the conversations taking place within the sea of light, which I referred to in Chapter 9. The interactions taking place at this level are increasingly being described as 'information exchanges', which serve up countless permutations of reality. These four forces are responsible for all life as we know it and are often referred to as the 'unified field'.

Whatever energy we are talking about we are only ever talking about a different manifestation of light; whether gamma rays, X-rays, ultra-violet rays, infra red, microwaves or radio waves, all are made up of light. The only real difference is their frequency (wavelength). It is the difference in their wavelengths that make them visible, invisible, audible or inaudible to us.

It's all about vibrations. According to the speed and the resonance of light, matter expresses itself in a slightly different way, offering us endless permutations and experiences. Once we understand that everything around us is light and we too are beings of light, it will come as no surprise that just as matter is able to influence us, we are able to influence it. It is our ignorance about our amazing power that most enslaves us.

So, stop what you're doing right now and take a look around you and begin to marvel at the amazingness of the world that you reside in and equally marvel at your own amazingness. There is so much we take for granted and it's becoming clear that most of it is invisible to us.

The visible range when looking at these four forces of nature is very tiny indeed. If we talk about the electromagnetic field, which goes from gamma waves through to radio waves, the visible range has been calculated as 0.005%. So tiny as to be considered insignificant when compared to the whole spectrum. In other words, what we perceive in relation to what's actually 'out there' is very limited. This tells us that sight alone cannot help us in our search for truth. And given that sight (if we can see) is our most sophisticated sense in terms of interpreting data, we can also assume that our five senses are not enough to accurately interpret the world. Although the other four do add more breadth and depth to our perception, we still find ourselves standing outside the complete spectrum of reality if all we draw upon are the five senses.

We have come to understand that our whole world - the dance of light and the different frequencies, in fact everything - is made up of atoms. However, these building blocks of reality have unveiled themselves as nothing more than space with bits of information floating inside. They are not the Newtonian wheels and cogs we once thought, locked together in different configurations, producing liquids, gases and solids. The story is much more subtle and sophisticated than that, as I hinted at in my explanation about the unified field.

Using powerful electronic microscopes we've been able to see the truth (in part) behind the magical and mysterious properties of the atom, which is why we now know that there is more space inside an atom than anything else. In fact, it's been calculated that there is so much space in atoms that if you took that space out of the atoms which make up all seven billion human beings currently on earth, what remains would fit into your local church! Incredible, but true; go and take a closer look at quantum physics and the mind-blowing mathematics that are taking us deeper and deeper into reality and you'll see the wonderful revelations which are afoot.

Believing is seeing – perception is everything

So if we've taken out all the space inside the atom, what's left? Information. That's it - the nucleus, protons, electrons and neutrons are all bits of information floating around in space, allowing and enabling countless possibilities, subject to how these bits of information are interacted with and utilised. It is at this atomic and sub-atomic level that we can really see that we live in a world of choice and unlimited potential and that the limitations that exist are largely in our minds, underpinned by our beliefs.

The perceptions that we hold are what govern our experiences. So if we want to be free from whatever enslaves us, we have to start recognising that it is 'I' who most stands in my way. My beliefs, attitudes and perceptions are what limit me, because the world I'm living in is offering me unlimited opportunity, every minute of every day. This is because the information contained at this quantum level is not neatly packaged and defined, but is in fact a set of possibilities and permutations waiting to be actualised by you and me. It is not sitting in a pre-destined state, guaranteeing an exclusive or certain path; it's much more dynamic and adventurous than that. It waits ready and willing to perform magic with me (and you) and for us to become co-creators in that eternal dance between mind and matter. This incredible insight cannot be seen or completely understood merely via the senses.

But I hear you say 'isn't it logic that has enabled me to understand all that you've said up to now?' Yes of course it has been but can it take us the whole way? No it can't. Logic, like the senses is priceless to the human experience but its real value cannot be extracted until its limitations are also understood. Logic is not all knowing and all seeing. There is in fact a level of 'knowing' that comes only through experience.

Logic is fabulous within the world of theory but it starts to operate outside its depth when we move into the realm of experience. The realm of experience does obey some of the rules of logic but it has a logic all of its own which by nature is paradoxical and so may on first inspection appear to contradict itself. However, the more you peer into its depths the more you'll see that the paradoxes exist because of the subtle interplay of the different layers that are inherent within the truth. Just as it's not immediately obvious that our world is made up of atoms and that those atoms are made of light, the same is true of the world of experience.

What first greets the heart and mind may appear to be one thing but on further reflection offers a set of insights that were not seemingly there. At times this may appear to be at odds with any initial revelation, but closer scrutiny quickly shows that it is not. Truth has an ebbing and flowing nature. Unless you sit and observe it for long enough you're unlikely to recognise the ebb and flow or to understand the purpose of each phase. The 'flow' brings one message to the 'shore of consciousness' and the 'ebb' can seem to take it away, sending something else in its place on the back of the next tide. This hypnotic movement, coming and then going, subtraction followed by addition, tells the story of how truth unveils itself. Its richness, diversity and depth cannot be understood all in one go.

Rarely is there a portion that one can digest at one sitting. Truth is kind enough to give us what we can manage; it's like a mother who knows that if we are presented with too much at one time it will simply cause indigestion and all the vital nutrients will not be absorbed. This is why truth ebbs and flows, testing out our capacity to consume its offerings. This is also why we need to step beyond the perimeter of logic to experience the wonderment of truth, as the insights and revelations on offer, often struggle to make sense in the mathematical, formulaic world. Mystery and magic are not always immediately obvious, as they are part of life's subtext - the real dialogue of the universe, which is better understood through the conduit of experience. So how can we access that experience?

The art of introspection
The answer is introspection. The door of experience is unlocked through the inward-looking habit. There is literally a mountain of evidence concerning the immense value of relaxation, prayer, meditation and contemplation. A good

place to start your own investigation is the work of Dr. Nataraja (The Blissful Brain) and Joan Borysenko PhD (The Power of the Mind to Heal). There are also others who are putting these reflective practices through the rigours of scientific testing to see if they do indeed make the human experience more fruitful. The results prove time and time again that such activities unquestionably do enhance our mental and physical health.

In fact, just about everything in the 'mind-body-spirit' system is positively affected by introspective practices. There is 'proof' that the brain, central nervous system, immune system, digestion, blood, muscles and tissues, the organs of detoxification, mood, perception, performance, relationships, self-image - the list goes on - are all enhanced in their functioning and expression. If you still need persuading, please take a particular look at the relatively new disciplines I've previously mentioned: neurotheology, noetic sciences, cognitive neuroscience and psychoneuroimmunology (PNI) and you'll see that relaxation, meditation, prayer, contemplation etc. all do quiet/enhance the mind and balance and harmonise the body.

The introspective realm is also where the seeds of logic and the senses can truly be harvested, taking you to the next level of awareness. So for those of you who want to understand all that metaphysics has to really offer I would highly recommend you take a voyage of self-discovery. There you will find the riches of inner space but remember, you will need practice, patience and perseverance. Don't be afraid of the unknown because it is within the unknown that all will be revealed.

Remember that valuable mantra I shared with you earlier in the book - knowledge takes you to the door of understanding, courage and application take you through, and experience and wisdom are waiting for you on the other side, to share their secrets.

Are we immune to our actions?

For hundreds of years Newtonian science has been used to explain the physical world, where man was thought to be 'in control', manipulating and changing the environment, yet somehow remaining unaffected by his actions. The recent developments, some of which I've outlined, in quantum physics, mathematics, biophysics and other cutting edge sciences are helping us to appreciate that something more intangible is at work.

Metaphysics has spent much time over centuries exploring the significance and impact of human intention and thought. The modern foundation laid by Einstein and Planck, in the 1930s and 40s, has helped us to understand that energy can indeed be manipulated by human intention and expectation; this work has since been explored and developed further by others including more latterly Lynne McTaggart, Rupert Sheldrake, Cassandra Vieten, Dean Radin and Gregg Braden, to name a few. The research to date shows us how consciousness and the energy inherent within it, has the capacity to affect all other energy systems as it dissipates into the world. Take the weather for instance, we are happy when it is sunny, down when it is dull; it is very easy to understand that the physical world affects us. What might surprise you, however, is that the opposite is also true. Our state of mind really does affect the patterns and behaviour of the physical world.

The spiritual science of metaphysics helps us to understand that for every law we have deciphered in the physical universe there exists a spiritual equivalent. The failure to acknowledge and understand these spiritual laws or to apply them to our lives is one of the reasons we have lost so much self-mastery. Until we understand that metaphysics is about the intimate relationship between thoughts, feelings and actions and how they impact on the natural world, we will continue to look outside the self for solutions to our problems and continue to blame others rather than to take responsibility for our own empowerment.

A useful example that can help illustrate how physical principles translate into metaphysical ones, which we can apply to our lives, is the passage of the seasons. We can see that nature delivers its changes within a certain time frame, which we call a season. Each season takes approximately three months to produce its effect, its change. Spring becomes summer, summer becomes autumn, autumn becomes winter and after twelve months, the cycle repeats. What we can learn from this is that the process of change is not something that yields its dividends overnight. The changes taking place as one season becomes another are largely unseen and subtle, but eventually the end product is very clear and tangible. I've discovered through my work, research and personal experience that just like the seasons, a period of consistent endeavour guarantees a marked change for the individual about every three months, with less obvious and gradual change happening all the time. This is why patience, perseverance and practice are needed to achieve our goals. So it's important to make consistent endeavour and learn to sit patiently, allowing the fruits of our actions to come in their own time.

Metaphysics is a living, breathing system - it is not a concept designed for endless analytical and theoretical discussions. It needs to be understood and then applied in our lives. How often have you cried out 'why me?' Doesn't it sometimes seem that despite your best endeavours, the force of events carries you to an unwanted destination? Why is this?

The answer is simple. We have not stopped to consider the connection between the physical laws and how they may apply to our thoughts, emotions and relationships. We have only applied them to our material existence. Those laws and principles are valuable templates for how we should live. So unless we pay proper attention to the conversion of the physical principles into metaphysical ones, we will continue to find ourselves slaves to a whole range of thought processes, feelings and addictive behaviours that deny us true peace of mind.

Nature – the mirror

As you can see, the subject of metaphysics is a vast one; however, its essence is simple. One of the ways to understand its simplicity is to spend more time observing the world around us – nature provides most of the clues and answers we seek. Then the so-called mysteries of life will begin to unveil themselves. The biggest mystery of all is how we have lost the humility to listen and be quiet, and in the stillness to become the observers of life. It is within this understated, reflective practice that the subject of metaphysics can really be understood and inspire us to act. This is why I said earlier that introspection is the key to experience and through 'being' in that way, we come to 'know'.

Hopefully by now you have come to understand that metaphysics is arguably best described as a spiritual science, which helps us to better decode human experience. All life forms are energy and all energy is subject to very clear, concise mathematical laws and principles. We have managed to decipher many of these principles and processes over the last four hundred years and as a result of our understanding and application of these laws we have been able to construct this incredible technological world we see before us - but many of the world's contradictions exist because we have in the process failed to appreciate how the physical laws have metaphysical manifestations and a whole set of consequences that go with them.

These metaphysical laws impact equally upon us, nature and animals and the reason for our predicament is our failure to understand that life is not a one-way street, where we can 'drive' things mindlessly in the direction of our choice without anything coming back the other way. I have been explaining throughout how everything is connected, so we cannot manipulate and control things without consequences for ourselves. It is time to review our often arrogant, narrow-minded view, which has served to embroil us in a world of dysfunction, hostility and limited thinking. The way to start doing this is simple. Sit and observe the course of nature. Nature is such an incredible mirror for us. It teaches us so much about ourselves - if we would only become students of our environment rather than its manipulators and polluters.

As you watch the course of nature, ask yourself, are you moving with it or against it? When we work in opposition to our natural environment, we also work in opposition to ourselves. Our interference with the planet compromises the natural order and natural laws and this in turn has created an environment, which no longer truly supports and sustains us.

Metaphysics – the virtuous cycle

So I am sure you can now see that what we think, say, do and how we are in the world will eventually find its way back to us. Below are nine points, which will hopefully inspire you to live with greater awareness, conscience and integrity, creating a life founded on compassion, which encourages service and kindness. To serve others is also to serve oneself.

I created a meditation based on the principle, of giving without expectation, called Asking for Nothing and Receiving Everything, some twenty years ago. This meditation has made quite an impact and in both its audio and video forms has been enthusiastically embraced across the world. I think it has touched so many hearts because it offers a message that altruism is actually a force for good, both for the self and others - 'everybody wins in a charitable world'.

1. It is our intention that determines the true value of our actions. In fact our intentions are the primary forces that shape the various experiences and outcomes, which manifest in our lives. In other words, the outward appearance of our actions means very little, it is what's 'beating at the heart' of our actions that really counts. So pay attention to your intention.

2. Our every thought, word and action emits a vibration; the latest sciences clearly show that we are influencing and shaping our environments mostly

'below the surface'. It is at the atomic and sub-atomic levels that we arguably have greatest impact. But the consequences of our actions are unquestionably felt at the macro level. The work of Dr. Masaru Emoto has repeatedly demonstrated our vibrational impact on water. His work has shown that water registers our emotions and thoughts - this 'recording' of our vibration on water, tells the much bigger story of how we impact on everything in our world, leaving a 'vibrational signature' wherever we go.

We are not immune to our mindlessness; on the contrary, our carelessness holds us back. It's time that we took responsibility for our thoughts, words and actions and understood the far-reaching nature of our energy. It's time to tread more carefully across the planet to ensure we 'add value' in whatever we do. Make a pledge not to be a negative contributor to our world. As you can see from what's going on in the world today, we are already suffering the consequences of negative equity.

3. A life of gratitude and true appreciation will always bear good fruit; we simply need to learn the art of waiting. Make patience and acceptance your companions and watch life surprise you every day. Can a seed bear flowers and fruits the day after it is planted? Can an acorn become an oak tree overnight? If we practise giving thanks for our lives, especially for those things we take for granted, then the magic and the beauty of life will serve us abundantly. To set a date of expectation whilst sitting and impatiently awaiting the outcome takes us down the wrong path, it helps to maintain our frustration and keeps us away from the very thing we seek.

Practise sitting quietly, joyously and patiently - let go of expectation and simply 'know' in your heart that the sweet fruits from the seeds of 'right action' are already on their way. No force is necessary.

4. 'The greatest fool is the one who doesn't learn from her mistakes'. Your history tells the story of the mistakes you've made and those same mistakes await you in the future if you have not learnt from them. If we look into the pool of time, the gentle ripples of what has gone before whisper the way forward. It's important to understand that life doesn't allow us to graduate to the next level of experience and learning until the gifts of the 'here and now' have been claimed and understood.

Only then are we equipped for what awaits us in the future. So when you're stuck in your life, ask yourself 'what has this situation come to teach me?' Whatever stands in front of you is always your teacher – the real question is 'are you really listening?'

5. It is imperative if you are to move forward in your life that all the things currently blocking your path are removed. Health is a life that flows freely. So many of us struggle to create newness because we are still standing in the stagnation of the past. We cannot move into a brighter, better future whilst we are standing in the mud of what has been. A brighter future needs the space and opportunity to germinate our best intentions.

So begin by de-cluttering your life. Understand that whatever you no longer need is occupying valuable space and is also blocking your path and therefore the flow of good energy. Find the courage to let go of the futile collection of 'stuff' you have gathered around you, otherwise you will only strengthen the dam that's holding you back.

6. All energy has purpose, value and meaning and as we are energy we too have purpose, value and meaning. If we lose our focus, our reason for being, we die. We become part of the community best described as the 'vertical dead', those who walk around as if they are alive when in fact they are absent from their lives, lifeless.

Meaning and purpose provide the spark which ignites the mind and energises the spirit. This union offers life-long learning, true appreciation of oneself and the opportunity to grow. So steer a course that is dear to your heart. Learn to love what you do and it will love and nourish you in return. It's not your title or position that matters, it's the 'way' that you do what's asked of you that unveils your true title and position.

7. You cannot attract happiness and well-being into your life if you don't believe you're deserving of it. Co-creation is, understanding that you have a part to play in the unfolding of your destiny. Life is not just happening to you, your contribution is its primary ingredient. So it's time to make a contribution that makes your heart sing.

Remove any incongruence wherever you can. The universe, as discussed, is a dance of vibrations - what we 'give out' will come back to us as a vibrational match. Everything is resonating and wherever there is harmony between the countless frequencies, there we will find attraction. In other words, you cannot create happiness whilst standing in a place of sorrow; you cannot create success whilst you're drowning in doubt and self-pity. You cannot attain the opposite to what you're thinking, feeling and doing.

Remember cause and effect is the primary principle of the universe. So be clear about what you want and construct a healthy obsession around it and that intensity of focus will attract it to your door.

8. 'Every moment is an opportunity to make yourself anew'. This is an eternal truth. Stop living a recycled past. Grab the now and make the lessons of yesterday your guide, not your dictator. You are not yesterday, you're what you make of yesterday. True health depends on movement. All energy works optimally where there is movement/circulation. So allow your experiences to be the fuel for your choices but walk with courage and faith so you can make the right choices for yourself.

    Learn to live with forgiveness for yourself and others. Count your blessings and find appreciation in all things. Living this way keeps you on the 'principled' edge of consciousness, allowing you to keep growing into your true purpose and potential. Underline this truth, 'if it's not moving it's dying'. This is why you must not allow yourself to get stuck in anger, fear, doubt, hate, low self-esteem etc., otherwise you cannot grow to be your very best. Invent yourself anew today.

9. Never exceed your capacity. Respect your limits. This means eat well, sleep well and think well. Find time for fun, laughter and an appreciation of the simple things. Respect yourself and your needs - then your energies will be replenished, enabling you to sustain your efforts and fulfil your ambitions.

    Remember you can't give what you haven't got, so avoid overtrading. When you give what you haven't got, something somewhere in the mind-body system suffers. Many diseases are a consequence of the stress caused by overtrading.

There are many more of these principles and laws which life repeatedly paints on the canvas of our minds. Practise being still and you'll begin to see life's many portraits and in return the meaning of every scene and the way forward will become clear with much less effort. Be a student of life.

Even if you're willing to embrace these valuable guidelines, there is something else that you will almost certainly need to make it to your desired destination… faith.

"Faith is taking the first step even when you don't see the whole staircase."
Martin Luther King, Jr. (1929 – 1968)

What is faith?

There is nothing a free and liberated mind cannot achieve - the whole thrust of this book is about how such an endeavour can be fulfilled. I've enlightened you about The Story of Health, N.O.S.E., The Three Aspects of Consciousness and Persuading the Body, Mind and Spirit, as well as underlining the crucial role of the Environment. I know from experience that if you apply the knowledge and learning offered in these areas then your victory is certain; it's merely a matter of when. That said, a certain amount of faith is also needed because faith, given time, will bend matter, circumstance and outcome to its will.

However, it's important to note that where there is faith there is nearly always doubt. Faith is not an absence of doubt. It is a determination, a quiet resolve that you will triumph in the face of your doubt. Many fail in this area of faith quite simply because they don't understand what faith actually is. They believe it's a cast-iron certainty about their position and in a few cases it is. But in most instances it's an uncertainty that is moving forward in spite of wondering whether it can indeed make it to the destination. It's like courage, which is not the same as being fearless. Courage is acting in spite of your fear. To be fearless is to have reached the final destination of courage. She who is courageous often enough will become fearless.

So he who practises having faith will eventually become unshakeable and develop a cast-iron belief; this is the final destination of faith. Once this definition is understood you can set yourself on a genuine path of faith and not chastise yourself for those times when your doubt tries to seize the initiative. So how does one walk the tightrope between doubt and faith?

Focusing with faith

Doubt is a very destructive force. Before you know it, it has dug the hole for your grave, lowered you into it, having secured the coffin lid, with the eulogy already prepared. Such is its ability to slay you. And once you are caught in the web of doubt you can easily remain its victim indefinitely.

In fact, until you realize that doubt is like a parasite with no real power of its own, only that which it draws from the host (you), you are likely to keep giving your power away.

Faith is the antidote to doubt. It is also a catalyst for change. Faith feeds your self-respect, self-esteem, self-confidence, and self-love. Without faith the very best resources, creative energies and talents we have are unable to fully express themselves. Faith galvanises our 'life force', our potential, opportunities and dreams, making what seems impossible, possible. This is why it is very difficult to be the best we can be without faith - doubt saps our strength, faith restores it.

To have faith means to keep believing in the possibility of a better tomorrow. To have faith also means to focus with belief - focusing on that which the heart most aches for. Faith is not an arrogant or conceited virtue, making countless demands and having unrealistic expectations. Faith is the realization that if I focus on my heartfelt desires and dreams with a sincere heart, with the purest motivations, then what I thought was out of my reach falls within my grasp. Do not underestimate the power of faith.

Faith is the basis of miracles, so utilise its power. Then what you thought may not be possible will emerge before you with such clarity and detail, you'll be mesmerised by its beauty. For those of you who may doubt the power of faith, experiment in the following way and watch what happens over a period of three months.

Find some time, preferably daily but at least four times a week (ten to fifteen minutes will be sufficient but by all means spend more time if you wish), when you can be on your own, without distractions, and select something that really reflects your heartfelt desires, some hope you have for the future. Maybe some desire for your career or your work or it could be how you would like to see a particular relationship progress. Whatever you choose let it be from your heart and let it be with the highest possible motives. To focus on things with purely selfish motivation is a waste of the force of faith.

Once you've chosen what it is you wish to focus upon, see that scenario on the screen of the mind unfolding in an idyllic way. Try making your visualization as clear and detailed as possible, 'feel' your way through the scene(s) as they emerge. The more you make 'conscious contact' with your hopes and aspirations in this way, the more they will materialise.

Whatever the heart and mind focuses on with sincerity, the universe conspires to create. This is why it is very important to focus, with the highest ideals, wanting the best outcomes for yourself and others because the power of your thoughts to conjure and create what's in your heart and mind is simply breathtaking. Remember our lives are self-fulfilling prophecies. Please practise with all your heart and watch what happens.

You will find that first of all, the more you see your heartfelt desire over and over again on the screen of your mind, the better you will feel inside about yourself, and secondly your life will start to mirror what's in your heart and mind - especially where your motivations are as noble and as sincere as they can be. So take up this challenge for the next three months and watch how faith creates wonders and the seemingly impossible becomes possible. This is metaphysics in action and is the basis of miracles.

Miracles are made

Most of us, if we search our hearts, would find that we are waiting for some miracle to happen, something that will come and make all that is wrong with our lives change and go away. We all, at some point in our lives, have pain, discomfort, fear, anger or some negative energy that disables us and at that point in time we most want a miracle to appear on the horizon.

'Miracles are made' is about understanding how we can make miracles happen, by harnessing the power of faith. As a result we come to understand that miracles are not the property of a fortunate few. In fact we all have the power to make miracles. First of all however, we have to stop waiting for one and understand it is in our hands to create them.

Making miracles relates intimately to the laws of metaphysics. It's applying practically the understanding that we do indeed live in a world of cause and consequence and that what we see unfolding around us is more than a game of chance and though we may not be able to trace every consequence back to its cause this is only because of the multiplicity and vastness of the web of action and reaction.

Think of how many actions you perform in the course of any one day and then multiply that by the actions of others and multiply that by all the different communities, societies, countries and continents. What you have is an almost unimaginable number of actions and consequences. It is because we don't understand this equation and the vastness of its expression, that most of what we see unfolding in front of us appears to be a mystery when in fact there is no mystery at all. What unfolds in front of us, moment by moment, is the 'cause and consequence' dynamic; but to truly comprehend it takes an open, reflective mind and the practice of loving detachment. Once we can understand that to every action there is indeed a reaction we have the basis for making miracles at our fingertips.

So in order to make miracles in your own life, you need to start by trying to live in the most noble ways that you can - this isn't about sainthood or perfection, it's about honouring your own truth, living your life in the kindest way, a way that is caring and compassionate and considers others. It's difficult to create wonders in your life when your life is riddled with contradictions, a lack of kindness, intolerance and hypocrisies. Living your life more thoughtfully - doing only unto others that which you would be happy to have done unto you, lays the foundation for making miracles.

You then find focusing on what you want in your life not only becomes increasingly easy and natural, but through the laws of cause and effect it is bound to come to fruition. Miracles are made is about understanding that if we work with the laws of cause and effect and understand that every action does indeed have consequences, then those laws are bound to deliver the treasure trove of our desires and ambitions because our positive focus ensures that.

However, it's important to remember that the law works both ways. When I think lowly of myself and sit in the cesspit of negative beliefs, recycling shame and guilt, shackled by fear and doubt, I can only create a future that looks like that. Equally when I treat people badly, withholding the love and respect that I myself ache for and they too deserve, then sooner or later the way that I have behaved will find me in some form or another.

It's time to embrace the metaphysical principles of life in a positive way and then life will positively embrace you. Understand miracles are made through the choices that you make, through the decisions you take. So start from now to live your life in the noblest way you can.

Honour your heart and do not hurt the hearts of others. Pursue your dreams but not at the expense of anyone else. Gather knowledge and through application make it wisdom. Focus with faith on where it is you most want to be, and miracles will indeed be made.

Remember, before you can experience the magic of creating miracles, you must know what you want and where you are heading. The biggest reason people fail to achieve peace of mind and happiness is they haven't answered these questions. They set out on a path and pursue goals that fit the social and cultural norms without ever asking the question 'is this the song that my heart is singing?' This is why I introduced you to the idea of the personal prayer, because it gives you a clear focus.

So by being still and practising listening you will hear the songs of your heart. Then you can spend time every day 'reeling in' your dreams. The more you apply a 'trance-like' focus to those dreams the more they will become yours. Sit regularly and watch your ideal reality on the cinema screen of your mind and patiently wait for the countless surprises.

What is really exciting is that there is now some movement to bridge the gap between modern day science and what many would call spirituality (which is the primary domain of metaphysics). This co-operation and sharing of data is a small step in the direction of synergy and is very welcome and certainly needed.

Bridging the gap between science and spirituality

Such are the advances in technology that we can now record the activity of a single brain cell. We can produce images reflecting the activity of different regions in the brain. We are also able to pinpoint the role of different individual chemicals in the brain and have identified their impact on human behaviour.

It was Hippocrates in the 5th century BC who first recognized the importance of the human brain in defining behaviour. However, it was Galen in the 2nd century BC who found the evidence to support Hippocrates's view. He worked with head injuries and performed countless surgeries and dissections, which led him to suggest that the brain was the seat of human intelligence. His work would later inspire the 17th century English physician Thomas Willis, considered by some to be the founding father of modern brain science. At the time, his work, The Anatomy of the Brain (1664), provided the western world with the most detailed insight into the anatomy, physiology and pathology of the brain. Since that time the uniqueness and the power of the brain has been unravelled even further.

The average brain houses more than a hundred billion brain cells - the neurons. It weighs on average about 6kg and is a reddish grey mass with the consistency of firm jelly. Each neuron has a cell body, which houses its processor, the nucleus. Branching from the cell body are numerous finger-like dendrites forming tree-like structures, creating the 'forest' we call the brain. As the dendrites extending from the cell body intertwine with other cells' dendrites, an infinite maze of connections is formed. Each neuron can make up to a thousand different connections with its neighbours and with cells in other regions of the brain. This interconnectedness allows electrical signals, which are essentially information, to travel within milliseconds from one area of the brain to another – see the work of Santiago Ramon y Cajal who won the Nobel Prize for physiology and medicine in1904. He presented the first microscope-assisted drawings of brain tissue, which appeared as a tangled mass of neurons. On closer inspection however, he found a highly ordered organism with different cell types arranged in different layers and the cells in each layer sharing a number of roles and functions. To give some idea of the staggering nature of the brain's abilities, it's been recently calculated that if every person currently in the world had internet access, the resulting network would still only be approximately one fifteenth of the size of the average human brain!

The workings of the brain are too vast and in some regards too complex to address in this summary but I believe understanding some of the primary brain functions gives an invaluable insight into our ability to change. For those wanting to delve deeper, I've already mentioned Dr. Shanida Nataraja and her excellent book The Blissful Brain (2008), which is a great introduction to neurotheology.

The thalamus is the gateway for all sensory input travelling into the cerebral cortex (the largest part of the brain – associated with higher brain function). It relays information to thousands of neurons synchronously. As well as being connected to the prefrontal cortex, the thalamus also relays information to the motor co-ordination centres in the cerebellum at the back of the brain via the neural circuits. Here the brain is involved in generating movements as well as fine-tuning them. So the thalamus is a key player in brain activity.

Another key player is the hypothalamus. The hypothalamus is responsible for the day-to-day running of the brain. The brain is very sensitive to even subtle changes in temperature, oxygen supply and the chemical content of the fluid bathing the neurons. All these factors need to remain relatively constant for the brain to perform optimally. The hypothalamus uses its extensive connections with both the endocrine system (hormone system) and the autonomic nervous system (ANS) to maintain the body's internal environment.

The ANS comprises two systems, the sympathetic (fight or flight response) and the parasympathetic (rest and digest) response. The hypothalamus is busy releasing hormones into the blood stream as well as releasing hormones that stimulate other glands. These hormones instruct the endocrine system which regulates all our physiological functions such as muscle, tissue and bone growth as well as digestion, the metabolism of food, appetite and even our sleep patterns. Its role is truly impressive.

The hypothalamus is also referred to as the 'mood centre'; this description starts to provide some clues into the impact of temperament on all these functions, because our moods determine how many of these processes are carried out efficiently, further illuminating the mind-body connection.

The emotional dynamic of the hypothalamus puts it alongside the hippocampus and the amygdala to form a powerful triad known as the limbic system, often described as the seat of emotions. The hippocampus is crucial to the formation of memory. It is where our most emotionally charged memories are stored. It receives inputs from all our senses and then assigns emotional value to these inputs. This is why a memory of a traumatic experience from five, ten, fifteen or even thirty years ago can evoke the same feelings in the present as it did at the point of trauma. Conversely, it is damage to the cells of the hippocampus that can cause persistent and progressive memory loss as exhibited in Alzheimer's.

The amygdala has extensive connections with the hippocampus, the thalamus and the prefrontal cortex (areas of short term memory and higher cognitive functions i.e. problem solving, attention, planning, empathy etc.). When stimulated the amygdala produces fearful, aggressive and violent behaviour; so if cells in this area become damaged or destroyed animals become tame and indifferent to danger or affection, and humans become incapable of any type of emotional expression.

The exciting leaps in neuroscience are really helping us to understand the interconnectedness of the brain cells and its layered forests of dendrites and how the various sections and layers relate to each other. It is the connections between neurons and how they can be switched on or off in line with the input received that illuminates our ability to learn, grow and change in terms of our understanding and awareness.

The flexible, malleable quality of the neurons' connections is referred to as neuronal plasticity. Every new experience, every incoming stimulus, brings about a change in our brain's configuration. Just as the strength of our muscles depends upon how much we use them, the strength of the connections in the brain depends on how often they are used. This is how our habits, patterns and tendencies are formed. This relates intimately to what we discussed in the previous chapter about The Journey of Becoming.

As early as 1890 the work of the renowned psychologist William James highlighted the importance of neuronal plasticity in human behaviour. It is his contribution that helped us to understand that the events and the experiences of childhood, if unchecked, will continue to drive human behaviour in adulthood. He described humans as 'mere bundles of habits'.

This is why so much of what we do is done without conscious thinking. Once the behavioural template is laid down and reinforced, those muscles (neuronal networks) are able to take over a specific range of tasks on the basis of what has gone before. When what we've enshrined adds value to our existence this is an invaluable asset. However, when the neuronal network is driving us down paths of negative, compulsive behaviour, the ordeal of such experiences can, at times, make the human experience feel unbearable.

Neuronal plasticity proves to us that a leopard can change its spots and that an old dog can learn new tricks. So, there's hope for us all! However we need to understand that new behaviour arises from the conscious process of learning. The repeated exposure to new experiences that emerges out of that learning moulds new neural circuits. Couple this with the avoidance of old experiences/stimuli and the old neural circuits are erased. In other words every positive action creates a new neural circuit and every time we avoid an old unwanted habit that old negative neural circuit is weakened. The combination of the two means positive change is always available to us, at any given moment.

Having offered some insight into the brain's workings and the intimacy that exists between its different parts, it is worth illustrating the divide of the left and the right hemispheres, which I spoke about in Chapter 5. You may remember that if it were not for the corpus callosum (which connects the two hemispheres via approximately two hundred and fifty million axonal fibres) they would be busy carrying out their different tasks independently, which would lead to a life of chaos rather than of unison. The truth is most of us are experiencing the former anyway because we've become 'trapped' more in one hemisphere than the other. The left hemisphere is bound up with the past and the future and is also primarily driven by logic (matters of the head). The right brain is preoccupied with the now, abstract thinking and emotions (matters of the heart). You might also want to explore the work of neuroanatomist Dr. Jill Bolte Taylor, who has done some excellent work in this area.

Although there still exists in some quarters a fairly pointless debate about which hemisphere is more dominant/important, the further you stand back and look, the more you can see that one hemisphere becomes limited and diminished without the other. For example, if one is only living in the past and anticipating the future the present moment, the 'now', is lost. Equally, if the 'now' ignores the value of past experiences and learning, then a life of repeated mistakes and negative reinforcement can rob the individual of the opportunity of re-birth, which each moment offers. I discussed this at some length when we looked at the Memoried Self, The Experiencing Self and the Anticipating Self.

It is when we live in the now, whilst being able to embrace the past and look to the future, that we afford ourselves optimal knowledge and the opportunity for a fulfilling life. This is also true in the matter of head versus heart. How can one be said to be more important than the other? Surely there is a time for both. I described it before as a dance. There is a time when the head needs to lead and a time for the heart; and wisdom is knowing the right time for each. Co-operation between the two hemispheres is vital otherwise we're left with a partial and limited description of the world. When the two hemispheres work as a team by sharing the information they've collected, that sharing leads to a more complete worldview.

As mentioned earlier, advances in technology have allowed us to peep into the brain. MRI scans (magnetic resonance imaging) have enabled us to measure the activity across groups of neurons, which is how we've been able to identify which areas of the brain are involved in specific tasks. This has also enabled us to understand the impact of lifestyle factors and disease on brain function. As we've combined this new knowledge with the detailed studies of individual neurons, their connections and their chemical signals, we are able to get a more complete picture of how the brain works and responds. Arguably for the first time we have a three dimensional view of human existence.

Although much more can be said on these matters (see the work of Susan Greenfield in her book The Private Life of the Brain; also I refer you again to Dr. Dawson Church, The Genie in Your Genes and the work of Dr. Bruce Lipton in The Biology of Belief) I believe there is enough data here to help you to understand that life is not simply 'happening' to you unless you abdicate responsibility for yourself.

Consciousness is not a 'victim' to matter unless the subtleties of consciousness are not understood and positively employed. This is why silence is so important. Activities such as meditation, prayer and positive intent allow for consciousness, via the brain, to dance a majestic dance with matter.

Understanding brain function and how that relates to the human experience enables us in every moment to write a new script. We can simply read the old text of yesterday and continue to remain under its spell or we can realize that consciousness has the opportunity through the incredible instrument of the brain to write a new more exciting play, one that matches our hopes, expectations and capabilities.

If we are to believe the many calculations made around consciousness, then most of us are barely awake. We live in a slumber of ignorance and peer at the world through eyes that are only partially opened. It's time to open our eyes and move into a state of focused awareness. It is a lack of positive intention and focus that denies us the miracles of each new moment. Professor William Miller Ph. D. and clinical psychologist Janet C' de Baca, Ph.D., in their book Quantum Change, explore personal changes and miraculous healings brought about by this kind of focused awareness.

Neuronal Plasticity has been described by neuroscientist Richard Davidson Ph. D. as 'enabling us to understand that things like happiness and compassion are no different from learning to play a musical instrument or tennis. It is possible to train our brains to be happy and fulfilled'. So Buddha was right when he said over two thousand years ago, 'thoughts are things' and what we invest them with determines whether they become 'creators of good or ill'.

So use these most precious of things, thoughts, wisely. Otherwise not only will they harm you (through their biochemical consequences) but they will harm others through your moods, attitudes and actions. What is the point of science if not to help us to better understand ourselves, and our world and lead to a life of positive change?

Make time to be still every day. Be altruistic where you can, give thanks for your blessings and treat all life with the respect you desire, for these are the actions that will best serve you, humankind and our planet. I've repeated this message numerous times on our journey, because it literally holds the key to everything you are looking for.

Metaphysics introduces us to what's really going on in the universe. It helps us to see our role and responsibilities more clearly. It shows we are not victims unless we opt out of our power to choose. Victory is ours for the taking and hopefully you've learnt that victory is not about winning, it's about doing the right thing. Only then does the universe conspire with us to create the very best outcomes. It's time to pursue the highest path… the path of right action.

I hope you can now hear the 'real' conversation, the one that's taking place at the most subtle level. Remember, the best way to 'see' is actually with your ears.

> *"The predominant thought or the mental attitude is the magnet, and the law is that like attracts like, consequently, the mental attitude will invariably attract such conditions as correspond to its nature."*
> Charles Haanel (1866-1949)

CHAPTER 12: EVERYTHING IS CONNECTED

"The truth is nearly always standing in plain sight."
Anon

The many gifts and benefits of this book

What I hope you'll take with you once you've completed this fascinating voyage is that there is indeed a panacea, a cure for all ills, and furthermore it's been staring us in the face for centuries. History has taught us, sadly, we are not very good at listening or learning from our experiences, which is why we keep going around the same loops time and time again. It has been said by numerous historical commentators that conflict and competition have provided us with many of our advantages and insights but I believe they've also in some instances, robbed us of our morals, values and our very humanity.

I have tried to demonstrate earlier in this book and also in its predecessor, Antiquity Comes Full Circle, that our egos have clouded our judgement to such an extent that we have often chosen sound over silence, immediacy over patience and even worse, war over peace. Unfortunately, co-operation and collaboration have been undervalued, treated with suspicion and therefore not pursued. Our 'collective blind spot' has been so huge it has eclipsed our conscience and common sense, yet how can co-operation and collaboration be surpassed when they can bring the best of what we know together in a non-competitive way?

Surely it's in that convergence of ideology (synergy), the pursuit of virtue and ethical and moral practice, that the answers to all our problems lie - both those of the individual and those of society?

I hope that when you put this book down you will feel enriched by its gifts. Here is a brief summary of some of the things I hope will always travel with you.

- Don't be afraid of your past - face those things you repeatedly avoid in a safe, sensitive and supportive environment and your heart and mind will be set free. Remember, what you don't resolve will continue to define you anyway. Such is the power of subconscious patterns and drives.

- Remember the mantra, 'Old friend… dear friend, what have you come to teach me?' Whatever stands before you is your teacher. So sit, listen and learn from the endless river of your experience.

- Health is like a four-legged table - mind-body-spirit-environment - and all four aspects need to be respected and treated equally. Otherwise the pursuit of well-being will always remain beyond your grasp.

- Develop an attitude of gratitude. The complaining habit cripples mind, body and spirit. Whereas the one who counts his blessings will find peace, joy and health. The power of thank you will ensure all your needs are eventually met.

- Develop an inward-looking habit. Take many adventures into inner space. The art of introspection and positive thinking deliver unlimited promise. Remember there is a 'knowing' that lives beyond logic and the senses and that knowing can only be experienced through the regular practice of silence. So make meditation, prayer, mindfulness or some other contemplative, reflective practice part of your life.

- The liberated mind is neither trapped in Self or Other - it moves easily and flows between the two and as a result the mind can ascend to the Lovingly Detached posture, that place of kind judgements and unwavering compassion, which with practice we are all capable of achieving.

- Change comes most easily through compassion. So be kind to yourself at all times and healing and wholeness will readily follow.

- Serenity is not freedom from the storm, but the ability to find peace within it. With our friends the Three Ps (practice, patience and perseverance) we can learn to meet life's challenges with grace, hope and optimism. The next time you are presented with something that seems bigger than you can manage, draw on the things that you have learnt here and you will discover that you are more than you imagined.

- 'When the cell is well all is well'. Meet the needs of your body in the best ways you can through: water, good nutrition, supplementation, exercise, deep restorative sleep etc. and the body will propel the mind towards its destination.

- Speak lovingly to your body daily and it will continue to find magical ways to enhance and maintain your health. "Dearest body" is the most important mantra to achieve good physical health and the conditions for good mental health will be enhanced.

- Remember, you are not defined by your genes - they merely offer you a doorway into life's infinite possibilities. Epigenetics has helped us to understand we are more than our biology.

- The power to choose is your greatest resource. Life is a marriage between destiny and free will. Don't give away your shareholding. You are the major shareholder in your life. You can't control everything that turns up in your life but you can certainly choose how you respond.

- Forgiveness frees you from the past. You can't change the past but you can change how it affects you. Forgiveness is the quickest way to set your heart and mind free.

- Virtues always travel in pairs. The delivery of your message is as important as the message itself. When you say the right thing in the wrong way, it is no longer worthy of the label 'truth'. Even truth when delivered in anger can become a vice. Do your best not to hurt the hearts of others and your own heart will be spared.

- Your reality is primarily shaped by your thoughts. Quantum physics has enabled us to see the intimate relationship between thoughts and our environment. We can either play our part or be victims of circumstance. Life is a self-fulfilling prophecy.

- The secret to health is the removal of waste. Avoid negativity and waste in your life wherever you can. Waste literally weakens the mind, body and spirit. So cultivate the habit of kind thoughts, positive relationships, of eating vibrant, diverse food and performing good deeds where you can.

Avoid unkind thoughts and toxic relationships, situations and actions.

- The relationship between the mouth and the mind is arguably the most intimate in human experience. If the body does not receive the necessary hydration and nutrients it needs, it cannot perform optimally. This in turn pulls down the mind and with it the spirit. If the mind is not fed a diet of positive, uplifting thoughts, it is unable to ascend to those majestic heights it is capable of and as a consequence the body is negatively impacted upon, and again, the spirit is affected. Meet the needs of both mouth and mind and your spirit will soar.

- Routine is power and practice makes permanent. This is a wonderful pairing that will assist your progress in magical and wondrous ways. Make them your allies and your victory is assured.

- Develop the habit of focusing with faith. Do not be afraid of doubt, as it may appear from time to time, but in truth it only comes to remind you of what you still need to do. Allow your doubt to help you maintain your focus. It doesn't come to disempower you.

- Once you've established a clear vision, make a plan around a set of non-negotiables. Those who are unwavering in their resolve cannot fail. Non-negotiables will hold you firmly on course whatever comes your way.

- Practise listening-in and you will hear the whispers of your heart, but remember your emotions are not always right. So scrutinize their validity before heeding them, because the head has magical and wonderful insights too. Introspection is the best way to connect with yourself and decide what course you need to take.

- A useful metaphor for getting to where you want to go in the best way you can, is to think of yourself as a tortoise. The hare always crosses the line first and so may appear to have won, but the hare has missed the point of the journey. The tortoise on the other hand smells the flowers, chews the grass, notices the beauty of the day - and so has won the race because she understood that experiencing the journey was the point of the race, not reaching the destination. Those who do the right things and appreciate the journey, not worrying about the destination, always win the race. Remember, the only destination is right action.

- Repetition is the key. The lessons we learnt about the anatomy of the brain and on the Journey of Becoming tell us that every 'right' thought weakens the old negative patterns and habits, setting up new neural communities which will propel us to our preferred destination. So realize the power to change your life does not reside with anyone else. It resides firmly with you.

- Synergy is an egoless pursuit for the union of knowledge. It recognises truth and justice are best found by not being attached to a particular point of view. Our egos and opinions merely get in the way. Wisdom has no allegiance to anything but itself.

- Remember The Three Gatekeepers, (Truth, Kindness and Benevolence). Ensure that you make them your companions in all your dealings and you will always find the best way through life's dilemmas.

- Believing is seeing. You've learnt that your perceptions and beliefs determine your reality. At every step, subject to how we see life's unfolding, we can either become victims of circumstance or masters of choice. Remember you don't see the world as it is, you see it as you are. So decide to see the best in everything and the best options and opportunities will unveil themselves to you.

Please keep coming back to this list because each point is like a piece in a jigsaw and the more time you spend looking at the pieces, the clearer the whole picture becomes.

"He who lives in harmony with himself lives in harmony with the universe."
Marcus Aurelius (121 AD – 180 AD)

The story of health revisited

Hopefully I've managed to persuade you of the need for a mind-body-spirit-environment strategy if you are to achieve wholeness and well-being. I've come at this from many angles in an attempt to illustrate the merits of this argument. If you've not yet been persuaded I hope you will at least research and test out the many concepts and principles I've presented you with in the laboratory of your own life. I believe the 'evidence' is overwhelming but I equally believe that no one should accept anything presented to them unless they can also validate it through their own experience.

I believe the reason that so much therapy is ineffective, or is short-lived in terms of its results, is because of the repeated failure to see the interconnectedness of life. Based on my experience, this is true whether the therapy is directed at the mind or the body. Generally the holism spoken of in the therapeutic arena tends to confine itself to neighbouring disciplines within any given field. So those claiming to offer a whole-person approach and who are practising a physical discipline such as acupuncture, Reiki, massage, Bowen Technique etc. are referring generally to their cousins such as naturopathy, diet and nutrition, chiropractic intervention, Pilates etc. It is rare to find a crossing of the borders and integration of seemingly unrelated subjects. Yoga is one of the few that genuinely crosses the mind-body divide, but even this wonderful discipline does not go as far as I've asked you to travel into and even beyond the human psyche.

The Story of Health, as I believe I've demonstrated, offers a holistic framework, which does cross the mind-body divide. It embraces the value of history, psychology, philosophy, science, religion, the arts, sociology, spirituality, meditation and even the technologies that have shaped so much of modernity. It asks you to see and understand the relevance of each of these forces and how each one has had a powerful say in the relationship we have with ourselves, and each other. How can we expect to understand who we are if we ignore the very things that have shaped us? How can any model provide us with solutions if it does not take into account all these factors?

Synergy renounces the arrogance of championing a particular point of view because it sees the merits and the flaws in each. Scientists, religious advocates, historians, philosophers, spiritual masters and therapists of all persuasions, often evangelically push their own message ahead of all others. Synergy knows that these largely singular messages miss the pluralism of truth and generally offer us countless mirages to pursue.

The real oasis that will genuinely quench your thirst is synergy because it provides the history that explains how we got here; it provides the spirituality needed with all its values and ethics to shape and maintain your inner world, your conscience, integrity and well-being. It also provides the scientific foundation that helps us to better understand disease and with that the secrets of health - leading to a mind-body approach that really works. Synergy also provides the psychological-social-emotional model needed to enhance our relationships not only with ourselves but also with each other and the planet. It provides a framework in which music, art, literature, architecture, in fact all creative intelligence can be better understood and used in ways that consistently enrich our lives. This is why, if The Story of Health makes sense to you, you need look no further than to a synergistic way of living. There you will find balance, peace and happiness.

The promise of a better tomorrow

Although we are quite a way from a world that is living by the synergistic code, there is some promise that a better tomorrow awaits us. In the following pages I would like to give you a glimpse into the future with some fledgling examples of where some degree of synergy is already happening and working. There are many more than the ones I've chosen to cover but I believe these examples prove how valuable synergy is.

The Reach Approach is not seeking to champion itself - it's a signpost, encouraging those with an open and listening mind to look at ways of integrating and collaborating the knowledge that's available to us, past and present. Too much energy is being wasted in the futility of competition and conflict. There is hope, but to take the next step we really need to look at ourselves and decide what we can do to create a better world. Change begins with each one of us taking responsibility. It's time to stop looking for someone else to create the change we most seek.

Anthroposophical medicine

Established by Rudolph Steiner in the 1920s, anthroposophical medicine is based on Steiner's concept that spiritual awareness is the foundation of individual health and of the health of society. Steiner believed that many of the oldest systems of healing, such as traditional Chinese medicine, Ayurvedic medicine, and Tibetan medicine, were based on a spiritual perception of the world that modern science has lost. Steiner wanted medicine to get back in touch with spirituality, and at the same time keep and make wise use of the gains that science and technology had made. Thus, conventional medicine needed to be extended beyond physical science to include a holistic spiritual science.

Anthroposophical medicine pulls together the best of allopathy (modern medicine) and art therapy, music therapy, massage, naturopathic remedies (such as mistletoe which has been used in the treatment of cancer) etc. Built on the Steiner principles, it is rich with the belief that no one discipline can be solely responsible for the healing of the body or the mind. This is why it makes use of art, literature, and music alongside conventional medicine in an attempt to tap the creative intelligence and unfathomable depth of the spirit. It should be noted that anthroposophical doctors are conventionally qualified clinicians who then go on to develop a fuller picture of the human organism - as a thinking, feeling and aware being.

Steiner's 'whole person philosophy' moves away from conformity in all aspects of life. This renunciation of 'norms' is also reflected in the schools bearing his name where 'individuality', nurtured within a social framework, is considered the best way to build a cohesive community and a fully functioning society. This philosophy and approach has proven to be very effective across the world, with over nine hundred schools adopting this more creative and holistic approach to education.

As the 21st century neurosciences suggest, healing that does not incorporate the mind will be handicapped by the negative thought patterns generated by a mind that is inadvertently working against itself. This is because we now know that such thoughts create neuropeptides and hormones, which hamper the biological workings of the brain and the body. Hence music, art and poetry can all help uplift and soothe the mind, which in turn soothes and heals the body. This approach to education and medicine is a simple and wonderful example of the need for the marriage of ideas and disciplines.

Orthomolecular medicine

The term orthomolecular, was first used by Linus Pauling (double Nobel laureate), in a paper he wrote in the journal Science, in 1968. The key idea in orthomolecular medicine is that genetic factors affect not only specific physical characteristics of the individual, but also impact on the whole of their biochemical story, including the brain and its associated functions. The term orthomolecular literally means identifying the 'right' (ortho) molecule to address those biological imbalances and by making the right biochemical corrections, the body is assisted in facilitating its own healing. This discipline has, over the last forty plus years, built a reputation for dealing with both mental and physical illnesses, such as: atherosclerosis, cancer, schizophrenia, various mood disorders, autoimmune diseases and clinical depression.

Orthomolecular medicine originally evolved in the context of treating and preventing psychiatric diseases, which is why some still refer to it as orthomolecular psychiatry. As stated, the primary goal of orthomolecular therapy is to provide the 'optimal' molecular environment for the brain and other tissues. To this end, diet, nutrition and the focused and sometimes intense use of supplementation are the essential tools employed to restore biological balance and health. So, by carefully altering the intake of nutrients such as vitamins (and their metabolites), minerals, trace elements, EFAs, macronutrients, as well as other naturally occurring metabolically active substances, a patient can sometimes enjoy a level of recovery where other medical interventions had failed.

This wonderful form of medicine is grounded in common sense and is founded on the obvious. If we are made up of food, water, air and light then any deficiency in one of these areas is bound to be reflected somewhere in the mind-body system.

The work of Hoffer and Pfeiffer (which began in the late1950s and focused on schizophrenia) laid the foundation for the journey this science would take. Already acknowledged at this point were the obvious biological disadvantages that poor nutrition would inflict on the body – for example a lack of vitamin C: scurvy and soft tissue damage; a lack of vitamin D: rickets and bone recession etc. But this was a science that took nutrition from its fairly exclusive focus on the body and shed light on its relevance and importance to the mind.

It became overwhelmingly clear that particular deficiencies not only affected normal biological functioning they also affected mental health. For example, Abraham Hoffer found that a deficiency in niacin (vitamin B3) was critical in cases of schizophrenia. This significant vitamin from the vitamin B family was actually found to markedly affect the mental health of those who were deficient in it. Two other nutrients, vitamin B6 and zinc, were also found to be central characters in this story. In fact, the more you explore this subject the more you can see how pivotal vitamins and mineral deficiencies are to our mental health.

Orthomolecular medicine is still, in current scientific terms, quite young, but the great work of Linus Pauling, Carl Pfeiffer and Abraham Hoffer continues to be developed worldwide with countless research projects and papers relating diet and nutrition very specifically to conditions such as: anxiety, hormonal mood swings, addictions, attention deficit disorders, eating disorders, Parkinson's

Disease, autism, memory issues and much more. To find out more, see the excellent work of: the International Society for Orthomolecular Medicine, The Food for the Brain Foundation, The Brain Bio Centre and The Mental Health Foundation, where some pioneering work continues to cross the mind-body divide. This research is beginning to show we cannot always fix psychological problems solely by talking, as some emotional problems are underpinned and even driven by our biology.

As we discussed earlier in the book, the role of water is a key player in mental health. We saw how a small decrease in the percentage of water within the body made a significant impact on cognitive functioning as well as on temperament and mood. This was originally mooted by Dr. Batmanghelidj and has subsequently gone on to be well researched by others (see the work of Armstrong, 2012 and Walsh, 2005). Now that the role of water is beginning to be better understood, it too is demonstrating that what have often been classified as mental health problems, are not always 'just in the mind'. Some exist in and are perpetuated by the body as well. So again, we see how physical substances are pertinent to good mental health and water is arguably the most important of all the molecules we put into the body.

Nutritional genomics – the future of medicine?

An interesting postscript to the innovative work happening in the field of orthomolecular medicine is what is taking place in the field of nutritional genomics. This even newer science, is actively studying the relationship between the human gene, nutrition and health. The increasing recognition that nutrients have the ability to interact, modify and influence molecular mechanisms, which in turn impact on an organism's physiological functions, has prompted this most recent development in the field of nutrition. This field of exploration into human health has two primary branches - nutrigenomics and nutrigenetics - both of which promise much.

Nutrigenomics: This branch of nutritional genomics is the study of the effects of foods and their constituents on gene expression. This fascinating discipline has focused its research on the molecular interaction between nutrients, food and the genome. Using systems biology, a map is developing around how the body responds and reacts at the genetic level to food and specific nutrients - and how by varying food and nutrient intake, those genes which when 'activated', make the individual more vulnerable to specific diseases, can in fact be 'switched off'. In other words our food and nutrient intake influences the biological expression of our cells. Our foods are said to have a 'dietary signature' and this dietary signature affects the metabolic pathways and also the body's state of balance – homoeostasis.

Added to this it has been identified that there are particular genetic markers, which respond quite specifically to the dietary signature of the food we are eating making us more vulnerable to latent genetic predispositions. One of the primary aims of this field, is to identify the markers, which make the individual more susceptible to specific diseases, such as: obesity, cancer, cardiovascular disease, Alzheimer's etc.

Running parallel to this field of research is neutrigenetics, which is looking at the 'single gene/single food compound' relationship. Basically, nutrigenetics is concerned with why one food, which may be beneficial for one person can cause harm to another.

One of the primary focuses of this discipline is to identify genetic susceptibility to diseases in order to offer what is in some quarters being called 'personalised disease prevention advice', which is offered based on the individual's genetic make up. Due to the great advances in genetic research, nutrigeneticists, via cheek swab or blood analysis, acquire the necessary DNA and through careful study and analysis of the genetic data, possible 'risk' genes are identified. Essentially, the researchers are looking for either positive or negative correlations between the risk genes and the various nutritional factors, in order that appropriate 'patient specific' treatment strategies can be devised.

There are a number of other sophisticated genetic methods and applications being employed such as, looking at how individuals absorb and process food stuffs, as well as looking at the consumption and transportation of nutrients to try and help us better understand the precise relationship between food, nutrition and genetic expression.

For those of you interested in exploring this subject further look at the work of Dr. Raymond L. Rodriguez and Dr. Somen Nandi from The Centre of Excellence for Nutritional Genomics and also see the work of The New Zealand Institute of Plant & Food Research.

Both these disciplines are helping us to better understand the 'personal' nature of health and disease, and should be considered as front-runners in the field of preventative medicine. They remind us that although there are undoubtedly things that are common to us all when it comes to health solutions, there is also a level of 'biochemical individuality' that needs to be understood and respected, if we are to find the best remedies and outcomes to match the genetic profile of the individual.

It should be stated for balance that nutrigenomics and nutrigenetics are still in their infancy but their contribution to human health is expected, over the next decade, to be substantial. What we do have though is enough data to illustrate that what we eat does in fact affect every system in the body, and food can be both medicine, or poison.

Nutrigenomics and nutrigenetics are arguably adding more texture and depth to the contribution orthomolecular medicine has made and are helping us to see how we can go even further in personalising dietary advice, through a better understanding of the genetic story of each individual.

I believe we are on the cusp of several revolutions, happening simultaneously across a number of disciplines. If we could just slow down, pay attention and observe, we would see that a host of things previously considered mysteries, are now in numerous ways revealing themselves. These revelations would serve us as individuals, and our planet wonderfully if we were only open to their message, that everything is indeed connected.

EFT (emotional freedom technique)

Emotional Freedom Technique is taking parts of the western world by storm, with more and more people celebrating its validity and life-changing power. Here we have another example of a methodology/intervention, which is built on a respect and appreciation of two seemingly opposing disciplines.

It pulls together the practice and the wisdom of ancient Chinese medicine, in the form of the knowledge of acupuncture meridians (dating from some fifteen hundred years ago) with modern day psychology and cognitive neuroscience. The basic premise of EFT and other disciplines like it such as TFT (Thought Field Therapy), is that if we use the body's wisdom and employ what psychology has taught us in the last one hundred and fifty years we can free the mind (and in some cases the body) from the ravages of trauma and disease.

I don't intend to expand on EFT, TFT, or their cousin EMDR (Eye Movement Desensitization and Reprocessing) as there is a plethora of information out there for those interested (see the work of Dr. Patricia Crane, Gary Craig,

Robert Smith and Nick Ortner), I simply want to bring to your attention that when we combine the best of what we have, we nearly always create something more potent than we could have predicted.

This odd alliance, which to many has simply become known as 'tapping', invites the user or the practitioner to tap sequentially on specific acupressure points on the body, whilst reciting carefully chosen positive statements, targeted at the emotional events the individual is troubled by. This in turn leads to an emotional/physical release in both mind and body. Time and time again sufferers report freedom from past trauma, Post Traumatic Stress Disorder, phobias, obesity, anxiety, irrational fears, physical pain and much more. Here again we see that the 'whole is certainly greater than the sum of its parts'.

EFT. is informed by two completely different schools of thought, which are nevertheless bound together in a system that works.

Psychoneuroimmunology (PNI)

PNI, as I referred to in Chapter 4, has crossed over into mainstream medicine/science as it has forced its credibility and credentials onto a largely resistant and reluctant audience. Medicine generally doesn't seem to be fully ready to embrace the mind's indisputable impact on the body. But PNI has shown it cannot be ignored. If we look at the rampant rise in all cancers, PNI has been a key player in helping us to understand how the natural killer cells (pivotal members of our immune defences) are directly affected by our thoughts, moods and attitudes. A direct correlation has been exposed, which shows how our feelings impact greatly on how well our immune and nervous systems function. The research has shown over the last thirty years how the natural killer cells respond very precisely to what is happening at the emotional level. In other words, if you are depressed your natural killer cells respond in a 'depressive' way – unable to function effectively. Equally, if you are happy and positive their efficiency is greatly enhanced, leading to optimal function and improved disease response.

Again there is a substantial body of research being done in this area, looking at the psychological/biological connection – see the work of Professor Steptoe and the Psychobiology Group, which is concerned with how social demographic and psychosocial factors influence the disease process.

This area of enquiry further underlines that thoughts and feelings are 'active' factors, impacting on our physical health and so we have an important part to play in our own healing story.

Positive thinking really works because there is a biochemical relationship that either enhances or diminishes brain and body function. Those at the cutting edge of medicine (cancer treatments are good examples of this) are now recognising that helping patients to change their thinking can greatly influence their sense of well-being and the outcomes of their treatment. This is not an alternative to treatment or cure - again we are talking about psychology and medicine working as one, rather than each championing their differing points of view.

PNI is slowly helping us to see that medicine and psychology will undoubtedly achieve better results by working together.

Epigenetics - a key player

Epigenetics, as you may remember from Chapters 1, 4 and 9, literally means 'control above genetics'. In other words, genes are not our destiny. They tell the story of predispositions and possibilities but they do not set us on an inevitable course that cannot be changed!

Let me take you back to the IEGs, the immediate early/experience genes, which have been an interesting development in this area. Epigeneticists have discovered that these genes, like the natural killer cells, respond to our thoughts and feelings, impacting on immune function, our energy levels and our moods. Here we see another mind-body interface, where our psychological reality impacts on our biological functioning. This is another reason why in Chapter 4, I spoke about our need to persuade the body, in other words our need to work with her, in order to achieve good physical and mental health, as both are intimately entwined. What the research around the IEGs has illustrated is the fact that our intention really matters. Focusing our minds in a positive direction makes us genetic engineers, because we can literally change those 'molecules of emotion', which in turn mould our minds and bodies.

Epigenetics is quite rightly taking the scientific community by storm. The essence of its contribution to synergy is that it is bringing psychology, biology and some aspects of spirituality to the table and a new script is slowly being written. It's not clear where it will take us but it definitely is re-writing some of our genetic assumptions about the 'fixed' nature of being human. In fact, it's going further, as we've seen with quantum physics, helping us to understand the infinite possibilities that every moment presents us with, as long as we do not buy into the lie of limitation. In the end we are what we think we are. Our destiny is to a very large extent shaped by the way we think. Epigenetics has underlined the powerful role of our beliefs and perceptions in the shaping of our reality. This is not merely shaping our minds, it is also changing the nature of the body and its functions. How can we continue to ignore the mounting data?

The mere twenty five to thirty thousand genes that construct the human being are not by themselves enough to explain our magnificence and incredible capacity. What else lies behind the wonder of 'I'? Maybe epigenetics will play its part in answering that question. What's for sure is that it's telling us genetics alone cannot explain the mystery of you or me.

Noetic science

You may remember I referred briefly in Chapter 1 to the role of noetic sciences in the enquiry of the unified field. Noetic derives from the Greek word noesis, which means, in its most basic and literal sense, "understanding," "thinking," or "relating to the intellect." It describes that which is comprehended through reason. The main focus of the noetic sciences is the inner universe rather than the outer universe. These researchers are primarily concerned with consciousness and unlike conventional science, they are actively looking at the role that consciousness plays in the dance of life. They believe that many of the unexplained phenomena may well be unveiled by understanding this dynamic.

Noetic investigations are being carried out across many scientific disciplines. Its investigators use scientific methods to study aspects of nature that are deemed 'frontier' because they are considered to be at the cutting-edge of scientific knowledge and so are not always the primary focus of conventional scientific research. The Institute of Noetic Sciences (IONS), a research and education organization in California, describes the range of noetic sciences this way:

"Noetic sciences are explorations into the nature and potentials of consciousness using multiple ways of 'knowing', including intuition, feeling, reason, and the senses. Noetic sciences explore the 'inner cosmos' of the mind (consciousness, soul, spirit) and how it relates to the 'outer cosmos' of the physical world."

This is a broad definition, including as it does research into the mind-body interactions, consciousness, the paranormal (often called psi research), alternative and complementary healing, subtle energy, information imprinting (in/on water or other substances), the human body-field, and other aspects of nature and human biology that are often routinely dismissed by conventional science.

There are a lot of unchartered waters in physics, medicine, biology, healing, and consciousness. For the most part, these unchartered waters, when traversed, reveal anomalies that call into question what we 'think' we know. Then we become aware that there are maybe other interpretations that need to be considered. These are the aspects of nature that scientists have caught glimpses of in their experiments or from repeated observations, but that fall so far outside the boundaries of conventional theory that these 'outliers' defy belief and so are often not taken seriously or worse still ignored. In fact, there are now so many of these anomalies that it's impossible to ignore them any longer.

Noetic scientists are amongst the researchers who are daring to venture into these unchartered waters to see if we can make greater sense of what the universe is repeatedly telling us, which from my research, observation and experiences, is to take notice of the part we are playing in life's unfolding. How can we continue to ignore the impact we are having on reality, when it's clear to see the impact that reality is having on us? The evidence is showing us that this is a two-way street and until we open our minds to that we will be poorer for it.

For those who are interested in this area, taking a further look into quantum entanglement and quantum physics generally will help you to have a better understanding of the impact that consciousness has on reality. As Einstein pointed out, the moment we are observing something we are affecting it and John Wheeler, the British physicist, postulated that the evidence would suggest that we are indeed living in a 'participatory universe'.

The wave-particle duality is a very good example of this. When a particle is in its 'natural' state (meaning it is not being measured or observed via experiments) it is said to be in a state of 'superposition', which means it is in every possible state it can be all at once. That's why it is said to be in a state of 'potentiality'. It literally embodies everything possible, in what is often described metaphorically as a fuzzy or 'smeared' cloud of probabilities.

Once the particle is being observed or we are performing an experiment it can show up only as a particle or a wave but not both, and furthermore how it shows up is determined by the kind of experiment that is being conducted to detect it. It is strange, but true that if an experimenter is seeking to explore the wave properties of a quantum particle, say an electron, then the electron shows up displaying its wave nature. If the experiment is designed to explore particles, the electron shows up with all the properties and dynamics of a tiny solid thing - a particle. Somehow it's as if subatomic entities 'know' what we are asking and so appear in our world in ways that best accommodate our questions. This is truly mind-boggling and I think further underlines the role of consciousness in these matters because the energy that the human 'presence' (consciousness) brings to these experiments unquestionably influences the outcome.

Here we can see that there is a 'conversation' of sorts taking place between the physical and the metaphysical. Would it not be better to explore that dialogue rather than deny its existence?

Neurotheology

I've spoken about this subject in various chapters and so it's not necessary to repeat it's many virtues. However I think it is worth saying that it is refreshing that psychologists, scientists and those with transpersonal leanings are now taking one another's differing perspectives into account, with an attitude of mutual respect.

Neurotheology, like the noetic sciences is also actively researching many of the subjective and introspective activities such as prayer, relaxation, mindfulness and meditation, to assess whether such topics should be taken more seriously in the process of health and healing. Did the scholars, prophets and the ancient masters such as Buddha, LaoTzu, Confucius, Muhammad, Christ, Guru Nanak, St. Augustus and many others, offer us the keys not just to health but to a more evolved way of being when they advocated – each in their own way - that an introspective habit was critical to an emotionally stable and contented way of life? I believe the latest 'evidence' backs them up. There really is a correlation between prayer, meditation and other positive, reflective practices and peace of mind.

Mindfulness has more recently brought much valuable quantitative and qualitative data to this debate, especially over the last decade. There are now a number of universities and other research establishments that have dedicated specific research to this subject, such as Bangor Univeristy, UCLA, University of Massachusetts, the Oxford Mindfulness Centre, the American Mindfulness Research Association and many more, demonstrating a serious interest in a subject that most people in the West hadn't heard of twenty years ago and would have ridiculed until recently.

There's also the interesting fusion of mindfulness with CBT (Cognitive Behavioural Therapy). Both seen as effective therapeutic tools in their own right and yet the evidence is suggesting they could be more powerful when combined – see the work of Professor Mark Williams and Professor Job Kabat Zin for examples of the therapeutic developments using mindfulness.

So spirituality is increasingly finding ways to sit alongside science and demonstrate how both can further enrich the human experience. Synergy again demonstrates that co-operation rather than competition has to be the new way for the 21st century.

Biophysics

Biophysics is rapidly changing the way we see the world. Here we can see two of the giants within science (biology and physics and their various offspring) collaborating in a way that expands our understanding and appreciation of the world around us. An excellent example is how physics has enabled us to see that we live in a world of light (see Chapter 9) and as I explained in Chapter 11, the world we live in lies mostly outside of our field of vision. That world of X-rays, gamma rays, sound waves, etc. is a world of light resonating at varying frequencies, which creates the rich tapestry of life that we largely take for granted.

In the data that has been unveiled so far, life can be seen as a symphony of light and we are beings of light and the things we consume, food, water and air, are forms of light that sustain our life force. Health is therefore about light frequencies that come together in a way that creates quantum coherence - when everything is resonating as it should, and so a state of harmony exists. Quantum dissonance (disease) is then naturally dispelled.

Biology (more specifically systems biology) has also shown us that human life is driven by photons. Everything in the body depends on the photon transaction. Green matter imbibes the sun's rays (photons), which are absorbed into the very fabric of the vegetation. When we eat that food-stuff it is broken down by our bodies into vitamins, minerals and micronutrients, but most critically it is broken down into units of light, which underpin and drive the biological processes alongside air and water. Here we can see both biology and physics helping to explain how life is propelled and sustained. We can also see the intimate relationship between the seen and the unseen. If we are to understand the visible, we also need to better understand the invisible.

So biophysics is teaching us that we are organisms of light, which is why we are so affected by our environments since everything is made up of light. This dual science offers us some understanding about what we need to do if we want to enhance our relationship with the body. It also is helping us to better understand the healing modalities because there is a correlation between the mind that thinks in the right way and therefore generates health and the mind that thinks in a negative way, and as a result promotes disease.

Cardiff University has been conducting research on wound healing where they have been able to demonstrate that the nature of the mind and one's thoughts and feelings have a bearing on the rate of healing. As I said earlier, The Institute of Noetic Sciences has gathered a vast body of research which not only supports these findings but goes much further, showing that there is evidence to support that hands-on healing, distance healing, in fact healing in all its guises, seems to be about the harmonizing of frequencies. So when a positive energy comes into contact with a negative energy (frequency), there is a neutralizing, or more accurately, a harmonizing of frequencies. And this is why it is postulated that what might have been previously described as miracles, is merely the harmonizing of frequencies. Is this such a bizarre claim, when The Story of Light is really understood, and we appreciate what is taking place at that invisible, metaphysical level?

You may also be interested in the work of the Institute of HeartMath, which has been busy for the last two decades researching the role of the heart in the relationship of the mind-brain-body system/dynamic. Some of the strategies and techniques developed by biophysics, have led to some interesting revelations about the pivotal role of the heart in relation to physical and mental health. On the back of these discoveries, HeartMath has created a useful set of methods and interventions for changing negative aspects of our behaviour and experience.

Yoga

Yoga is arguably the best example we have today of the value and importance of synergy. This is such a vast subject that I'm not going to attempt to cover its diversity and complexity here as that would take a whole other book just to cover the history and the different types of yoga (some of which I covered in Antiquity Comes Full Circle). If your appetite has been whetted by what I have covered in this book, then I suggest this is a topic you may want to look more closely at, as it has a lot to offer the mind-body-spirit-environment model.

The evolution of yoga has been a very winding, undulating road that has taken place over thousands of years. Its journey from the East to the West has brought many changes to it. It could be argued that the plethora of different schools of yoga has served to confuse the picture further. And yet the essence of yoga is about union, about connection. Union - union with what? For some this is God or the Divine, for others it is about a meaningful connection with one's body and with one's spirit or alternatively a connection with truth. Whatever one is seeking union with: God, the planet, humanity, oneself, others or the truth, yoga seems to offer the potential for access to any and possibly all of these.

Yoga originally was about the intimate relationships between mind, body and spirit - using breathing, mantras, body control and intense mental focus to develop and harness the power in those relationships. Additionally it taught, and in some cases still teaches, that if that connection is finely tuned the practitioner can be connected to the cosmos and glimpse the truth of reality. Its primary premise is that union with self fosters better union with everything else. It's fascinating that yoga, despite all its changes, and the dilution of its messages by different egos, cultures, personalities and even time, has still managed to hold onto its essential message, 'all answers begin with me'.

The subject of yoga embodies the mind-body relationship and offers through its practice a better understanding of everything including the Divine. It essentially teaches us that by finding harmony (union) between all things we are most likely to find the truth in ourselves and about the time and space we inhabit.

The Reach Approach

These examples of synergy I think illustrate where our attention needs to go if we are looking for lasting solutions for both our personal woes and the demise of our planet.

I could easily have continued making the point for a greater synergistic model with many more examples from disciplines I have not specifically mentioned here, such as: NLP, acupuncture, Qi gong, herbalism, shiatsu, homeopathy, reiki, spiritual healing, nutri-energetics, (working with the human body field), in fact the list goes on. I have omitted more than I have reported on simply because I'm not trying to advocate on behalf of any particular discipline. This is not the point of this book. I'm not even advocating that The Reach Approach is the path you should take. What I am saying is if you are looking for a panacea and you don't take into account the four key variables (mind, body, spirit and environment), then in my experience you are unlikely to find a sustainable solution(s).

The Reach Approach, as I said, is merely a signpost towards synergy, as we do not claim to provide all of the services someone would need to find health and well-being. What we do though, is provide individuals with a compass and a clear map so that they can actually work out what is the best arrangement for them. Our speciality is putting together a programme that is specific to the needs of the individual.

Someone might come to see me suffering with anxiety and panic attacks and on closer inspection of their life, it becomes clear that their hydration is poor, which will undermine brain function. They have unresolved issues, which keeps them tied to negative thought patterns. Their life lacks any meaning and purpose and so they are drifting aimlessly in self doubt and they have limited social contact, which keeps feeding the idea that they are not liked or valued. Someone who presents in this way is unlikely to find just talking enough. They undoubtedly need to express themselves but no amount of talking will address poor hydration, only drinking water will do that.

In this same example, conversation might be enough to help them understand that they need to change their self-talk, but only a clear strategy and resources to enable them to do that, is likely to change those negative thought patterns. If their life lacks meaning and purpose, again talking about this is a good starting point but in the end what they actually need is to work out a plan, which identifies their talents, ambitions and desires and provides them with the framework and practical support for fulfilling their potential. Also, given the nature of anxiety and the biochemical factors often involved, they may need some form of nutritional intervention and/or herbal/homoeopathic remedies to help regulate their temperament.

So you can see with this one case, a presenting problem often has many other strands that need attention, if the person seeking resolution is to really be helped. This kind of scenario is one I see several times a week. A range of people may present the same situation but each would require personalized responses in order to achieve the same outcome. This is because the underlying reason for the presenting problem is nearly always different and is why a 'one size fits all' approach rarely works.

The right question

When we began this journey I contrasted the different approaches in the talking therapy arena. This was not meant to champion a particular approach, nor was it designed to condemn the many therapeutic models out there that are making a difference. My primary aim was to say the debate itself is flawed. This is the case both in the psychological arena, as well as with those treatments that concern themselves primarily with the body and its dysfunction(s). We are, in my view, focusing on the wrong question. What we should be asking is what is the best combination of therapeutic options available given the nature of the individual's problem/concerns? Equally important is to realize that the answer to that question should not be confined to a purely psychological remedy, nor indeed a purely physical one. I hope you can now see this for yourself - because it's time to change our approach. It seems to me that we are in danger of remaining dogmatically tied to what we 'think' we know and therefore do not have the courage to venture into the unknown.

It's time for us all to open our minds and allow our awareness to expand and grow. It's time for us to stop 'overlooking the obvious', simply because it has become easier to stay where we are. It's time for us to find the courage to take the many small leaps of faith that are needed to fly beyond our perceived limitations.

It's time for change and the change that you seek begins with you!

I leave you in love and in hope

Our journey is now complete. I hope you are at least considering the merits of what I've presented in this book and will begin to question the modern premise that progress is always better and competition always brings out the best in us.

Hopefully, like me, you're tired of a world that is less kind, more selfish and too busy defending its opinion rather than pursuing the truth. Whatever changes truth may require of us it's time to face and embrace them with open arms. I hope I've done enough to persuade you of what I said in Chapter 3, 'The Only Destination Is Right Action'.

So let us at least try to be the best we can be.

"Our problem is that we make the mistake of comparing ourselves with other people. You are not inferior or superior to any human being....you do not determine your success by comparing yourself to others, rather you determine your success by comparing your accomplishments to your capabilities. You are 'number one' when you do the best you can with what you have."

Zig Ziglar (1926 - present)

CASE STUDIES

The rocking chair of regret

I belatedly decided to add this section because the approach I've advocated throughout the book has worked for literally thousands of individuals, not only those who've benefitted from the face-to-face work, but also those who've used our website and other resources. I think hearing some of their accounts would be extremely helpful and inspiring, because these are real people who in most instances had given up, having tried many things before ever coming to mine or Reach's door.

I coined this phrase 'the rocking chair of regret' having worked with an elderly man, who when I first met him, (he was eighty three), was sitting in a rocking chair. In our first conversation, he listed all his regrets but said he didn't want to die without meeting arguably the most important person he'd never met... himself! I remember that image of him rocking backwards and forwards as he spoke and it haunted me for days. It was the sadness in his eyes, the way he was slumped in the chair and the tone of his voice that touched something deep inside of me.

He asked me if there was any chance of this meeting with himself before he died, because he increasingly felt not meeting 'him' would be his greatest regret. I said to him that I couldn't promise this, but what I could promise was if he faced what he needed to with an honest heart, the truth would come and embrace him, and that's what he proceeded to do.

Over the next twenty-one months we took a beautiful journey together and shortly after his eighty fifth birthday, we met for what I knew would be the last time. And as usual, he was sitting in his rocking chair and I remember he had his back to me when I entered the room and before he turned to face me he said, "I really wouldn't mind now if I died, because the one person that I'd never met is now present in my life. And as I've connected with him, I've been able to make peace with my past."

This was such a poignant moment. I remember my eyes moistening because I knew the truth of what he was saying because I'd experienced the changes in him, but I also felt he was saying good-bye. As we parted for the last time and looked into each other's eyes, I realized he had avoided that 'rocking chair of regret'. He was now able to move on in contentment and I could see that etched on his face.

Two days later I received a call to say he had died and I remember punching the air, because I knew he had left in the way that he had wanted to and tears of joy rolled down my cheeks. He told me in that last meeting that I had changed his life but the truth was that he had changed my life in an equally powerful way. I will never forget the message he left me with – a leopard can definitely change its spots. An old dog can learn new tricks. There just simply has to be a desire for such a change, a flicker of hope for it to be different, and it can be.

In the ten case studies that follow, some of the individuals' names have been changed to protect their identities whilst others have preferred not to use an alias.

Their stories are true, written by them. Their accounts are moving and clearly illustrate how a 'one pronged approach' is rarely enough especially when one's challenges are substantial and complex. I have had the pleasure of walking alongside each of these individuals and I would like to thank them all for allowing me to share their stories.

I hope these accounts will move and inspire you as they did me.

Case study 1

Subject: Anglo-Asian female, 42 years old.

I began my journey with The Reach Approach as a very disconnected 25 year old young woman. My Father had passed away when I was age 6, and I was raised by my Mother who was battling with her own pain and grief. From then onwards my life was a very lonely, isolated and confused one, and the way I learnt to cope with life was not to allow myself to feel, as at times the pain was too much to bear. Hence somewhere along the line I decided that not to feel was the best option in order for me to survive and so I shut down emotionally. This however resulted in me making bad choices in my life and putting myself in stressful situations that were damaging for my health and well-being.

I still remember that first phone call. In my hour of need, I was given Easton's details by someone who was also taking The Reach Approach journey. He was so attentive during that phone call, and his caring nature came across very clearly. Then we met, and the hope I felt from him was incredibly uplifting. He was kind and reassuring and helped me to understand that we all have the capacity to change. It's about having access to the right resources and support. And although this felt beyond my capacity at that point, I did feel a sense of hope. I'm not sure I'd ever felt that before.

As my journey progressed I began to become aware of my self-limiting habits and behaviour. I was offered numerous tools to help expand my awareness and develop positive routines in order for me to establish the emotional connection and well-being I had been yearning for.

Slowly but surely Easton created the environment for me to open up to him, and to myself. My journey with him has brought many highs, as growing in self-awareness is immensely empowering. However, there have also been lows, and in those times of crisis I always felt held and understood and the process kept pointing me in the right direction, showing me how to deal with my life's challenges in a non-destructive way - continually reminding me that I was my own greatest resource, which, although it took time, I began to believe.

I was introduced to many new concepts for health and well-being and the interconnection of the mind/body relationship was one of them. I found The Story of Health particularly helpful for pulling it all together.

Metaphysics was another new concept to me, and this knowledge helped me take responsibility for my life. By having this new understanding and applying these new tools I began to feel a hope and strength that I had never experienced before.

Now, two marriages and two children later, I can honestly say I am no longer confused about my life. I know why I am here, and I know how to heal myself and work towards fulfilling my life's purpose. I used to be a person who would have an idea or vision, and would make it happen at all costs. Now I have learnt not to force my way through life, and instead to trust that if I live by certain values and principles, my life will in turn reflect all that I am. One of the life mantras that stayed with me is 'the only destination is right action' and through learning from my mistakes, experience has taught me that this is indeed true.

I feel I now have an internal compass of my own, directing me towards my peace and happiness, and each year the compass is strengthening. The external terrain of life is unpredictable and having such an internal guide is an incredible resource to have at all times but especially in times of challenge. For me this compass is a combination of knowledge, understanding and practical applications like stillness, prayer, meditation, hydration, nutrition and affirmations, to name a few. These have become my friendly companions.

I am eternally grateful for having found The Reach Approach. It has transformed my life and helped me to create an inner strength and clarity that continues to guide me now. I have now taken the journey from being one who was badly damaged and distressed to someone who is helping others to find their way. I consider this to be a gift and an honour.

Dee Smith

Case study 2

Subject: White Caucasian male, 55 years old. The journey to the self is different for all of us. For some, it might feel like a 'fast track' event that flashes by in the blink of an eye, while for others, it may seem like a never-ending marathon without a finishing line in sight. Neither way is wrong or right. They are both equally valid journeys that pertain to an individual's own unique capacity to imbibe, absorb and practically put into place the foundations of change.

There is however, one commonality that links both journeys, and that is the requirement of courage. I've never considered myself courageous, or even been aware that this quality existed within me, but looking back now from my current position of relative security and happiness, I can clearly see my own 'unseen hero' at work… a hero that never veered off course, and gently guided my life to a place of stability and calm. It's hard to put my time with 'Reach' into words, primarily because until it was recently pointed out to me that I was 'waking up', it had never even occurred to me just how much my life had changed, and… how far I had come on the journey of self-transformation. For me, the whole concept of change up until this point, was an entirely elusive concept in my head… for others, but not for me. When I first came to Reach in 2007, all I wanted to do was numb my pain and justify a delusional position of righteousness, which was fixed firmly in my head. Looking back, it was a ridiculous position to take, but when one is closed down and shut off, any sense of rationality is totally lost.

The truth was that at 49 years old, lifelong dysfunctional traits had once again run their course, and blindly trashed and broken everything that was good and meaningful in my life... a beautiful, supportive and loving relationship of 17 years... a fantastic career within the performing arts... a beautiful home and enviable lifestyle... and... a wonderful spiritual path full of valuable principles and ethics.

It was the lowest point of my life and I was too arrogant and angry to see it. All I wanted to do was rage against the injustice of it all and convince myself that I was unaccountable for my situation. Initially, my Reach counsellor took on the role of a listening board, allowing me to 'vomit' my pain and life story over and over again. This was always done with great care, patience, love and respect... no matter how angry or hurt my dialogue became... I was heard.

I must have sounded like a broken record, because for the first year I did not listen to a thing that was being said. I was arrogant, blind and dishonest... and... such was my alter ego, that I became entrenched in the belief that I alone had been wronged and that the whole world was against me.

Later this discourse turned to a kind of righteous anger... like, I had a 'right to be angry' without being accountable for any of my actions. I wasn't looking honestly at my own contribution to the problems, but always seemed to be justifying my position. I had become a victim. I've since understood that 'victimhood' is part of the transformational process - a phase on the journey for us all. One cannot go from being a damaged soul to a place of being healed without passing through it.

For me... it allowed me to develop a very important bit of myself – a 'conscience'. As I progressed further, 'my conscience' allowed me to start talking more maturely and realistically about my situation, and for the first time I started to see things from the other person's perspective. I still wasn't listening properly, but a strange thing happened during this period. I broke down. I guess, this was the point when the 'real me' finally turned up, because from here on in, the flood gates opened and a torrent of grief and life long suppression poured out like a never ending tidal wave.

Feeling the emotion of grief for the first time was both a frightening and liberating experience, and I moved quickly into a place of loss, hurt and sadness where I found myself re-visiting my whole situation from a place of newfound humility. I was starting to 'listen' for the first time in my life. Instead of endlessly talking, something inside told me that if I wanted to make my life better, I needed to pay attention to the advice being offered and actually put the Reach ethos into practice. I can only describe this process as akin to building a new house with solid foundations.

The principle pillars being - mind, body, spirit and environment - with each pillar being dependant on the other for an all round balanced growth. I guess I must have been gradually improving, because with the encouragement of my counsellor, I went to University and obtained a first class Masters degree. Since then, although rocked by periods of self-doubt, I have made slow but steady progress. By recording and re-listening to each session, the application of these fundamental cornerstones is taking a definite foothold in my psyche. Through the process of trial and error, they are beginning to transform my life to a point of real change… and… the possibility of a brighter future with values, principles and ethics. Given where I started from, and how damaged, blind and closed down I was, this feels like nothing short of a miracle from my perspective. It's important to emphasise that none of this would have been possible without the unfailing support, love and guidance of my therapist and ally, who has been nothing short of a 'rock'.

Without his unshakeable belief and ability to see the best in me, my life might have taken a very different course.

I've learnt many valuable things along my journey, but perhaps the most important lesson for me so far, is the understanding that by giving and helping others less fortunate than ourselves, we bring immense benefit and joy to the self… and thereby gently nurture the art of appreciation and deep gratitude for everything that life has to offer. Something else important that made a real difference to me was summarized in this way…

"The measurement of a person is not where they end up, its where they end up in relation to where they started from."

Bernard Adams

Case study 3

Subject: Afro-caribbean female, 44 years old.

"There is always light that can be found even in the darkest moments." This has proved to be one of the most important lessons I have learnt on my Reach journey.

Another profound lesson has been, "when the student is ready the teacher will appear."

It was a Friday morning at work, my day for paperwork. My colleague and I started a conversation about peaceful places we have visited, which evolved to a discussion about a person, Easton Hamilton, who had helped her at a time of need. She gave me his number and by instinct I called him. He was fully booked so I was unable to get an appointment, however at that time my life was not in the mess it was about to get into. I believe even though my attempts to make contact with him did not lead to a meeting at that time, it was as if destiny/God knew what was waiting for me and this contact would become important at some future date. And this did prove to be the case. In fact, it saved my life.

I was in an emotionally abusive relationship, however I didn't see it or rather didn't want to see it because there was no physical abuse and so in my mind there was no abuse. The harsh words here and there, the on-going insults and the put-downs were not abuse. Now I know it was abuse! And it had damaged me.

However, my eyes were fully opened when the emotional abuse turned physical -not towards me but towards my son. When my husband hit my son for something trivial to do with homework from school, I watched the joy leave my son's eyes and it was at this point I knew I needed to do something. This was when I called Easton for help. I rang him in a state of utmost distress about what had happened. His question to me at the time was, "if it is so bad, why don't you leave?" and my answer was "I don't know." Now I can honestly say I was afraid, not of what my husband would do, because if he had tried to touch me I would rip his eyes out, I didn't want to give up the comfort of my home. I remember saying to Easton that I wanted him to see my son. He said he'd be happy to do that but it's nearly always better to be working with the parents first because the child has to keep going back into the same environment, and if nothing has changed any progress is undermined. That was not what I wanted to hear, but life has a way of continuing to put you in the same position until you eventually are forced to see what you have been busy denying.

One day out of the blue, my husband said "I don't want to be married to you anymore."

A vicious divorce followed, my ex-husband (it is such a joy to say that - my ex), got me fired from my job, then the house got repossessed, he took the car so I was on the street, no job, homeless and no car with my mother and two sons. We were given a single bedroom by a relative, where all four of us slept for six months (I cry at this point of my story, ironically because this is where I was most grateful because we had a roof over our heads and were not sleeping on the streets). I kept my sanity by the grace of God and by talking to Easton. He helped me by continuing to remind me of The Story of Health. He kept my focus on getting the basics right. This was exactly what I needed because I was all over the place. He allowed me to feel the hurt and the pain but always directed me to the resources that could help me heal. I needed both things. I needed to be angry, scream, cry and go round in circles, but I also needed the guidance and support. The Reach Approach is full of resources and I was never very far from something that would help.

One of the fascinating things we did was something called Dark Room Work. I can't believe the revelations that this unveiled. Issues that I would have rather remained hidden, came floating to the surface and things that I thought were my enemies I discovered were actually my friends. This is where I learnt about Old Friend, Dear Friend – this idea that the things that hold us back and we run away from are not in fact our enemies but our friends. This at first seemed peculiar to me but it was through this process that I learnt the truth of it and freed myself from the idea that the best way to deal with my demons was to avoid them. This had never worked anyway.

I also remember doing exercises like finding things to be grateful for even then in my darkest moments. At first I thought this is silly - look at your circumstances, what do you have to be grateful for. I remember the first time I tried it. I started by being grateful for a roof we did have over our heads and then I kept finding more things to be grateful for. Then out of the blue I got a house to rent. My problems didn't all disappear, they were still there but I found courage and faith to deal with them. Everyone including me was surprised at my attitude and resolve but I knew it was the work that I was doing that was saving my life. And the power of thank you was clearly playing its part.

Having said all this, the thing I still struggled with the most was personal responsibility, which The Reach Approach is built on. I didn't like this much because I preferred the game of blame but it became clear this was keeping me stuck. I was willing to be the victim or the wronged one and not willing to acknowledge any personal responsibility. I didn't always like what Easton said on this subject, mainly because it was inviting me to look more deeply at my circumstances. Somewhere in me I knew it was the truth, but I still didn't want to hear it.

I later conceded that this was right and the moment I acknowledged my responsibility I was able to let go of the blame, victimhood and most importantly I was able to find my self-respect and voice. I am free of all that now although I still occasionally catch myself pulled by those feelings but I now can look at the situation or circumstance and recognize I have the choice to feel and behave differently and I am not defined by my circumstances but my reaction to those circumstances.

I am now happy, emotionally happy, I don't have as much materially as I did before but there is a joy that seems to come from within that makes me laugh often, as I live with an inner knowing, which values me rather than what I have. My contact with Reach has been a blessing and a pleasure. This amazing meeting is one that I will never forget and will bless that day forever.

The horrendous journey I've been on has now taught me so much about myself, other people and the world. I have managed to find the blessings amidst the pain and I am grateful for that.

My challenge now is to continue on this journey of becoming the best I can be.

To Easton and Reach I will continue to be forever grateful.

Deniese Wilson

Case study 4

Subject: Asian woman, 47 years old.

My journey, my story, my experience with Reach has always been part of me, it was just a matter of time before I opened myself to the truth.

My first session I will never forget, I was uncertain, I wasn't expecting much, I remember walking in and spotting a box of tissues, thinking to myself do people actually cry at these meetings?

It was the first time I heard myself verbalize my feelings, my thoughts. I tried to listen but the noise, the chaos of clutter in my head was deafening. I knew then I needed help. Towards the end of the session I can only describe what I was feeling as a homecoming event. I had been out in the cold for so long I had forgotten how the warmth of the truth melts our hearts. An unsaid sacred connection had been made, and yes I came out with tissues and trust, the sincerity of acceptance was mind blowing.

Reach has always valued and loved the seeker in me, giving me the best tools to deal with life. At the beginning it was the heavy-duty stuff. There was a lot of excavation work, some of the foundations had to be re-laid and strengthened before I could build. It was painful, heart breaking at times, it even brought me to my knees and in a few instances I found myself flat on my face. But how else do we connect with the source of our pain, discomfort, unease? How else do we find our purpose, that unspoken message that lives inside each one of us? I realize that at no point was this process harming me and what I was feeling was the beautiful pain of relief. I began to understand the concept of 'naming it' and 'owning it' before it was possible for surrender and empowerment to take place. My initial resistance was replaced by joyous enthusiasm as I discovered that in trusting myself and the process, I did indeed find my message(s) and my purpose.

My aim was to now build anew, with integrity, honesty and truth. I loved this idea of The Three Gatekeepers and this set me on a different course.

As with most renovation projects, they are sometimes slowed down due to unforeseen circumstances. Mine was, due to ill health. I felt like a crying child who had lost her mother in the crowd. And for a time, I lost some of my faith and hope. But as I looked up from my despair, there she was with welcoming open arms, a heartfelt embrace, wiping the tears away. In that embrace I remember feeling a sense of peace, gratitude and complete surrender.

Thank you Reach, for being my mother, for turning up at the time of need when I had lost my way. You have provided an abundance of riches which have served me countless times. For anyone who hasn't looked at their fabulous website, please go and do it at your first opportunity (www.thereachapproach.co.uk). The combination of my journey with my therapist, and these wonderful resources has been a medicine like no other. This work has given me the chance to reflect, to be grateful, to visualise my purpose, what a gift, a life changing inspiration. The investment of love and hope from Reach has been consistent, never leaving my side, helping me improve all aspects of my renovation.

My tears and fears these days are mostly filled with gratitude, wonder and divine love. I love the organic growth; the richness of learning, it is so deep sometimes, words are not enough. We all have the capacity and the courage to reconnect with our authentic nature if we are willing to embrace the truth about ourselves and reality.

I have been on a roller coaster of life lessons, and continue to be. Reach has held my hand even when I have sometimes let go, the love has remained... open and welcoming. That's Reach - it's a relationship of positive change, acceptance and truth. I give thanks from deep within.

"The wound is the place where the light enters you."
Rumi

Namaste

Case study 5

Subject: White female, 44 years old.

Looking back, it's hard to believe who I was, how I was and how my life was when I first came into contact with Reach. I was thirty years old. My husband had just had an affair and left me and our two very young children, which had hit me extremely hard. I was living in a different country to my own family and felt very isolated and so alone. On top of that I had just been diagnosed with cancer and having had some operations, had just started a regime of chemotherapy. I wasn't equipped with the tools to cope with any of this and was handling it all very badly. I was on anti depressants and was on the run from everything that was happening to me. Rather than looking after myself, I was engaging in completely destructive behaviours, doing anything I could to distract myself from how my life had turned out. I had reached rock bottom, I didn't care whether I lived or died, and I was so out of touch with myself that I didn't even realise that this is where I was.

A dear friend, who realised much more so than I did, that I was on the path to destruction, encouraged me to call Easton and make an appointment. I will always be grateful to her for this. As far as I am concerned, that gentle persuasion saved my life. Although the journey I have taken with Reach has at times been difficult and challenging, the rewards have been immense and I do not believe I would be here today if I had continued on the path I was on.

My journey started with Life Mapping, which was enormously beneficial in helping me to understand what exactly had gone wrong and when and why this had happened. It helped me to begin to unravel the mess that my life had become. It was never an exercise in wallowing or self pity, but proved to be truly enlightening as we picked through the debris of my past to see how this past was still shaping and influencing my present and thus my future. Going through my past in this way, always being encouraged to look through eyes of compassion and understanding, was invaluable in helping me to identify and begin to let go of the sense of shame and failure that I had unknowingly carried around for so long. I have always been a perfectionist and as such was my own worst critic. Life Mapping helped me to realise that actually, given my upbringing and it's influences, I had only ever done the best that I could. This message took a long time to sink in, the critic in me not wanting to let myself off the hook, but from the moment I started to even entertain this, things began to change.

Shame work was challenging but I had so many revelations through this process. It was an amazing experience, to look deep, and to realise that I was holding on to so many negative thoughts and beliefs about myself that were shaping everything I said, thought and did. Liberation began when I realised that these perceptions didn't belong to me anymore, never actually did in the first place. Its hard to describe the freedom that comes when you can begin to let go of the burdens of the past - holding onto the lessons that the past has to offer but letting go of the negativity and the shame that so often tends to linger most strongly.

I can't say I ever looked forward to our sessions when we were doing Dark Room work. I have always been somebody who needed to be in control and I didn't like the fact that I was delving into the unknown. But given the choice I would do it all over again as it enabled me to connect with myself at a deeper level than had ever been possible for me. It helped me to identify and connect with those parts of me that had still not healed and were blocking my way forward. I think we could have talked forever and never discovered some of the things I learnt about myself in this part of the journey.

The beauty of the Reach Approach for me was that from a very early stage I was presented with the tools that would help me to change and encouraged to use them. I don't think I was the easiest of clients as my pattern was always to initially resist. It took a long time for it to actually sink in that although knowledge is important and necessary, without application it can actually just be another tool to beat yourself up with and I was very good at that! I know everybody takes this journey in their own unique way but looking back I could have saved myself a lot of unnecessary struggle if I had taken that leap of faith a little bit earlier! It's one of those things that you just can't know until you've experienced it. And once I experienced the true benefit of regular and consistent application it very quickly became one of my non-negotiables. It has made too much of a difference to my life for me to ever let it go.

It's an interesting exercise to sit here and reflect on my journey through the Reach Approach. Thinking about it, positive change actually began very quickly for me. Easton was unwaveringly accepting, loving and supportive. You just can't come into contact with that level of acceptance and care and not begin to change even in spite of yourself! The further I went on my journey the more I truly realised that change is always, always possible for all of us. Whatever it is we are struggling with there is always a way to turn things around. Reach always offered a way to do this and what is more it invariably worked!

I am such a different person now to who I was then and immeasurably more content, more fulfilled and more at peace. I more recently went through a second experience of cancer and handled it so differently to the first time. I was able to move through it with so much more ease and positivity. I looked after myself well through the treatment and never lost sight of myself and my hopes and dreams for the future. I am through the other side of this now and l am looking forward to the rest of my life with hope, optimism and even excitement in my heart. Who would have thought it was possible!

Selina Leigh

Case study 6

Subject: Asian male, 52 years old.

My Reach Journey – how it transformed my life within a year – what could it do for you?

I lived an enviable lifestyle:

I had a loving wife and two wonderful children

I was a Sales Director and travelled the world on business

I had a Lexus company car, expense account and bonuses

I was a part-time Children's DJ & Entertainer

I lived in a good size home and had regular holidays abroad

I was gregarious, extrovert and the centre of attraction in social gatherings

I was blessed with a very youthful appearance, slim body and was rarely ill

My life was perfect, right? Wrong! For 10 years during my 40s, I felt that even though 'I had everything' I felt a huge sense of 'something was missing'. I couldn't figure it out and so kept myself busy and just continued my 25+ year fast-paced/high-pressure corporate life-style. When I walked through the door of Reach, I was on the precipice of burn-out and on the road to a heart attack or something similar.

All my life, I considered the world of counselling and psychotherapy as being applicable to weak-minded individuals who just needed to 'pull themselves together'. The very mention of words like 'holistic', 'spiritual' or 'enlightenment' etc. would instantly make me think of tree-hugging, open-toed sandal wearing hippies and I would consider this arena as namby-pamby and mumbo-jumbo.

However, as soon as I discovered Reach (thanks to my patient wife!), I rapidly ate a large slice of humble pie (if not the whole pie!) and encouraged everyone I met to at least dip into the vast resources available on the Reach website and to embark on the Reach Journey if they felt they had any unresolved issues or simply wanted to feel better about themselves.

I initially embarked on my personal 'Journey of Truth' to deal with the guilt and regret around my mother's passing away from Alzheimer's disease. The timing was such that I had simultaneously resigned my then corporate sales position. My wife urged me (which she had been doing for many years) to contact Easton Hamilton; I am eternally grateful that I took this first step. He encouraged me to read the following handouts ahead of our first meeting; The Reach Approach, The Story of Health 1, 2 & 3, NOSE 1 & 2 and Persuading the Body 1, 2, 3 & 4. I immediately related to the Story of Health's equilateral triangle diagram and understood that the corporate environment, that I had spent so many years in, accumulating kudos and status, was in fact lowering my spirit and that this could lead to serious ill health. I also realised that I had been neglecting my body in terms of hydration, sleep, exercise and nutrients. With such gaping holes in my Environment and Body aspects, I could not even begin to contemplate the higher plains of Mind and Spirit!

I quickly decided that it would be far more beneficial for me to take the Reach journey rather than just deal with my issues in relation to my mother. I needed to apply self-care and be a better husband and father. I started my journey during January 2011 and my transformation, as a result of applying the outcomes of my sessions along with Reach's methodologies is captured from a 'before' and 'current' point of view as follows:

BEFORE	WITHIN 12 Months of Starting My Reach Journey
• **Environment** - Immersed in corporate 'business model' of relentless targets, growth and efficiency - Typical working day hours; 8 am - 8 pm - Trains, Planes, Automobiles, Hotels lifestyle - Enjoyed part-time Children's Entertainment shows but quite often performed tired and did not value the kudos relative to the corporate world - Family did not always get the best of me since I had already expended my energy outside home	• **Environment** - Monumental improvement in relationships with my wife and children. They finally have the best of me as their husband and father. - Peaceful and nurturing home environment - Self-employed, running my Children's Entertainment business. 'Connecting children to their joy and happiness' is extremely uplifting and altruistic. - Relatively relaxed lifestyle, with much greater balance and freedom
• **Body** - Although I was slim, I hardly exercised - I had not slept well for years - High blood pressure and high cholesterol - Feeling tired and somewhat haggard - Okay diet	• **Body** - Consistently drinking more water and taking vital nutrients - Achieving restorative sleep, particularly since giving up alcohol - Exercising regularly, including yoga - Feeling more energised

• **Mind**
  - Constantly active, no Still Time
  - Harsh, cynical, critical and un-emotional
  - Uncompromising, Unforgiving, Ruthless, Controlling and Ego-centric
  - My way or not at all
  - Impatient and quick to criticise
  - No real connection to my Indian identity and roots
	• **Mind**
	  - Considerably more patient and sensitive
	  - Slow to criticise and quick to praise
	  - Abundance of gratitude & thanks, kindness, compassion and humility
	  - Unafraid to show emotion (including tears) and share feelings
	  - Realisation of true self, including ethnicity and heritage
	  - Still Time and Meditation are my goals
	  - Forgiveness is another goal

• **Spirit**
  - Lacking sense of purpose in life
  - Lack of altruism and benevolence
	• **Spirit**
	  - Spirit is soaring as the Reach journey continues to de-layer my acquired self and negative drivers
	  - Changing my work environment to focus on bringing happiness to children has had a significant knock-on effect on many aspects of my life

Reach has quickly become the foundation for my way of life due to its highly integrative and all-encompassing approach.

Easton's contribution in helping people to be 'the best they can be' is immense and yet the work is done with never-ending humility, integrity and benevolence. Having compared the Reach approach with other offerings within this arena, my attraction to Reach was that it is free of ego, self-publicity and figurehead worship; in my experience this cannot be said of many other individuals, movements and organisations.

Reach resources

The staggering abundance of Reach material, blending wisdom from the past with modernity, comprehensively covering every aspect of counselling, psychotherapy and personal growth (most of which is freely available on the Reach website) should not be taken for granted; the huge quantity of material is equally matched by its consistent first class quality and high standard.

During my Sales & Business Development days, I was responsible for producing technical product & services marketing material such as brochures, presentations and press releases. I know how much effort is required to produce professional material, from concept to final form, which engages the reader with succinct information in the form of text that flows well and layout that utilises relevant photos & images. I therefore truly admire and respect the amount of effort and careful thought involved in the generation & dissemination of Reach material in the form of website information, handouts, audio mp3/cds, videos, books and apps. The information is not just 'thrown together'; the content and construction is well thought out and inter-connected with relevant reference to related information. The messages contained within the Reach material are intelligently articulated in plain-speaking language, which does not patronise or over-load the reader.

My journey has not just taken the form of therapy and mentoring sessions. My progress and growth has been greatly aided by the aforementioned materials, which have accelerated my development (particularly handouts and audio materials). Reading and listening to the material several times throughout the journey time-line has deepened my understanding and appreciation of the information. This coupled with the application of the knowledge and methodologies, through carrying out the exercises and tasks set between sessions, has been extremely beneficial in achieving good personal growth in a number of key aspects of life; not only benefiting myself but equally importantly benefiting my wife and children as well.

Concluding remarks

I would encourage anyone who is cynical and in doubt with respect to the benefits of taking this journey, as I was in the past, to take the courageous first step and embark on their own process of self reflection and discovery. I have benefited significantly by applying the knowledge and wise counsel offered to me. The most important part of the equation "Knowledge + Application = Personal Power" is application; without consistent application, I would not have been able to reap the rewards from my journey. Having taken the Reach medicine, my life has transformed beyond imagination within a relatively short time period.

I would like to once again thank my wife for bringing me to the door of Reach after 10+ years of patient waiting and to Easton for developing my self-awareness so that I can conquer my demons now (rather than facing them at my mortality) and lead a more fulfilling and up-lifting life.

Sat Panesar

Case study 7

Subject: White male 51 years of age.

"You're not anxious, you're angry...."

That was pretty much how the conversation began with Easton and I wondered could it be true? I felt betrayed, I was in deep emotional pain, I was confused, I was hurting, and I had been told by a counsellor previously I was suffering with chronic anxiety as the panic attacks consumed my every waking moment, late into the nights and at times throughout the night.

But no one had ever said, I was angry.

The anxiety, Easton explained, was the smoke screen; the issue is your unresolved anger… and I simply didn't believe him.

At 26 years old I had been diagnosed with cancer, my then girlfriend had just found out she was pregnant with my son and we had a two year old daughter and I was told I had a 60% chance statistically of surviving 5 years. I was also diagnosed with chronic anxiety and was given six sessions through the NHS and someone sat in front of me as young as me and in training who was attempting to alleviate my fear, depression, anxiety symptoms which were all consuming. I suffered with tachycardia, free-floating anxiety, disorientation, and was becoming agoraphobic too. The theme of 'not being safe' travelled with me daily. My body would shake uncontrollably; I constantly wanted to run to safety as this wave of panic paralysed me time and again.

Yet, in all that time, no one had said, "Stuart, you're angry" - instead I was given beta blockers 160 mg, enough to slow down an elephant and it took me ten years to wean myself off the medication and yet that undercurrent of anxiety bullied me at various times for over 20 years.

They say, adversity carries with it an equivalent seed of hope and I can say that is true because I am still here some 24 years later and living testament of a completely different life.

I was never really the same person after going through treatments and seeing what I saw which was all those around my age pass away. I sought refuge through meditation, yoga, and other holistic therapies such as, nutrition, aromatherapy, reflexology and gained several diplomas over a period of 7 years, as I sought ways to help myself.

I then began a small practice and taught yoga at The University of Birmingham and this paved a way of life that became healthier and undoubtedly contributed to my survival and yet I remained firmly rooted in that survival mode.

I had become the best survivor I knew, I had learned to become an expert in managing the symptoms of anxiety, by which time my girlfriend had become my wife and my children had begun junior school and I had changed practically every area of my life and yet I was falling apart by trying to keep it all together and the changes I thought I had made were on reflection no more than learning how to cope and manage symptoms.

My marriage broke down over a long period of time and I held onto that for many more years than I should have, purely out of fear and then my worst fears became my reality and I was alone with my two children and completely broken and the skills I had gained over a decade no longer served me.

I sought help by ringing a friend who knew a counsellor who said she was fully booked but she had the number of someone else who could help.

I introduced myself on the phone and although the conversation was brief as I put the phone down I broke down in tears and sobbed uncontrollably - as I can only describe the experience as being really heard by a complete stranger who turned out to be Easton Hamilton.

Imagine that you are slowly drowning and someone reaches down for you and in one moment, pulls you up and you come up for air and that gasp, that relief as you breathe in.

I felt that someone had reached for me quite unlike anyone had before and I recognised something within the voice at the other end of the phone as a knowing exactly where I was. It wasn't exactly what he said as I couldn't clearly remember the conversation after I put the phone down, it was something else and I just kind of knew I had been heard and more importantly answered.

I eventually put a face to the voice and met with Easton and began what was to become a unique relationship, one that has taken me from perhaps the brink of devastation to one of victory over adversity and that story still continues as I write this synopsis - my reason for writing the above is to explain where I was at the time to give you a comparison to where I am now and how that came about.

When we hear truth from another person who has been through their own challenges, we hear it in a completely different way from someone who has merely read through an academic paper, because we hear their empathy and we can see someone who stands before us as a living testament to overcoming something equally devastating.

I have learned over these last few decades that what people say and what they do rarely match. I have heard many people who have a script already in place and repeat the same empty words without actually living it themselves.

However, I will say that there has always been something incredibly solid about the Reach philosophy and I can honestly say Easton is perhaps the only man I have ever met who lives what he says and because of that I trust him totally as he has never let me down through moments of utter despair and doubt when so many have stepped aside and have run.

I learned that our bodies have a wisdom built in and although the body listens to what we say it also waits for the 'evidence' and responds to a whole synergy of things when it comes to health and well-being.

I have learned that it responds to hydration by giving us signals of coherence and well-being, it responds to the nutrients we swallow such as probiotics, essential fatty acids and a whole host of nutrients, described as part of a non-negotiable strategy, because they give us a greater sense of well-being and assist the mind in fulfilling its potential.

I have come to realise through personal experience that when we go through the Reach process that this process is perhaps one of the most challenging experiences as it invites us to ask questions that have been hidden away in the deep recesses of one's mind for sometimes a lifetime. Those moments where you have said to others "I am depressed, anxious, and I just don't know why" - beneath those feelings are a whole legacy of usually traumatic experiences that have been tucked away hidden from the conscious part of the mind.

So we express the 'reaction' to those experiences throughout our life in the way we live and never really knowing why we do what we do and even more frustrating not knowing why or how to change those often self-destructive patterns.

Easton says, "One of the secrets to health is the removal of waste" and that just doesn't mean a week long detox in a health farm; it is much more than that. It's about removing waste in all its forms from your life… a total de-cluttering, which involves removing those habits, defences that we have hidden behind for a lifetime. Like any detox process it can sometimes make us feel not so good for a while, I think they call it the healing crisis, which is aptly named.

The truth is the Reach Approach asks each of us to open that box of secrets containing pain, uncertainty, regrets, resentments, and so much more and one by one removes them if they are no longer serving us, until one day, clarity and insight is revealed in the most amazing way. All of this is done in a safe, sensitive and supportive environment… so I always felt heard and held.

Once we see things as they really are and we become no longer afraid to face them we can take them apart and those bullies within our own minds that have made their presence felt usually at our weakest moments now begin to fall away.

Questioning those beliefs we have about ourselves that have passed down from our parents, education, culture and other relationships and circumstances, is not a negative process – one to be afraid of. It is our social conditioning that leads us to run away from things, but as I've discovered, if we run away, those things simply remain with us affecting us in a host of ways.

One by one the elimination process takes place and if you are able to stay the distance, as Reach offers no quick fix, you will come out different and certainly stronger, with the support and validation of someone who has travelled this path ahead of you. Your life, without any secrets makes you feel whole. I discovered an authenticity that left me feeling relief. I now understood why Easton would often say, being the best you can be is all that really matters… it's not about perfection, it's about reaching your own highest point.

So, from that place of strength, insight, wholeness, I have been able to co-create my intention of having my own natural health centre, I've been able to support my son with every ounce of my being through 7 years of illness, ending up in intensive care. I have come through a divorce without resentment, and watched my dad pass away on the day my son came out of hospital for the last time.

I say this only to show you, for someone who was diagnosed with chronic anxiety to have been able to do this is perhaps a miracle in itself and so I encourage those of you who have this feeling that "all is not well" to take the advice written in this book and apply the principles daily and perhaps even make contact with Reach -as today I am living testament to the continual affirmation I was given which has always remained, "Your kind is rare."

When I was told for the first time I was 'someone' and my existence was acknowledged, I looked behind me to see if Easton was talking to someone else as I believed I was nothing special; for most of my life although it is difficult for me to admit, but I felt like nothing.

Yet today I know I am the strongest man I have ever met and I know I am unique, not in a conceited way as that is true of each of us, but in a way that has helped me to change, achieve and grow in the direction of my dreams… once lost. If I were to sum up my experiences with the Reach Process it was one of offering me hope and that is all I needed to build from and I still do so today.

So hope, for me, was the beginning of a journey, which gave me confidence in my ability to define who I am, no longer by anyone else's definition or affirmations. If someone had offered me strength, compassion, humility, forgiveness, clarity, and a sense of self-worth as the by-product of a difficult and sometimes painful past, I would have taken that path without hesitation.

I have achieved that by the way I live my life as I am living my life forgiving again, again and again and I have gained insight into compassion for myself and others through a clear understanding of human nature and that came about as a direct result of going through the experiences I have lived through and finding meaning and clarity through the Reach process.

God bless.

Stuart Morris

Case Study 8

Subject: White male, -37 years old.

It's hard to know exactly where to begin when trying to capture in words the magic of the journey I have undertaken as a result of The Reach Approach, so I shall begin at the beginning.

The first time I met Easton I had travelled 3 hours on the train from Aberystwyth where I was at university. I had just turned 21 and two of my best friends had both begun therapy with him because of difficulties in their lives.

Faced with similar difficulties – cripplingly low self esteem, severe bouts of depression and a fairly sizeable drug problem – they had both told me that Easton had basically blown their minds (that's how we talked, we were young people!) and could be of tremendous help to me. Seeing the change in them, and their budding enthusiasm for the process of personal growth and development, I was more than happy to make the six hour round trip to gain access to that kind of help.

Over the ensuing ten years (almost to the day, in fact, as I write this) my life has changed immeasurably. Everything I have ever managed to achieve in my adult life owes a debt in some way to seeds that have been sown through The Reach Approach and the unique relationship I have been lucky enough to form with Easton. He has displayed incredible wisdom, kindness, boundless patience, empathy, humour, incredible faith in me, and an unbelievable honesty which has inspired me to try and do the same for others, and perhaps most importantly, for myself. One of the most useful concepts that helped me radically change my relationship with myself and those around me was: The Story of Health. It was so refreshingly simple and yet I'd never seen the obviousness of it until it was explained to me. How can one expect to be balanced and well when their life is falling down around them? And yet this is what I expected. I look back now and think, how crazy!

This beautiful, clear model has helped me deal with all that life has thrown at me – from health difficulties to complicated personal relationships, and helped me face these situations with my head held high. I have been drug and alcohol free for 8 years now, and this is directly attributable to the work we have done together. I had no idea that hydration was so critical for both my mind and my body. I started to understand how the cleansing it brought allowed me to think more clearly and begin to make better choices in my life. As a student my diet was not all it should have been to say the least and I hadn't made any connection between this and my mental and physical health! As I write this I'm realizing the incredible education I've had about the interconnectedness of life. The simple changes in my diet helped facilitate other changes in my mind and my life. And as a result I have a very different outlook, which is more positive. I still have moments when I lose my way – the difference is I now have a compass.

One of the many high points on my therapeutic journey came when my mother and I went to see Easton for a few sessions together. We had both undertaken our own therapeutic journeys but frequently ran into problems with each other. We had both suffered some fairly major trauma during my childhood, and we often argued bitterly, despite our best efforts and intentions. Our relationship has been completely transformed by the process, and is now incredibly mutually supportive and beneficial. I think it's fair to say that most people would have thought that it would have been impossible for us to achieve the kind of friendship we have now, and of all the many blessings I have received through my work with Reach, this is perhaps the one I am most grateful for.

I feel incredibly fortunate to have begun this journey at the very beginning of my adult life, although it is not over for me as I feel I'm still blossoming. Ten years down the line from that first meeting my journey is very well established. It is proving to be better than I could ever have hoped it would be, and that certainly wouldn't have been the case without the incredible work of Reach.

Paul

Case Study 9

Subject: Afro-caribbean male, 47 years old.

It is my pleasure to be able to write my story and how my connection with Reach changed the direction of my life. I can honestly say that my life has changed beyond what I even imagined was possible.

When I first came into contact with Reach I was broken, I felt completely hopeless, beyond desperate. At least when there is desperation it feels as though there's something still to fight for. All my fight had gone. A friend of a friend had been seeing a Reach therapist and I was still aware enough to be able to see how things were changing for him and there must have been the smallest spark of hope living in me that there maybe was still a chance for me.

For well over two decades I had lost myself in drug use and depression and my mind was a chaotic mess of negativity. I had so lost myself that I couldn't even call it low self-esteem, but of course that's what it was. I'd come from a violent and abusive background, which I'd escaped from at the earliest opportunity but that had meant that I felt set adrift from my family at the age of 16. Since that time I'd been surviving, certainly not living. Many destructive relationships under my belt, no job or sense of direction I arrived at Reach's door.

I can honestly say I find it hard these days to even imagine being that lost, that broken, that depressed. What amazed me first of all and for quite some time was that my counsellor actually understood how I'd got to this place and explained it to me, step by step. I'd just thought I was some kind of loser, a real failure. There was no acceptance anywhere I went; I just stood outside of anything I wanted to be a part of. But miraculously, I started to realize how it had all happened and that I was not a loser, I actually had something worthwhile to offer.

Next I was truly amazed by the things I was asked to do. Drinking water had never been part of my life, nor had I ever wanted it to be but again I came to realize and experience for myself that unless I started to cleanse my body, my mind had no chance. Now, nothing would persuade me to give this up! Similarly, I'd paid no attention to what I ate and it seems so obvious now, but I learned that there actually is a relationship between what you eat and how you feel. Food had never been a high priority, either in the family I grew up in or subsequently.... and the revelations went on and on. It was more like going on a course on 'how to live your life' and I can't even express in words the difference it made to mine.

Of course I had to face a lot of stuff I'd been running away from for years. This was difficult and very painful and part of me wanted to leave it buried forever but I do know that 'you can't heal what you conceal' – one of Reach's catch phrases that has never left me. I don't really know how I found the courage to keep going back for more but I am so grateful that I did.

Little by little my life was changing for the better. I did work very hard on forgiving mainly myself but also those who'd hurt me along the way. This was something I resisted for a long time but it became clear to me that I couldn't move on until I let go of all of my anger and resentment, my shame and sense of inadequacy.

One of the hardest things I realized I had to do was to create a different environment for myself. The 'environment' part of The Story of Health I came to understand was just as important as the mind and body parts. For me, I had to think about finding new and more positive relationships, seeking out those individuals who wanted what I now wanted – to be healthy, happy and productive in my life. This part of my story is a work in progress but it is beginning to happen and I feel blessed that I have a small but beautiful group of people in my life who genuinely want the best for me – and vice versa.

I am studying too! I love history and I've got my 'A' level and am soon to begin my degree. I volunteer as well but I hope that soon I'll be able to earn an honest living. This is my greatest desire... and I am busy invoking this every day.

I could write so much more and yet as I read back this summary of my experience with Reach I have tears in my eyes because I know I have travelled such a long way and I couldn't have done it without the immense wisdom, patience and real care of my Reach therapist. Thank you is just completely inadequate and yet it is all that I have for now... so thank you from my heart.

Simon Brown

Case Study 10

Subject: white female, 48 years old.

When I first started my counselling I was so chronically tired and crippled with anxiety I wonder how I actually made it to my appointment. Thinking back, there have been a number of appointments I didn't make because panic got the better of me. But thankfully, that eventually stopped.

To be honest, I didn't even really know that my problem was anxiety or panic, I just thought there was something seriously wrong with me because I couldn't seem to tolerate what other people took for granted. I couldn't bear being away from home most of the time; when I was out I was always planning a quick exit so that I could return home. It seemed as though the only safe place was my house. I didn't want to go away for the weekends anymore or see anyone and I had become so lonely, my life felt completely empty and yet it was also completely full - of fear.

I actually hated myself. I could feel it deep, deep down, this self-disgust for being so weak and stupid. After all, I was a grown-up, my kids were virtually grown up and here I was not being able to run my own life without always having to have someone there as my 'safety net'. My self-talk was so condemning and yet I didn't even notice it any more.

Probably the most important thing I learned when I started on my road back to health with Easton was that I couldn't get well until I chose to be kinder to myself. I just didn't feel I deserved it but in the end I had to concede that nothing else was working. He gave me a handout called Change Through Compassion and it clearly showed me how there was no way out of my horrible life unless I changed my attitude towards myself. Looking back, that was a turning point. Not that it happened overnight. But it did start to happen, slowly.

It then started to dawn on me, through Easton's patient explanations, that my health problems were connected to my state of mind. I'd had IBS for years and just tolerated the pain and discomfort, limited diet and embarrassing toilet habits. I had no energy but put that down to getting older and running around after the children for years. But looking at it now, that was ridiculous. I was still a young woman and yet I could barely walk up the stairs without a great effort. The doctors couldn't find anything from their endless tests but deep down I knew something was badly wrong.

So incredible though it seemed to me at first, even my fatigue and IBS were related to my fears and anxieties. I now know how toxic anxiety, stress and panic are to the body. Easton patiently explained many times how the chemicals produced in the body as a consequence of fear become toxic and this means that the body, especially the immune system, is bound to struggle to be fit and strong when there are poisonous chemicals swimming around in the blood stream and infiltrating all my cells and systems. I didn't understand all the science at first but I did really get the connection. If I could calm my mind and make friends with my fear, this would definitely help my exhaustion and the IBS.

I started following a programme of self-care, which included water, a much improved diet of vegetables, fruit, pulses and juices, and certain supplements – CoQ10, vitamin B complex and a multi mineral amongst them. I eventually began to grasp the art of positive thinking and relaxation and gentle exercise became a part of my life. Little by little I started to feel alive again.

But I also had to dig up what the cause was of all my fear. I say had to, I didn't really have to but I knew instinctively that to properly get better I couldn't leave anything festering inside me. I felt rotten inside and I knew this had to change if I was ever to live the life I wanted to.

I started to realize that my childhood had been cold and un-nurturing, I always felt I wanted to impress my parents, get them to be proud of me, and yet I'd never felt I could. Nothing was ever good enough. I loved them and yet they had played such a powerful and negative part in making me feel so unsafe, so completely unworthy and unable to do anything well enough. I began to see through the therapeutic process how the Three As were pretty much absent altogether. Attention, Affection and Affirmation – that handout was so shocking to me. I just hadn't experienced this as a child or actually ever, in any relationship. Not that I blame my parents any more – the game of blame as I learned, doesn't get you anywhere and I know they did their best.

I came to understand if I was to move beyond fear, panic and ill health, I had to be my own parent, develop a loving kindness towards me. I had always hated my fear but I now see how fear originally was just trying to protect me and to be a friend to me. The Dearest Fear video was so beautiful I listened to it over and over again - I have worked very hard on rebuilding that friendship, strange as it sounds – even to me - and it has made such a huge difference to my life.

I feel as if someone has turned the energy dial back up. It took a long time to be turned up properly but I am proud to say I now live my life free from fear the vast majority of the time, I go out when I want to, see friends and most of the time feel really well. I still work on relaxation and reassuring my body that I do love it and want to take care of it properly. I am a very long way from where I started and feel very close to my goal of actually living instead of just existing.

This story is mine, even though it still sounds like a fairy tale to me sometimes. The Reach Approach is so thorough – it covers every angle – and so if you're prepared to do the work, you can't fail to improve your life, especially when the person helping has so much belief in you!

Bettina Bauer

Sustainable solutions

I've had the privilege of working with thousands of clients, on a one-to-one basis, in couples, families and groups, and in the context of numerous workshops and training. I could have presented a book filled with literally hundreds of case studies demonstrating the effectiveness of a synergistic approach. But what I hope I have achieved with this small sample is a sense of how when dealing with the complexity of the human story, one has to address more than the presenting concerns because there is an intimate and delicate relationship between all the different bits of one's life and if you do not tease your way through that, it's easy to prematurely pat oneself on the back for a job well done. What is the point of giving someone a solution that may well help in that moment but is unlikely to sustain them through life?

Our hurried approach to just about everything in the modern world has found its way into how we care for ourselves, and each other. This has been equally reflected in the helping professions. So the many techniques and methods currently available, claiming to offer a solution, prize themselves on the speed they can be achieved rather than the sustainability of what's offered.

I am not suggesting that the way I work is a miracle cure. I am suggesting that it is capable of creating miracles but only if firstly the individual understands how their life is connected to everything around them and how by using this understanding they can make themselves well or continue to maintain their sickness.

In addition to this understanding there has to be a willingness to do the work. Knowledge, plus application, equals personal power and liberation. These ten case studies are examples of individuals who fulfilled both these things and as a consequence have either taken back the reins of their lives, or are claiming them for the first time.

If you feel your life is not flowing in a positive direction and you are a victim to circumstance, please realize there is a lot you can do about this, but you have to take responsibility for your life. I hope these accounts will inspire you to do just that....

"The willingness to accept responsibility for one's own life is the source from which self-respect springs. "

Joan Didion (1934 – present)

BITE SIZED INSIGHTS

This is a list of catch phrases and slogans, which encapsulate many of the principles I use in my work. I refer to them as bite sized insights, because, in a short, snappy way, they remind me and those who are taking this path, of the primary concepts that are needed to fulfill one's potential and arrive at one's preferred destination. They have become part of the Reach vocabulary and are largely unique to this model but I think apply generally to life.

I think you will find them useful as prompts and reminders of much of what you've read in this book. They will almost effortlessly take your mind back to seminal moments and important concepts. They will also remind you that peace of mind and positive change are only ever one thought away.

It's not necessary to learn or remember these phrases and statements because my experience has taught me that the more you immerse yourself in this material, the more they will grow on you anyway, over time. I've added them here, as I believe they will be a useful resource, helping you to change the way you think and assist you on your journey…

There is no future in the past

When the cell is well, all is well

Focusing with faith

Miracles are made

The only destination is right action

Living with ambivalence

Charity is really good for the soul

The secret to health is the removal of waste

Where the mind goes the molecule will follow

A mind full of gratitude has no room for complaint

The three Ps

Courage and application are the keys

Knowledge plus application equals personal power

Dearest body

From pain to power

Non-negotiables

Old friend, dear friend

Change through compassion

Practice makes permanent

Routine is power

Resolution creates space, time and energy

The paradox of progress

The power of choice

Victory or victimhood

Virtues always travel in pairs

Define or be defined

An inventory of incongruence

Knowing to doing

Doing to being

N.O.S.E.

Self-care is the key

The three As

The journey of becoming

Key principles for growth

Order creates peace

The power of thank you

Waste weakens

Understanding your blind spot

The art of appreciation

Reacting or responding

The story of health

The journey of enough

Who are you when no one is looking?

The three aspects of consciousness

Personal prayer

Persuading the body

We are vertical rivers

Forgiveness and gratitude

Remember the message not the messenger

The discipline dilemma

The memoried self

The experiencing self

The anticipating self

Your delivery is as important as your message

Remaining regrets

The story of light

The promise of practice

Dearest past

Healing habits

Still time

The wonder of water

Thank you for the gift of

Sustainable solutions

Asking for nothing and receiving everything

Listening-in

Listening-out

Giving without counting

You can't heal what you conceal

The problems and the solutions live in the same place

Dearest fear

Are you really listening, or simply waiting to speak?

Everybody wins in a charitable world

Patience is the mother of wisdom

Change is a process not an event

FURTHER READING

1. Alston, B. (2007) What is Neurotheology?
2. Batmanghelidj, F. (2008) Your Body's Many Cries for Water: You're Not Sick; You're Thirsty.
3. Bland, J. (2014) The Disease Delusion.
4. Bloom, W. (2011) The Power of Modern Spirituality: How to Live a Life of Compassion and Personal Fulfilment.
5. Bolte-Taylor, J. (2008) *My Stroke of Insight*.
6. Burtt, E. A. (2003) The Metaphysical Foundations of Modern Science.
7. Carper, J. (2000) Food Your Miracle Medicine.
8. Church, D. (2009) The Genie in Your Genes.
9. Clayton, P. (2004) *Health Defence*.
10. Connolly, P. (2014) A Student's Guide to the History and Philosophy of Yoga.
11. Doidge, N. (2008) The Brain that Changes Itself.
12. Emoto, M. (2010) Messages from Water and the Universe.
13. Evans, M. and Rodger, I. (2000) Healing for Body, Soul and Spirit: An Introduction to Anthroposophical Medicine.
14. Ferguson, L. (2013) Nutrigenomics and Nutrigenetics in Functional Foods and Personalized Nutrition.
15. Fuhrman, J. (2011) *Eat To Live*.
16. Gerhardt, S. (2004) *Why Love Matters*.

17. Hoffer, A., and Saul, A.W. (2008) *Orthomolecular Medicine for Everyone*.
18. Holford, P. (1997) The Optimum Nutrition Bible.
19. Holford, P. (2010) Optimum Nutrition for the Mind.
20. Houghton, C. (2010) 'Switched On': Harnessing the Power of Nutrigenomics to Optimise Your Health.
21. Jackson, T. (2011) Prosperity without Growth: Economics for a Finite Planet.
22. Kirsch, I. (2009) The Emperor's New Drugs.
23. Klemm, W. R. (2014) Mental Biology: The New Science of How the Brain and Mind Relate.
24. Lipton, B. (2005) The Biology of Belief.
25. Maté, G. (2004) When the Body Says No: Exploring the Stress-Disease Connection.
26. McTaggart, L. (2003) *The Field*.
27. McTaggart, L. (2008) The Intention Experiment.
28. Nataraja, S. (2008) The Blissful Brain.
29. Pauling, L. (2006) How to Live Longer and Feel Better.
30. Pert, C. (1999) Molecules of Emotion.
31. Sheldrake, R. (2011) The Presence of the Past: Morphic Resonance and the Habits of Nature.
32. Sheldrake, R. (2012) The Science Delusion.
33. Singer, M. (2007) Untethered Soul: The Journey Beyond Yourself.
34. Radin, D. (2009) The Noetic Universe.
35. Ramachandran, V.S. (1999) Phantoms in the Brain: Human Nature and the Architecture of the Mind.
36. Ramachandran, V.S. (2012) The Tell-Tale Brain: Unlocking the Mystery of Human Nature.
37. Walsh, B. E. (2005) Unleashing Your Brilliance: Tools & Techniques to Achieve Personal, Professional & Academic Success.
38. Williams, M. and Penman, D. (2011) Mindfulness: A Practical Guide to Finding Peace in a Frantic World.

ABOUT THE AUTHOR

Easton Hamilton is the founder and director of Reach, a private therapy practice based in the UK, which specializes in helping others to attain optimal mental and physical health, through the therapeutic integration of modern psychology with cutting edge science as well as ancient philosophies, principles and various systems of healing.

Reach is twenty-five years old, with practitioners UK wide – and through its popular franchise scheme, has a growing number of international satellite practices around the world. The Reach Approach is a holistic model developed by Easton and it was conceived out of his tireless research and many thousands of face-to-face client hours accumulated from thirty five years of helping others to resolve their issues and fulfill their potential and purpose.

A qualified psychotherapist, hypnotherapist and holistic practitioner, Easton has dedicated his professional life to working with those who are looking for lasting solutions to the many and varied problems encountered in modern life, including: addiction, depression, anxiety, stress, eating disorders, relationship problems, self-esteem issues, acute and chronic illnesses, dissociative disorders, just to name a few.

His truly integrative approach to wholeness and health properly recognizes that a struggling mind will impact negatively on one's physical health and the status of one's physical health will equally impact on the mind. The main thrust of Easton's philosophy is that we will fall short of true health and wholeness if we try to find balance, harmony and contentment by looking in only one place i.e. through the vehicle of one kind of healing system. If you only attend to the needs of the mind or you attempt to 'fix' the body but ignore the needs of the mind, then sustainable health will continue to elude you.

The Reach Approach, as this book attests to, offers a profound and complete answer to the ills of the human condition. It is a synergistic approach to well-being, which initially evolved because Easton found that despite what existed in the helping arenas, there was nonetheless a 'void' that somehow did not meet the precise needs of the individual. Each helping organization or system was concerned with their bit of the equation – such as alcoholism, depression, eating disorders, cancer, diabetes – but there was no coherent approach which demonstrated how the mind-body system works interdependently as well as independently. And so a model, able to address all aspects of what it is to be human - mind, body, spirit and the environments in which we play out our roles - was needed.

Easton's own life journey has not been without significant challenge and through his personal experience and that of countless others who have walked the Reach Approach path, Easton has carefully integrated many related and seemingly unrelated disciplines – including: psychology, biology, history, philosophy, spirituality, cognitive neuroscience and many more - and developed the tools we all need to live our lives to the full so we may rise up and be all we are capable of being.

Easton and Reach continue to be part of a silent revolution, which concerns itself with the empowerment of individuals and their communities through research, education and personal development practices. They are busy promoting the best ways to achieve self-improvement, mindful-living, increased personal awareness and spiritual growth.

Why not join this silent revolution today!

"I see a world in the future in which we understand that all life is related to us and we treat that life with great humility and respect."
David Suzuki (1936 – present)

If you are interested in finding out more about The Reach Approach, visit the website at: www.thereachapproach.co.uk

LIVING WITH AMBIVALENCE

By now you will have realized that peace of mind and happiness are not always found by being free from the storm. They are found in the mind that is at ease with itself, despite its contradictions and ambivalences. As I've illustrated, the mind can either be hell or heaven. It all depends on the nature of your thoughts and feelings and more importantly how you respond to them.

You have learned on our journey that it's our responses to our thoughts and feelings that most shape our reality. The hypercritical, uncompassionate mind is the one that can make heaven into hell. It can even find fault and blame where there is none - such is its expertise. It considers itself omniscient - all knowing - and it need not take advice or consider other options, because they'd be inferior anyway - such is its ignorance and arrogance.

Whenever we choose condemnation over compassion and blame over personal responsibility, we create our own prison in which we become trapped by thoughts and feelings that torture us. The reason many of us defer to the hypercritical, uncompassionate mind is that somewhere inside of us lives the feeling that this is what we deserve and so we are not worthy of something better. This feeling lurks deep inside, annoyingly reciting this toxic mantra and sadly over many years we've learned to accept and come to believe this recital.

There's an easy way to break this pattern and establish a mind that is at ease with itself and therefore free from the internal storms. The method is simple - learn to live ambivalently. What does this actually mean? Well, it's about accepting your contradictions, flaws, dualities, your inconsistencies, fears, doubts and bad habits. The more you accept these 'less desirable' parts of yourself and choose not to judge them harshly the more you'll be able to find peace of mind, happiness and well-being. It is our relentless war of attrition with those less desirable parts that binds us to internal turmoil and external chaos, sustaining our inertia in the process.

So whilst you attempt to implement the synergistic code I've presented you with, lovingly embrace where you are right now. Living with your ambivalence allows you to relax and let go of the tensions and anxieties that conflict creates. The stress of conflict literally diminishes mind, body and spirit and poisons us at every level (remember, waste weakens).

When we can accept our flaws and contradictions, that shift in consciousness frees that energy bound up with conflict, enabling us to find clarity, relaxation and eventually joy. Doesn't it make more sense to treat your less desirable bits as if they were your friends rather than your enemies?

All those things you relentlessly give yourself a hard time about, accept them as parts of yourself in transition. They are those parts of you that have not yet become all they are capable of being. So don't criticize or condemn them. Is it fair to condemn a child who has not yet learned a skill? We need to understand that some parts of us are more evolved than other parts. Our lives are wonderful opportunities for the growth, and learning necessary to help those less evolved aspects flourish. This growth is best achieved with a compassionate mind and an accepting heart.

Allow your mind to move in the following direction… (Remember to allow the dots to act as pauses to allow you to really reflect on the meaning of each phrase).

Ambivalence and duality are natural states…. It's time to embrace the truth of that and walk the road of acceptance…. Something deep inside of me says I can do this…. I can accept those parts of me that are not yet healed, resolved or even as aware as I'd like them to be…. I understand that some of me is not evolved, compassionate, fearless, understanding, or as generous as I'd like…. I accept that I am failing in some areas of my life and that's ok…. This does not tell the whole story…. I'm not defined by those shortcomings…. In fact I find that when I accept and embrace these parts of me I become more understanding of the whole….

It's time to broker a truce between the damaged and broken bits and the bits I feel more comfortable with…. As I increasingly understand that I am a work in progress and mistakes are inevitable, then getting things wrong is more easily accepted.... And the need to hide and cower before my nemesis, shame, falls away.... And so I worry less about how I am perceived by others.... I feel myself stepping outside of my limitations where I can, and where I'm still not ready, that's ok too.... There's such a wonderful sense of peace in this place.... Accepting my ambivalence and all that comes with it is definitely the way forward.... I give thanks for this discovery.... I now promise to keep moving forward in this way.... As a result of my acceptance, I feel an overwhelming sense of peace....

Make a pact with yourself today to accept your shortcomings, to accept where you're still 'not getting it right', to accept your feelings of disappointment, both with yourself and with others. Realize that through this acceptance you'll come to know what peace of mind and joy really feel like. They both exist in the mind that has learned to live with its duality and ambivalence.

There you will find contentment....

"Your task is not to seek for love, but merely to seek and find all the barriers within yourself that you have built against it."

Rumi (1207 – 1273)

Printed in Great Britain
by Amazon.co.uk, Ltd.,
Marston Gate.